Effective Sustainability Strategies: How to Build Them

Effective Sustainability Strategies: How to Build Them

Elisa Gomez Gonzalez

SOCIETY Publishing

www.societypublishing.com

Effective Sustainability Strategies: How to Build Them

Elisa Gomez Gonzalez

Society Publishing
224 Shoreacres Road
Burlington, ON L7L 2H2
Canada
www.societypublishing.com
Email: orders@arclereducation.com

ISBN: 978-1-77469-012-3 (Hardcover)

ABOUT THE AUTHOR

Born in the Canary Islands, **Elisa Gomez** has always been aware of the immense potential and limitations that resources provide to communities. Following her passion towards the environment and sustainable development mechanism, she completed the Madrid Environmental Sciences degree and later completed a Master's degree in International Sustainable Development and Corporate Sustainability.

She has worked for a wide range of industries and sectors as a sustainability consultant and analyst implementing international standards, achieving certifications, and ensuring the management processes were effective. The sectors englobe oil and gas, construction, telecommunications, and software design.

Moved by a great passion towards her work, she decided to quit the corporate environment and set up her own company, Better Together (www.bettertogether-sustainability.com) an online sustainability company that specializes in simple, effective, and understandable sustainability practices for all types of companies. They focus especially on Startups and SMEs, as these are growing; ensuring that they are sustainable right from the start without the burden of complicated, time-consuming, and expensive measures.

TABLE OF CONTENTS

LIST OF FIGURES

LIST OF TABLES

LIST OF ABBREVIATIONS

ASTD	American Society for Training and Development
ATFP	L'Agence Tunisienne De La Formation Professionnelle
BOTA	Botswana Training Authority
CDSB	Climate Disclosure Standards Board
CITES	Convention on International Trade in Endangered Species
CLG	Corporate Leadership Group
CRM	Customer Relationship Management
EfS	Education for Sustainability
EIB	European Investment Bank
ESD	Education for Sustainable Development
E-TVET	Employment and Technical and Vocational Education and Training
EVPs	Employee Value Propositions
FIVET	Federal Institute for Vocational Education and Training
GAP	Global Action Program
GCED	Global Citizenship Education
GRI	Global Reporting Initiative
HRD	Human Resource Development
HRM	Human Resource Management
IADB	Inter-American Development Bank
IAG	Inter-Agency Groups
IAGs	Internationally Agreed Goals
ICCS	International Civic and Citizenship Education Study
IDPs	Individual Development Plans
INDCs	Intended Nationally Determined Contributions
IWRM	Integrated Water Resources Management
KPIs	Key Performance Indicators
KRAs	Key Results Assessment

LTIs	Long-Term Incentive Compensation
MDGs	Millennium Development Goals
MDPs	Management Development Programs
MENA	Middle East and North Africa
MSF	Multi-Stakeholder Feedback
NAFTA	North American Free Trade Agreement
NCHRD	National Center for Human Resources Development
NEA	National Employment Agency
NGOs	Nongovernmental Organizations
NSSC	Netherlands Sector Skills Council
OECD	Organization for Economic Co-operation and Development
PMS	Performance Management System
PwC	Price Waterhouse Coopers
SDGs	Sustainable Development Goals
SDSP	Sustainable Development Skills Profile
SENAR	Serviço Nacional De Aprendizagem Rural
SETAs	Sector Education and Training Authorities
SMEs	Small and Medium-Sized Enterprises
SSA	Sub-Saharan Africa
TDI	Technology-Delivered Instruction
TESDA	Technical Education and Skills Development Authority
TREE	Training for Rural Economic Empowerment
TVET	Technical and Vocational Education and Training
UNCED UN	Conference on Environment and Development
UNCSD UN	Conference on Sustainable Development
WSSD	World Summit on Sustainable Development

SYNOPSIS

This book will run you through the entire process of setting up a sustainability management system, that everybody feels accountable and responsible for as well as highlighting how it can build resilient mechanisms towards natural disasters.

The first chapters will set up the scene describing how sustainability is currently being implemented, what are the trends and challenges. These initial chapters are very important as they contemplate the main assumptions and characteristics of current practices, which will enable the reader to better understand the measures presented afterward.

The last chapters focus mainly on how sustainability practices can be implemented effectively into different departments within businesses to assure a good deployment of efforts and allocation of resources.

EXECUTIVE SUMMARY

Sustainable business examples are progressively showing up on the radar of organizations around the globe because of current trends and communication efforts. An effective company or association is very much reliant on its investor's needs and expectations. Investors are interested in sustainability, impact, and added value.

A reasonable association meets the desires of diverse partners. A genuine feasible association is capable of bringing together monetary, social, and natural contemplations. Such businesses are effectively ready to meet the desires of both internal and external partners, for example, investors, clients, government, employees, and groups to guarantee long-term success for all.

In any case, most businesses neglect to execute feasible objectives. Regularly, businesses neglect to execute sustainable business practices because of insufficient reconciliation with business methodology, absence of help from authority, constrained comprehension, and inclusion of workers at all levels, and additionally, nonappearance of frameworks and procedures that enable a systematize support.

Sustainability can enable businesses to prevail with regard to current economic business trends. Albeit numerous businesses dedicate themselves to sustainability and frame a strategy, its implementation, and coordination depend upon effectively embracing the following:

- Empowering and driving economic business practices at all levels of the association.
- Creating effective frameworks and procedures.

PREFACE

Sustainability management systems have proven not only to benefit the company that applies them but also to the world as a whole. Sustainability is slowly but steadily being incorporated into public policies, governments, private sector companies, and even freelancers. The world has begun to believe that we can actually operate and perform in a way that is respectful to the environment, society, and the economy enabling us to develop sustainably.

This is not merely a trend or the hot topic for the coming years, but it is a crucial aspect of we want to continue prospering a thriving. A great part of sustainable management practices relies on people. People that work with a purpose; feel engaged, accountable, and responsible for their actions. People that want to make a difference for good. These people together form teams that work with purpose, feel engaged, connected, accountable, and responsible for their actions. This group of people forms companies, businesses, organizations, and overall a community of people that have in mind to be sustainable and to provide the best for future generations.

The purpose is the main driver for millennials in choosing a workplace and a career, this shift from other generational trends implies that companies and the workplace industry globally need to face a transformation. Millennials which will shortly constitute the biggest generation in the workplace have a broader understanding of sustainability. Not only a broader understanding but they go one step further and actually reject working for companies that do not create value and have a positive impact where they operate. Their understanding of sustainable development together with their immense technological capacity nowadays set the perfect scene for all types of companies and organizations to start implementing sustainability management systems.

With sustainability management systems, renewable technology development goes hand-in-hand. Thus, along with an overview of what is happening around the world, this book covers the trends, future expectations, and forecasts.

Typically, sustainability management systems or sometimes referred to as corporate social responsibility (CSR) are very much dependent upon international standards, regulation, legislation, and certifications which are very much industry-related or country-related. This means that they are heavily influenced by the culture, the economic positioning in the market, and the countries legal and political trends.

Moreover, globalization has enabled access to products and services where they were not available before. All of these changes and limitations have created a difficult scenario for companies, where implementing sustainability measures imply allocating a great part of the budget and result in very time consuming for employees.

The main aim of this book is to provide simple, effective, understandable, and applicable mechanisms for all readers. To enable and empower them to implement management systems that are adapted to the reality and expectations of their business.

In this book, you will find all of those mechanisms and resources needed to ensure that sustainability is well embedded into a company through Human Resources Practices, Marketing, and Communication, Procurement, and CEO Leadership.

This book is for all those that want to effectively implement sustainable management and culture into their current business practices. The book runs simply through all of the steps to design and create a strategy according to the needs and expectations of all the stakeholders, ensuring everyone involved feels accountable and responsible for their piece of the pie.

It is also intended for all those studying or professionals that work as sustainability consultants or analysts to broaden their perceptions of sustainability implementation in a millennial digital world.

INTRODUCTION

Sustainability emerged from the need to protect and ensure our environment, our society, and our economic system assumes responsibility and works to cause as little harm as possible. Sustainability as a concept stepped onto the world stage in 1992 at the World's first Earth Summit in Rio. Since then, awareness, and the application of sustainable practices have been on the rise.

This book will include the background information needed to understand sustainability management systems and their integration into businesses fully. The reader will be provided with the benefits, risks, and disadvantages of the different methods to assure comprehension and analytical thinking are stimulated.

Renewable technology development goes hand-in-hand with sustainability management systems. Thus, this book covers the trends, future expectations, and forecasts as well as a thorough overview of what is happening around the world.

A simple methodology will be presented to effectively approach the integration of sustainability in all types of businesses. Case studies, practical examples, and templates will be provided in each phase of the methodology, enabling the reader to assess and implement sustainability as they read along. Relevant supporting information will be provided at the end of each chapter on specific topics to take into consideration.

Promoting and empowering people into incorporating sustainability is my personal mission. I strongly believe in the positive impact it provides and in the added value that it enables for all. Sustainability does not have to be complicated, expensive, or unrelated to the business activity. The numerous benefits its incorporation provides to all types of companies are always worth the journey.

In the end, the main goal of sustainability, in my humble opinion, is to do and use business as a force for good.

Chapter 1

Sustainability: Introduction

Everything starts with posing the rights questions. For sustainability we need to ask ourselves:

Who does what, when, and why? How does the company get the assets expected to endure and flourish? My emphasis here is on overseeing what I call the "physical measurements" of sustainable sustainability: the utilization of energy; the sources of energy, water, and materials; the decrease of waste and the environmental impact of a company's creation; and the effect of the utilization of whatever the company produces. The key inquiry to be tended: How does a company figure out how to lessen its negative effect on nature?

Sustainability effectiveness lies within the fate of the board. Sustainability must be coordinated into the core of what companies do. In the 20th century, companies focused on including universal activities, supply chains, data innovation, refined advertising, implementing procedures, ensuring money flow, bookkeeping, and new types of gathering forms.

Today, companies all through the globe are endeavoring to decrease their carbon footprint, limit atmosphere pollution, and sustainable hazard, upgrade strength, and incorporate sustainability into their tasks. The issue is they do not have the foggiest idea how to do it.

Organizations, governments, and charities are remembering they have to take these activities, yet their ability lies in their very own center capacities, not in creating sustainability designs and evaluating operational hazard inside this specific circumstance. To have important change on sustainability, companies, not-for-profits, and governments must carry it into the customary texture of authoritative setup.

Over the long haul, we ought not to require a "sustainability department;" each department should turn into a sustainability operating unit. Dealing with the physical components of sustainability should now be added to standard working methodology so all chiefs become sustainability supervisors. Huge thoughts, eager objectives, and delightful approaches do not convert into on-the-ground change until companies change.

The master plan issue we are trying to deliver at last comes down to the test of worldwide sustainability: how might we make a high throughput economy without decimating the planet? We are, actually, looking at sparing the planet for our kids.

The issues at the core of the sustainability issue are perplexing, worldwide, and fundamental, and cannot be effectively unraveled. These difficulties require activity by partners at all levels. Be that as it may, making an interpretation of these thoughts energetically requires far more prominent hierarchical limit than we right now have. We may realize how to construct a LEED-certified energy productive structure, yet do we realize how to look after it? Frequently, we don't. This hierarchical test is not generally recognized; it is not the flashiest issue that environment promoters are pointing out. In any case, companies are starting to comprehend that they cannot just make a sustainability department and anticipate that the issue should be unraveled. A significant number of our best heads realize they have to deal with the physical components of sustainability. There is ever more extensive acknowledgment of why sustainability is required, yet there is not yet a profound comprehension of how to do it. What we have to do is figure out how to fabricate that limit. As a scholastic, you will not be astounded to peruse that I accept the information we need must originate from scholastically thorough however applied research.

As an understudy of the board, I realize that every company and the authoritative condition is novel, yet there are examples and practices that can be distinguished and comprehended.

Under what conditions improve at lessening their utilization of energy and changing their wellspring of energy from high carbon to low? When do interests in shut frameworks building get made and when are they evaded? What sort of chiefs pays attention to environment components and what type believes it is a joke? In companies intensely subject to an all-inclusive production network, what techniques have succeeded and bombed when attempting to impact the conduct of providers?

As we gain more from the "bleeding edges" of sustainability the board, I additionally will be keen on the preparation and instruction needs that we distinguish. This will be added to our educational program in undergrad and graduate investigations in sustainability. Current courses should be adjusted and new courses should be created. I additionally anticipate that customary fields, for example, building, business, law, open organization, and general well-being, should add sustainability issues to their courses also.

There has been a propensity for some sustainable backers to concentrate on representative political fights, to some degree as a method for picking up consideration and instructing people in general. The appreciation for imagery goes back to the beginning of the advanced environment development.

The present unquestionably increasingly advanced variant of vehicle covering signals incorporate endeavors to strip benefits assets from petroleum derivative organizations and suing energy organizations for the environmental harm they have caused. It worked with the tobacco organizations; why not the oil organizations?

It may work in some sense, and it surely assumes a job in state-funded training. Be that as it may, the genuine work is persuading individuals to quit smoking and to utilize renewable wellsprings of energy. Strolling in the city of New York or urban communities anyplace on the planet, I see a lot of individuals smoking. The tobacco organizations appear to do OK.

Driving down those equivalent lanes is a lot of vehicles controlled by petroleum derivatives. We are altogether dependent on petroleum derivatives, and non-renewable energy source-based energy is integral to our day-by-day lives. I concur that putting resources into petroleum product organizations is an impractical notion, yet regardless I fill my tank with gas. Those organizations get our cash one way or the other.

The genuine work is getting an electric vehicle framework fabricated, propelling battery, and sustainable power source innovation, and actualizing these new advancements. I am keen on figuring out how to energize and speed up genuine change. Representative signals have a task to carry out; however, we ought not to mistake emblematic motions for operational reality. Companies and social orders can be exceptionally delayed to change, however, after some time they do advance. In the previous century, a great part of the change has been in light of the improvement of new advancements. We have to adapt considerably more about our planet's environments and significantly more about the effect of our innovation on our planet. I accept that with insight, care, and new innovation, we can achieve a type of financial advancement that accomplishes both development and environment quality. In any case, it will be troublesome work, and it will not be accomplished rapidly.

Chapter 2

Sustainable Development Strategic Topics

CONTENTS

In 2019, preceded by political insecurity, there was an increase in environmental impacts/degradation and quickening paces of biodiversity misfortune. While the scale and multifaceted nature of the sustainability challenges we face is overwhelming, there is likewise an explanation behind good faith. We are seeing remarkable administration and advancement driven by urban areas, districts, and organizations, rising urban activism and promotion by Generation Z, and quickly developing mindfulness about issues, for example, plastic contamination. We anticipate that this developing force should drive truly necessary advancement on basic social and sustainable issues in 2019. Just because, we are additionally sharing further investigation of five areas: nourishment and agribusiness, innovation, pharmaceuticals, and social insurance, energy, and utilities and budgetary administrations. In our part inclines, we research the key issues confronting these quickly evolving enterprises and talk about rising arrangements.

Current endeavors stay deficient to change our course towards risky atmosphere change. A quickly warming atmosphere and inability to enough diminish ozone-depleting substance discharges the pressing requirement for a more prominent spotlight on flexibility measures. Quick, enormous scale interest in successful arrangements is expected to keep an unsustainable weather change from coming to conceivably cataclysmic levels.

2.1. RISING GLOBAL EMISSIONS

Falling costs for both sustainable power sources and flammable gas have brought about unobtrusive emissions decreases among top producers, for example, Europe and the United States.

In any case, none of the four biggest worldwide polluters (China, the United States, the European Union (EU), and India) are at present on track to do their part in worldwide endeavors to arrive at the Paris Agreement objectives.

Specialists report that worldwide ozone-depleting substance emissions rose by an expected 2.7% in 2018, arriving at a record-breaking high. This speaks to the second year of remarkable increments after a concise time of moderately stable emissions due to eased back monetary development.

Universal media center keeps on staying around outflows from power age, where the best progress is being made. Be that as it may, farming and transportation are additionally significant supporters, and just restricted consideration is being given to these areas and other littler producers.

The most recent IPCC report featured the seriousness of effects we are now encountering at 1°C warming and expressed that 2°C of warming is currently considered profoundly hazardous.

Nations have consented to provide details regarding their emissions like clockwork beginning in 2024, as per the new Paris Agreement rulebook concurred at COP24 in December 2018 in Poland.

China proceeds to intensely put resources into sustainable power sources, electric vehicles (EV), and energy capacity, yet its absolute outflows are anticipated to keep moving until 2030. India's outflows are foreseen to top in 2033.

Air contamination identified with utilization of non-renewable energy sources stays a significant worldwide issue. In excess of 3 billion individuals are breathing savage smoke in their homes from utilizing dirtying stoves and fills.

The EU has attempted to keep up outflows decrease energy, in enormous part because of Germany neglecting to change away from coal. In the meantime, the US carbon dioxide outflows rose by 3.4% in 2018, the greatest increment in 8 a long time.

"To have a chance of limiting warming to 1.5°C, greenhouse gas emissions must be cut in half by 2030 and be net zero by 2050." Diana Liverman, University of Arizona, lead author for the IPCC 1.5°C report (Figure 2.1).

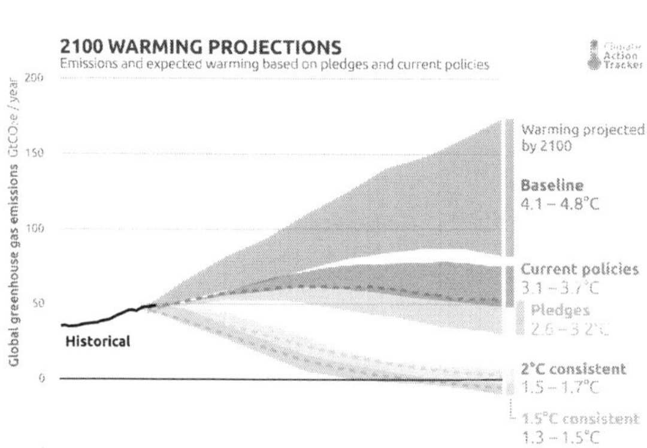

Figure 2.1. 2100 warming projections.

Source: *Climate Action Tracker.*

2.1.1. Adaptation Investment Is Urgent

The effects of 1°C warming are unmistakably more serious than anticipated. Extraordinary climate is causing billions in harm yearly, with flooding, storms, and dry season in Asia coupled with seething flames in the United States, Canada, Greece, and Sweden. While a few atmospheres relief and adjustment ventures are complimentary, as a rule, they are going after restricted government reserves.

Worldwide effects to urban situations are now evaluated at $314 billion every year and are anticipated to increment to more than $415 billion yearly by 2030.

Serious out-of-control fires in California caused billions of dollars in direct harm and protection payouts in 2018.

Warmth waves hit Europe in 2018, affecting financial execution and diminishing control age from wind turbines, featuring the dire requirement for additional interest in atmosphere flexible energy foundation and horticulture.

As per new gauges by FAO, dry seasons in Asia caused over $48 billion in lost harvests and domesticated animals somewhere in the range of 2005 and 2015.

A perilously warmed atmosphere is prompting recharged discourse among specialists about the upsides and downsides of geoengineering mediations. Geoengineering, for the most part, falls under two classifications: the expulsion and capacity of carbon from the climate and sunlight-based radiation the board, which is the impression of the sun's beams once again into space or on the other hand obstructing a little segment of daylight before it arrives at Earth. While there are numerous advocates of geoengineering arrangements, the science is still generally dependent on hypothetical models and has been reprimanded for being possibly risky and for exhibiting policymakers with the guarantee of a silver shot that may ease back endeavors to decrease emissions.

The New Carbon Economy Consortium is an activity of scholastic organizations, national research facilities, and NGOs hoping to utilize rising advancements to change the economy by emphatically using carbon. The United States and Norway are at the front line of the drive for carbon catch what is more, stockpiling (CCS), yet so far, the European Commission (EC) has been tepid about this innovation. Y Combinator, the tech hatchery celebrated for kick-beginning organizations like Airbnb and Dropbox, is currently emptying a huge number of dollars into financing geoengineering arrangements.

Geoscientists, environmentalists, and urban organizers are attempting to improve soil to retain higher measures of carbon dioxide in both farming and urban situations. Other incipient innovations getting subsidizing incorporate hereditarily designed phytoplankton, direct air catch, marine cloud lighting up, and electrogeochemistry.

Regardless of expanding enthusiasm for geoengineering arrangements, a developing number of specialists are cautioning about potential risks related to the innovation, counting obscure and conceivably disastrous reactions, significant expenses, and the fracture of worldwide endeavors on ozone harming substance decrease.

"Geoengineering is the brave-new-world of climate mitigation. While the scientific jury is still out on risk and effectiveness, what's already becoming clear from our initial research is that any silver-bullet climate solution brings with it an additional 'moral hazard' that it may desensitize the general public to climate risk and sap their motivation to support decisive mitigation." Victoria Campbell-Árvai, a Research Scientist at the University of Michigan's School for Environment and Sustainability (Figure 2.2).

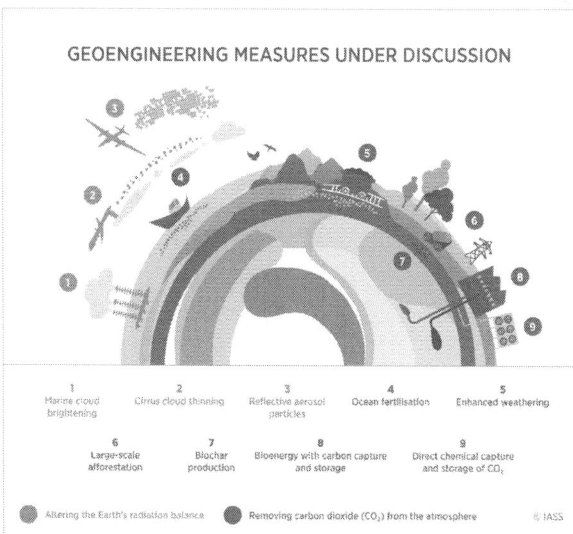

Figure 2.2. Geoengineering measures under discussion.

Source: *IASS.*

2.1.2. Future Expectations

We hope to see billions of dollars of extra harm and a lot more lives lost because of extraordinary climate occasions. Versatility, adjustment, and obligation with respect to framework that is badly arranged for progressively outrageous climate will be front what is more, place for the two governments and business. Organizations will quicken activity to build atmosphere readiness in both direct tasks and their inventory chains. Geoengineering advancements could see more prominent speculation from the private area furthermore, restored exchange at the strategy level.

1. **Organize Interest in Atmosphere Strength and Adjustment:** Organizations need to build the versatility of their stockpile chains and direct tasks. This will require interest in atmosphere hazard evaluations and situation arranging.
2. **Shape Strategy and Campaign Governments for More Atmosphere Activity:** Organizations need to have a progressively dynamic influence in national and worldwide endeavors to execute the Paris Agreement and apply more noteworthy weight on governments to restrict a worldwide temperature alteration. This implies supporting for activities like a cost on carbon, forceful arrangement of renewables and EV, and atmosphere brilliant farming arrangements.
3. **Increment Collaboration Efforts to Scale Low Carbon Economy Solutions:** Quickly decreasing ozone harming substance outflows and expanding the versatility of framework may be accomplished through multi-area joint effort. Organizations need to work with corporate cohorts, governments, NGOs, and others to use the assorted aptitudes required scaling low carbon economy arrangements in all enterprises.

2.2. CITIZEN POWER

Citizens demand a more sustainable, equitable world from companies and institutions. Engaged citizens, joined by an increasing number of Gen Z teens, are taking to social media and the streets to demand action from governments and businesses on pressing social and environmental challenges.

Savvy companies are tapping into shifting consumer values and empowering people to act on important issues like climate change.

2.2.1. Power to the People

Around the world, a small but growing number of citizens are rising up to challenge institutions, companies, and governments to deliver a more equitable and sustainable society. They are increasingly using social media and other digital technologies to spread the message, elevate important issues, and mobilize people. Civil disobedience movement Extinction Rebellion—a UK-born action group that calls for mass economic disruption using non-violent direct action and civil disobedience to prevent catastrophic climate change—has now spread to more than 35 countries around the world.

Americans took to the streets in 2018. Millions protested against gun violence, gender inequity and the separation of children from their migrant and asylum-seeking parents.

One in five Americans have protested in the streets or participated in political rallies over the last 2 years. Of those, 19% said they had never before joined a protest march or a political gathering.

In one of the biggest movements for women's rights in India, 5 million women lined up across the length of the southern state of Kerala to demand an end to outdated social norms that prevent women of childbearing age from entering places of worship.

In France, thousands of working-class protestors known as the gilets Jaunes (yellow vests) have taken to the streets to protest the newly-introduced green taxon diesel—highlighting the need for a more just energy transition—and call for an increase in the minimum wage.

Employees at multinational firms are increasingly making their voices heard, with Amazon employees protesting the sale of facial recognition software to law enforcement and unsafe work practices.

Meanwhile, over 1000 Google employees signed letters protesting the company's involvement with AI military development for the Pentagon, as well as its decision to aid China's online censorship. "Empowering Action at Home": A study of 30,000 people in 35 countries found that 62% of customers want companies to take a stand on issues such as sustainability, transparency, and fair employment practices."

"A majority of global consumers are concerned about climate change, but only a handful of these feel empowered to take action in their own lives. Global companies, like IKEA, have an important role to play in inspiring and supporting more people to take action." Pia Heidenmark Cook, Chief Sustainability Officer, IKEA Group.

2.2.2. Gen Z Coming of Age

Conceived when the new century rolled over, Gen Z is as of now entering the workforce and will overwhelm recent college grads to turn into the biggest age of purchasers by 2020. While many are still too youthful to even consider voting, Gen Z is now significant influencers, locks in organizations and governments on a scope of social and environmental issues.

Youth turned marching through Main Street for COP24, the UN Climate Change Conference in Poland, and sent a record-breaking message calling for worldwide pioneers to meet the 1.5°C objective as 125,000 postcards spread out on Aletsch ice sheet in Switzerland.

In Australia, a large number of youngsters from in excess of 20 urban communities left their homerooms to fight the Australian government's inaction on environmental change as a major aspect of the Strike 4 Climate Action, roused by 15-year-old Swedish understudy Greta Thunberg.

The understudy drove March for Our Lives saw in excess of a million Americans take to the avenues supporting for more grounded weapon guidelines.

As acts of mass violence proceed over the US, American secondary school understudies are putting pressure on financial specialists, for example, Vanguard, and BlackRock to drop firearm producers from their speculation portfolios.

An ongoing report found that 68% of youngsters matured 14–18 in the UK have taken an interest in volunteering or different types of social activity.

A multi-year-old young lady reached Warriors basketballer Steph Curry on Twitter to inquire why his Under Armor shoes were accessible for young men, and Curry and Under Protective layer helped the issue in under 24 hours.

2.2.3. EMPOWERING ACTION AT HOME

Individuals progressively need organizations to make significant move on environment and social issues. Driving organizations are discovering approaches to empower individuals to make simpler, sustainable, practical changes to their lives.

An investigation of 30,000 individuals in 35 nations found that 62% of clients need organizations to stand firm on issues, for example, sustainability, straightforwardness, and reasonable work rehearses.

Research by IKEA and GlobeScan found that a lion's share of shoppers needs to lessen their carbon outflows, however many are reluctant to pick less advantageous or, on the other hand, progressively costly choices.

Organizations including Patagonia and IKEA are implanting manageable advancement into their plans of action with the objective of engaging residents to lead more sustainable lives.

Unilever backup Ben and Jerry's is using blockchain to engage clients to carbon counterbalance each individual scoop of frozen yogurt.

Worldwide office-sharing organization WeWork has gone sans meat at its 502 areas—with meat never again served at staff occasions and WeWork workers not ready to cost meat dinners—in an offer to diminish carbon discharges.

2.2.4. Future Expectations

Resident drove activism will keep the weight on governments and organizations to address squeezing social and environment issues. Desires for organizations to address issues, for example, environmental change, single-use plastics, and gender equality value will likewise keep on developing. Clients, particularly youth, will progressively move their loyalties to organizations they see to convey social and sustainable incentives to society.

1. **Convey an Incentive to Society:** In 2019, organizations need to reassess the sustainable and social effect of their center products and administrations and move their plans of action towards producing long term an incentive for society on the off chance that they are to stay aware of moving customer desires.
2. **Increment Straightforwardness:** So as to construct trust and reliability in 2019, organizations should grasp progressively extreme types of straightforwardness. Blockchain and web-based social networking will be fundamental apparatuses.
3. **Engage Purchasers:** Driving organizations ought to put resources into building brand control by empowering customers to make manageable way of life changes that are both helpful and cost-aggressive.

2.3. SECURITY THREATS

Exchange wars, cybersecurity breaks, and environmental change undermine worldwide security and financial soundness.

The worldwide network is confronting difficulties on universal exchange, the effects of environmental change and the developing seriousness of digital fighting, which are all affecting advancement on reasonable improvement.

Governments and worldwide organizations are progressively powerless against cybersecurity breaks, debilitating their companies just as resident trust. Exchange pressures undermine a debilitating worldwide economy, while environmental change and different variables heighten clashes in the Middle East, Central America, and Africa and uproot millions.

2.3.1. The Cyber Battleground

From state-supported cyber-attacks, to psychological militant cells, and the developing advancement of solitary programers, the dangers of cyberwarfare are developing. Expanded digitization and mechanization, particularly IoT and distributed computing, make greater open door for cyberattacks. Hacking development keeps on outpacing the security incorporated with existing innovation. Government guidelines fall insufficiently behind.

The World Economic Forum's Global Risks Report 2018 recognized cybersecurity breaks as probably the most serious hazard to mankind. In its Top 10 dangers digital assaults are positioned third as far as Likelihood.

New deep fake innovation permits the production of carefully controlled recordings that can approach flawlessly copy anybody, from heads of state to military commanders.

Malevolent chatbots are getting progressively far reaching. Assaults presently start with fundamental content-based bots, however, could begin to utilize human discourse bots to capture exploited people over the telephone.

The year 2018 saw various prominent digital assaults hit enormous organizations including Facebook, Google+, British Airways, Marriott, and T Mobile. WhatsApp, a mainstream auxiliary of Facebook, was utilized to spread disinformation by Russian programmers in the number one spot up to the 2018 Brazilian political race and may have assumed a job in the appointment of Jair Bolsonaro.

Confronting analysis over the abuse of its foundation during national decisions in Brazil, the US, France, and the UK, Facebook has declared designs to increment advertisement straightforwardness and safeguard against remote resistance in front of the 2019 Lok Sabha surveys in India.

"Countries need to work together to tackle challenges that extend beyond their own borders. Countries should cooperate to reduce trade costs further and resolve disagreements without raising distortionary barriers. Cooperative efforts are also essential for enhancing cybersecurity, tackling corruption, and mitigating and coping with climate change." International Monetary Fund, World Economic Outlook 2018 (Figure 2.3).

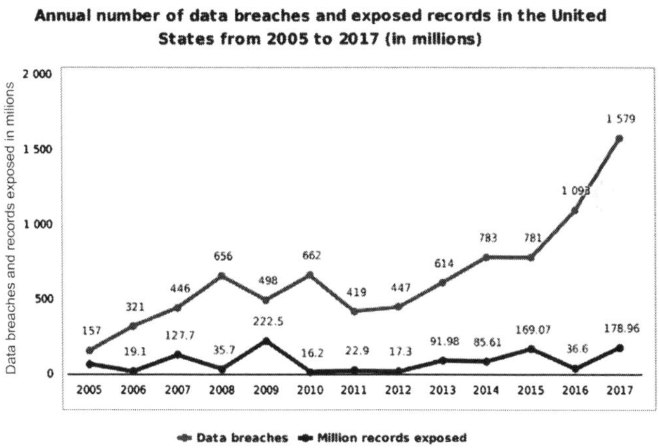

Figure 2.3. Data breaches.

Source: *Identity Theft Resource Center.*

2.3.2. Exchange Tensions Threaten Global Economy

The Trump administration is endeavoring to decrease imports from nations with which the US has an exchange shortage, upsetting exchange arrangements with the EU, Canada, and Mexico, South Korea, Japan, and, above all, China. Progressing pressure between the world's two biggest economies over exchange is expanding the probability of a worldwide financial downturn by 2020.

The breakdown of two-sided exchange talks and the acceleration of duties and other protectionist resistances by the US and China is starting to hurt the two economies.

Exchange pressures could decrease universal development by around 0.5% by 2020, the IMF reports.

The CFO of Chinese telecoms organization Huawei was captured in Canada over potential infringement of US endorses on Iran, shocking China, and confusing exchange arrangements between the world's two biggest economies.

As of composing, the US has made a deal to avoid following up on its ongoing danger to expand taxes on the $200 billion value of Chinese imports from 10% to 25%.

2.3.3. Environmental Change Tops Global Security Threats

Environmental change is progressively perceived as the main worldwide security risk. Atmosphere-related security dangers incorporate effects to fundamental assets, for example, rural yields and drinking water, which can thusly intensify existing clashes, as has happened in Syria and Yemen. Further effects incorporate direct harm to foundation and networks from out of control fires, tempests, and flooding, and consequences for human well-being brought about by ozone harming substances, and related toxins. These effects can dislodge networks, expanding the number of worldwide outcasts and raising geopolitical strains.

Atmosphere-related dangers, for example, dry spell, crop disappointment, typhoons, and rapidly spreading fires, are huge supporters of contention and dislodging of huge quantities of individuals in Syria, Yemen, Kenya, and Sudan.

The most recent National Climate Assessment directed by the US government presumes that environmental change is "exhibiting developing difficulties to human well-being what's more, security, personal satisfaction, and the pace of monetary development" and accordingly presents noteworthy national security dangers. Right now, more than 65 million individuals are uprooted internationally for some reasons counting struggle, starvation, and catastrophic events, which is the biggest number ever recorded by the UN Refugee Agency. The World Bank predicts that over 140 million individuals will be dislodged by environmental change alone by 2050.

2.3.4. Future Expectations

The worldwide network will see much more prominent union of geopolitical and reasonable improvement motivation, with declining financial, physical, and computerized dangers in 2019. Environmental change impacts on worldwide security will turn out to be more conspicuous. The expanding number of cybersecurity breaks and exchange clashes are probably going to compound geopolitical pressures and cost the worldwide network billions of dollars. A potential worldwide financial downturn may slow advance on sustainability in the event that organizations decide to react by decreasing their sustainability spending plans:

1. **Put Resources into Cybersecurity:** The two governments and businesses are neglecting to stay aware of programers. All organizations need to expand interest in cybersecurity, and tech organizations specifically need to attempt to work all the more intimately with governments to assist them with sanctioning guidelines to all the more likely protect the two organizations furthermore, residents.
2. **Draw in Governments on Exchange:** Enormous organizations need to cooperate, and with exchange relationship, to utilize their impact with governments and multilateral companies to endeavor to balance out the present unstable exchange relations between the US and other huge economies, most strikingly China.
3. **Dissect Geopolitical Dangers:** Organizations that dissect geopolitical patterns will have the option to more readily envision, what is more, be readied, for interruption regardless of whether this comes in progressively capricious and entangled ways.

2.4. SAVING ECOSYSTEMS

Energy develops to handle plastic waste as biological systems are confronting phenomenal dangers. Our property and marine environments are confronting phenomenal dangers. Species are vanishing at disturbing rates, land corruption is undermining the prosperity of a large number of individuals, and compounding air contamination is costing a huge number of lives every year, and plastic contamination in seas and ashore is arriving at perilous levels.

China's choice to boycott plastic and e-waste imports has tossed waste and reusing markets into unrest, uncovering the greatness of plastic contamination, and raising the criticalness to lessen and reuse unmistakably more materials.

2.4.1. Biodiversity at Breaking Point

Appraisals of the Earth's biological system present a depressing picture. While mindfulness about biodiversity misfortune is developing, consideration paid by organizations and different companies to the issue stays restricted.

As per the most exhaustive evaluation of worldwide biological system well-being in late decades, biodiversity is declining at a disturbing rate crosswise over a large portion of the characteristic world. Species are vanishing multiple times quicker than their common rate of termination. In its Living Planet Report, WWF finds "detonating human utilization" was the primary purpose for a monstrous drop in worldwide sustainable life populace in later decades. Somewhere in the range of 1970 and 2014, misfortunes in vertebrate species—warm-blooded animals, fish, and birds of land and water, and reptiles—found the middle value of 60%.

Air contamination levels are arriving at basic levels. WHO evaluates that 9 out of 10 individuals inhale air containing significant levels of toxins, and around 7 million individuals bite the dust each year from presentation to contaminated air.

In excess of 75% of land, zones are currently considerably debased, which adversely impacts the prosperity of more than 3.2 billion individuals.

Sustainability specialists accept that the worldwide network has made constrained progress on SDG 14: Life below Water and SDG 15: Life on Land. They are among the sustainable development goals (SDGs) that get minimal consideration from business and different companies.

"Earth is losing biodiversity at a rate seen only during mass extinctions" Living Planet Report, WWF (Figure 2.4).

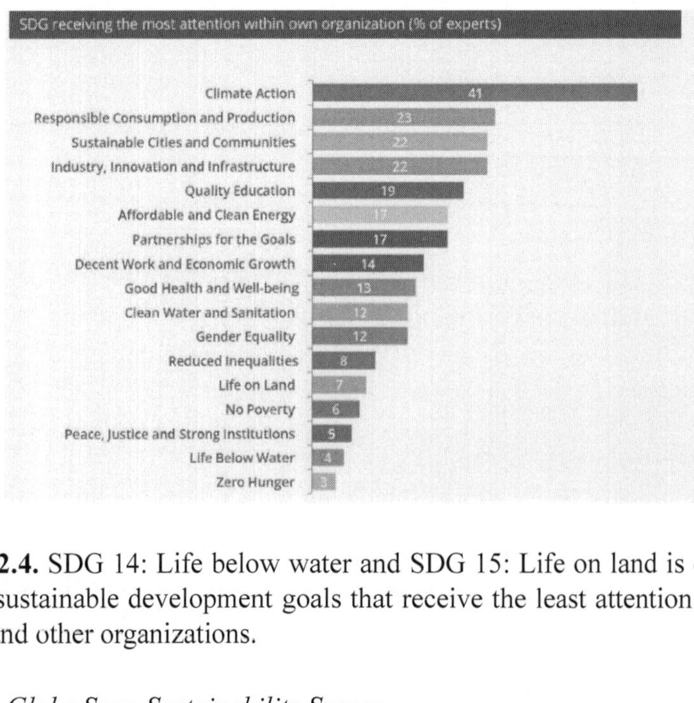

Figure 2.4. SDG 14: Life below water and SDG 15: Life on land is currently among sustainable development goals that receive the least attention by businesses and other organizations.

Source: *Globe Scan-Sustainability Survey.*

2.4.2. Waste and Plastic Hit Headlines

Worldwide mindfulness about plastic contamination and its effect on our biological systems proceeds to develop. A few significant worldwide alliances have been declared to handle the issue. Organizations are encountering developing weight from customers to diminish plastic waste.

Before reporting a boycott in January 2018, China imported more than 66% of the world's plastic waste. Nestlé is working towards plastic waste issue by making an Institute of innovative science research, which will concentrate on improving recyclable, biodegradable, and compostable packaging.The New Plastics Economy Global Commitment unites organizations, government, and common society behind a dream for accomplishing a round economy for plastic. The 290 companies that have marked the responsibility speak to 20% of all plastic packaging delivered all around. UNEP's Global Plastics Platform means to drive cross-fringe joint effort and learning among nations and urban communities.

Marine plastic issues are increasing expanding unmistakable quality in Asia. Course Capital what is more, Ocean Conservancy reported at any rate $150 million of venture capital for waste and reusing advancements that keep plastic waste from entering the sea from Asian nations.

WWF reported a 3-year, $7.5 million No More Plastics in our Ocean activity supported by the Norwegian government to propel a worldwide administration answer for marine plastic contamination (Figure 2.5).

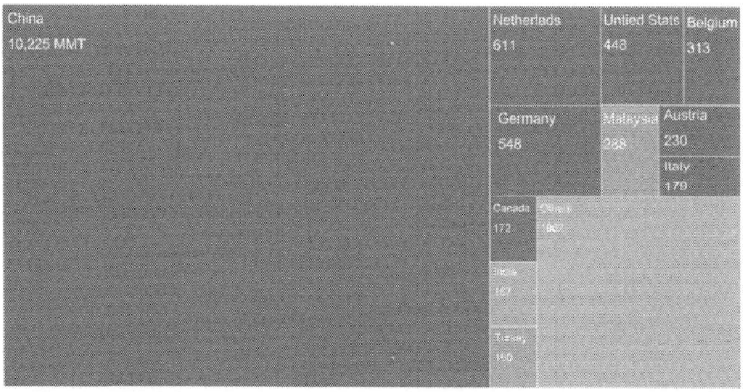

Figure 2.5. Plastic waste imports, millions of metric tons, 2016. For many years, China was the main importer of plastic waste, which changed in 2018 when it announced a ban.

Source: *National Geographic.*

2.4.3. Future Expectations

Worldwide mindfulness about waste and plastic contamination will keep on developing. A number of coordinated efforts have just been reported however a lot more prominent exertion will be required to handle the issue. China's choice to boycott wastes imports will proceed to put pressure on governments and organizations to search for fundamental arrangements on a worldwide scale. While mindfulness about biodiversity misfortune contrasted with other practical improvement issues has been low, a developing number of NGOs are attempting to transform it. Open and private companies the same will confront developing desires to have an increasingly dynamic influence in saving area and marine biological systems.

1. **Address Plastic Waste Over the Whole Value Chain:** Organizations crosswise over numerous ventures—not just the ones legitimately capable for the greater part of plastic waste (nourishment and agribusiness, retail, and so on.) yet additionally those less related with plastic contamination (innovation, pharma, and so forth.)—will confront developing pressure by governments, clients, and different partners to address plastic waste. Organizations need to research their whole value chain to execute arrangements that would diminish waste and plastic contamination.
2. **Biodiversity as a Material Issue:** Not many organizations distinguish biodiversity as a material issue, yet as mindfulness about land and marine environments emergencies develops, organizations will be relied upon to research their effect—and reliance on biodiversity.
3. **Put Resources into Round Arrangements:** Putting resources into round arrangements along the whole value chain gives one of the best pathways for organizations to address waste issues and improve the sustainability of their tasks.

2.5. NEW LEADERSHIP

Urban areas, locales, and businesses keep on sloping up authority as trust in national governments struggles. Worldwide governments are bearing a continuous emergency of trust. Non-state entertainers, for example, city and provincial governments and the business network, are venturing into the authority void and making a move to make a progressively manageable, impartial future.

2.5.1. Doubted Governments

Crosswise over significant European powers, the US, Canada, Russia, Australia, and Latin America, trust in governments stays low. This has been filled by expanding political polarization and deficient reactions to issues, for example, disparity, and environmental change.

Trust in national governments in a lion's share of European nations stays low, counting the UK, Germany, France, Spain, Italy, and Russia.

Latin America likewise has low degrees of trust in government with Brazil, Argentina what is more, Colombia all scoring under 50%.

The US Administration is bearing an immense emergency of trust—the first occasion when that such a huge decrease in trust has happened outside of a monetary downturn or national calamity as indicated by Edelman Trust Barometer.

In China, state-controlled assessments of public sentiment demonstrate high trust in government, yet this information has been raised doubt about by specialists who express that the administration's dictator control has brought about expanding doubt and loss of social capital.

Specialists evaluated national governments as having the least fortunate performance on tending to sustainable advancement out of any worldwide organization.

2.5.2. Urban Communities and Regions Lead

With worldwide pioneers neglecting to make a satisfactory administrative move on a scope of issues—counting atmosphere alleviation and adjustment, sea plastics, waste, and well-being—urban areas, what is more, provincial governments are assuming the job of sustainable advancement pioneers.

In the US, trust in neighborhood governments is at its most elevated since 2008. California leads subnational endeavors to control environmental change, with objectives to move to 100% sans carbon power by 2045 and to become carbon impartial by the same year.

Around 27 worldwide urban communities, including London, New York, Sydney, and Rome, have as of now arrived at top outflows and have effectively diminished their emissions for the most recent 5 years while keeping up powerful monetary development.

San Francisco now occupies 80% of its loss from landfills. It additionally joins New York, London, Dubai, and 20 other worldwide urban areas in having an objective a zero-waste objective. Company for Healthy Cities is another coordinated effort between a worldwide system of urban communities, WHO, and Bloomberg Philanthropies to spare lives by anticipating noncommunicable ailments and wounds.

In excess of 20 worldwide urban communities including London, Los Angeles, Paris, Mexico City, Seoul, and Tokyo have promised to guarantee a significant region of every city is zero emissions by 2030 and to buy 100% zero-discharge transports from 2025 onwards.

Ukrainian urban areas have built up an objective of moving to 100% renewable energy by 2050, in an offer to address environmental change and increment energy autonomy.

2.5.3. Business Leadership Is Increasing

Business is progressively venturing into the void left by worldwide governments, setting aggressive new social and sustainable objectives, and participating in radical straightforwardness endeavors that help to fabricate trust and believability with the two shoppers and workers.

In excess of 500 worldwide organizations are making a move on science-based atmosphere targets. Innovation organizations including Salesforce, Autodesk, Lyft, and Arm have framed the step-up coalition with the objective of using rising advances to lessen ozone-depleting substance emissions overall industry areas.

Driving Japanese insurance agency Sompo Japan Nipponkoa has set SDG targets for each territory of its business, including an objective to create products and administrations identified with fiasco avoidance and alleviation.

Around 150 organizations have focused on 100% sustainable power source through RE100. What is more, 23 multinationals have resolved to zero outflow vehicles through EV100.

Google as of late met its 100% sustainable power source objective, joining Apple and Microsoft.

Illustrious Dutch Shell has declared that it will interface official compensation to its carbon decrease objectives.

"With several governments dialing back from global commitments and reducing environmental protection, we need- and are seeing-the non-state actors step up to the challenge. We need a New Deal for nature and people." Kavita Prakash-Mani, WWF (Figure 2.6).

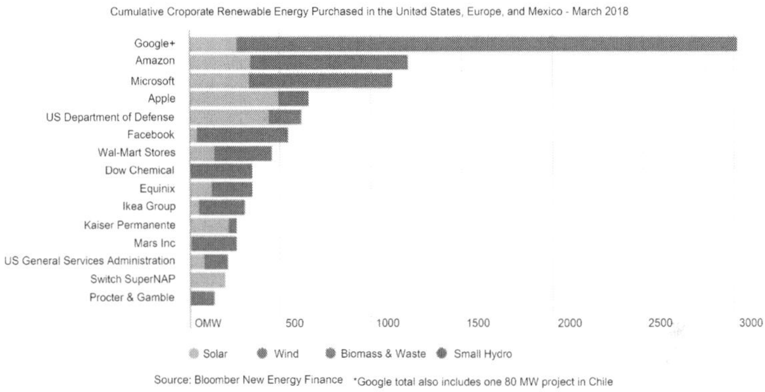

Figure 2.6. Royal Dutch Shell executive remuneration and carbon reduction goals.

Source: *Royal Dutch Shell.*

We hope to see proceeded with low degrees of trust in national governments and fortifying authority and aspiration of urban communities, provincial governments, and organizations. Proceeding with vulnerability in Europe due to Brexit and expanding polarization in the US is probably going to additionally hose trust in the political frameworks.

Buyers will be expanding hoping to organizations to act in agreement to their qualities and all the more effectively advocate on social and environmental issues.

Set intense objectives: Business should keep on inclining up administration and aspiration on conveying social and environmental advantages to society by setting and providing details regarding execution against intense sustainability objectives.

Increment straightforwardness: One of the best approaches to build trust is making information—on everything from decent variety to official compensation and carbon discharges—open and available to the general population.

Chapter 3

Strategic Trends Per Sector

CONTENTS

3.1. FOOD AND AGRICULTURE

"Demand for food poses one of the biggest dangers to our planet. It's the leading cause of deforestation, destroying countless habitats and threatening wildlife to the point of extinction."—Tanya Steele, WWF UK Chief Executive.

There is a critical need to make our nourishment framework unquestionably progressively feasible. Developing populace and related nourishment utilization is fueling biodiversity misfortune on an extraordinary scale, with 40% of the world's once-forested land now cleared for human horticulture and settlements.

Biological systems ashore and in the sea are being crushed by plastic packaging—an enormous level of which originates from nourishment and drink items. Entertainers in the nourishment esteem chain, from cultivators to retailers, are giving expanding consideration to both nourishment furthermore, plastic waste—investigating ways packaging can be decreased without settling item time span of usability or sanitation.

3.1.1. Adjusting Packaging and Food Waste

Plastic packaging is progressively in the media spotlight, with shoppers requesting activity from organizations on single-use plastics. Food industry producers are feeling the strain to diminish both plastic packaging, just as food waste. Research shows that shrewd and economical packaging can help decrease nourishment waste, and a developing number of organizations are putting resources into new innovation arrangements.

The worldwide expense of nourishment waste is assessed to be nearly $1 trillion per year, with up to 25% of private waste emerging from deficient packaging.

While some accept single-utilize plastic packaging has prompted an expansion in the measure of nourishment waste, many contend that without plastic packaging the expense of nourishment waste could rise.

There are a developing number of organizations putting resources into maintainable packaging. Kroger has collaborated with Apeel Sciences that makes a defensive film from rural side-effects and waste, and Florida-based SaltWater Brewery is utilizing a biodegradable and compostable six-pack ring configuration produced using wheat and grain.

UK retailers, Tesco, and Waitrose, have propelled new supportable packaging to expand the time span of usability of avocados and Morrisons are because of preliminary a film packaging arrangement which can stretch out timeframe of realistic usability by dependent upon two to four days.

New businesses in the US handling the test of nourishment waste got over $125 million in funding and private value interest in 2018.

"An issue of packaging is an issue of food waste, and an issue of food waste is an issue of hunger and food availability—we need to find and focus on the balance."—Jackie Suggitt, Director of Business Initiatives, ReFED.

3.1.2. Singling Out the Kids

The pace of corpulence in kids and teenagers has risen ten times comprehensively in the previous 40 a long time, with nourishment advertising being one of the most perceived givers. Kids in created nations keep on being raised in a stoutness advancing condition, encompassed by cheap and influentially showcased fatty nourishment. Youngsters are presented to twice the same number of low-supplement nourishment as sound nourishment advertisements; with examine exhibiting that such presentation impacts affect kids' weight control plans.

WHO has discovered that current strategies and guidelines focused on nourishment advertising to youngsters in many nations are "especially lacking," with kids still uncovered to unsafe business messages advancing nourishments high in fats, salt, and sugar.

Weight specialists are thinking about the case against the nourishment business in the light of developing examination recommending that an ascent in lousy nourishment neuromarketing that could commandeer a youngster's cerebrum.

Of the evaluated £296.6 million spent on nourishment showcasing in the UK every year, just 5% is allotted to leafy foods.

The Peas Please activity is proposing another Veg Ad Fund to guarantee vegetables get comparable degrees of showcasing speculation as marked chocolates, cheap food outlets, and soda pops. The crusade will dispatch in 2019 and has support from significant general store chains.

McDonald's as of late reported goals to consent to stricter wholesome rules and capable advertising, utilizing inventive promoting to help serve more organic product, vegetables, entire grains, lean protein, and water in Happy Meals.

3.1.3. Dietary Diversity

Biodiversity is basic to guaranteeing sound biological systems; nourishment security, and sustenance, be that as it may, nourishment frameworks are a key driver of biodiversity misfortune around the world. In spite of nearly 7,000 crops being consumable, most of the world's worldwide energy admission originates from just three: rice, wheat, and maize. The subsequent monoculture, combined with expanded pressure on agrarian land for domesticated animals cultivating, is fueling biodiversity misfortune on an uncommon scale.

Living Planet Report by WWF recognized human utilization to be behind an uncommon loss of vertebrate species.

Somewhere in the range of 2010 and 2050, the natural impacts of the nourishment framework could increment by 50–90%, coming to past planetary limits if no activity is taken.

Shoppers are progressively mindful of the effect of diet on biodiversity. One out of eight Britons is presently veggie lover or vegetarian and a further 21% guarantee to be flexitarian.

India has for some time been a worldwide pioneer, with roughly 20% of the populace being veggie-lover, yet progress is likewise being made in China, where veggie lover eateries are starting to multiply in significant urban areas, and meat deals are starting to decrease.

Retailers are urging customers to receive progressively manageable eating regimen. Tesco is collaborating with WWF to urge customers to purchase moderate manageable nourishment.

Walmart and Unilever are teaming up with neighborhood governments to stop loss of biodiversity in their sourcing locales.

3.1.4. Feed Behind Our Food

Animal feed is an imperative, yet inconspicuous, contribution to the nourishment business that has noteworthy suggestions for ecological wellbeing and nourishment security. Horticulture is mindful for 14.5% of every single outflows, with feed generation bookkeeping for 45% of this aggregate. In numerous nations domesticated animals generation is quickening deforestation, biodiversity misfortune, and water shortage.

While the utilization of most nourishment waste in feed is illicit in the EU, it is advanced in other portions of the world. In Japan and South Korea, around 40% of nourishment waste is reused as animal feed.

Weight from promotion gatherings and even pig ranchers to relegalize heat-treated swill in the EU is expanding, with explore proposing this would altogether decrease land utilization.

Organizations, for example, Calysta, Protix, Ynsect, and Evonik are putting millions in creative recognizable feed fixings. This incorporates bug-based protein, oil from characteristic marine green growth, feed added substances like amino acids, and protein got from methane-eating microscopic organisms.

Pet nourishment speaks to as much as 30% of all meat utilization in the US, furthermore, there is a developing requirement for maintainable other options. Wild Earth is as of now, the greatest player, making pooch and feline treats from parasite and lab-developed mouse meat (Figure 3.1).

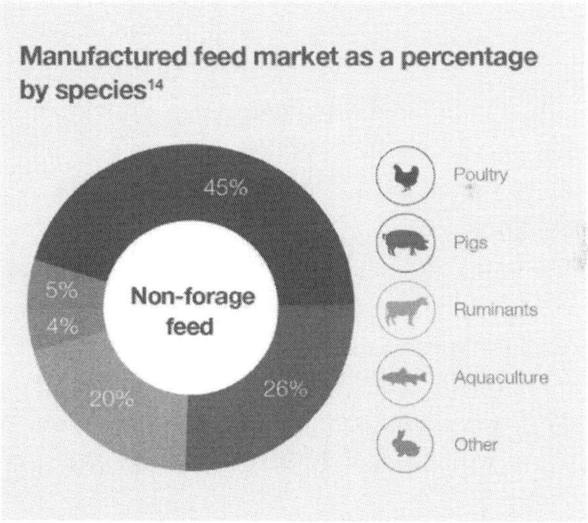

Figure 3.1. Manufactured feed market as percentage of species.

Source: *International Feed industry.*

3.1.5. Future Expectations

Issues identified with waste and packaging will keep on drawing in examination in the coming years, putting pressure on organizations and other key partners to search for fundamental arrangements. Poor industry principles in regards to showcasing of low nourishment, unhealthy nourishments, and refreshments to youngsters will likewise create progressively escalated discussions—with an expanding number of organizations making the willful move to raise industry guidelines. Securing biodiversity, health, and plant-based weight control plans will likewise be a bigger concentration for promoters, business, and customers.

Actualize circular arrangements: Producers to retailers need to grasp round intuition to address current foundational impediments. This methodology looks past setting eager reusing focuses for packaging and contemplates endeavors to upcycle nourishment waste into new items—where waste items from one piece of the framework become contributions to another.

Improve perceivability of concealed issues: The nourishment security banter has to a great extent concentrated on the homestead part and on exchange, with different portions including agri-inputs, handling, coordination, and discount moderately covered up. Inside these regions, sustainability issues, for example, biodiversity misfortune, water shortage, and human rights breaks can regularly go unnoticed. With customers requesting morally sourced and excellent items, nourishment organizations must handle the perplexing test of production network perceivability and should look to the ways that trend-setting innovation, for example, blockchain, can empower this.

Promoter for shrewd approach: Nourishment and refreshment organizations have a significant task to carry out in working with policymakers to catalyze change. For instance: supporting for stricter guidelines in regards to publicizing to kids; affecting the structure of store return plans for plastic assortment; and ensuring new strategies (for example, the US Farm Bill) consolidate activity with respect to the squeezing need to improve soil wellbeing.

3.2. TECHNOLOGY

"In 2019, there will be increasing focus on opportunities to apply technology to help a range of industries drive smarter decisions and resource efficiency, develops circular economy solutions, and drive improvements in supply chain responsibility practices."—Suzanne Fallender, Director, Corporate Responsibility Office, Intel Corporation.

The tech division needs to grasp straightforwardness what's more, city duty to satisfy its latent capacity. Cultural trust in the innovation division is declining—driven by significant information protection ruptures, charge evasion, the utilization of innovation stages by rebel players to undermine vote-based procedures and an absence of sufficient government guidelines what's more, oversight.

However, against this background of doubt, tech organizations have kept on pushing forward with developments that drive financial development and assist humankind with handling squeezing social what's more, ecological difficulties. The area remains at an urgent minute where changes will be important to modify trust and understand the part's maximum capacity to move society toward a progressively reasonable future.

3.2.1. Moral Code under Fire

For long the most confided in part, trust in innovation organizations and their administrations (particularly enormous Internet organizations) has been declining, showing reputational and business dangers for the segment. Innovation organizations are progressively tested by customers and different partners to exhibit the positive social effects of their items and administrations on the networks in which they work. Rising innovations, for example, self-ruling vehicles, blockchain, and AI remain the most inadequately comprehended furthermore, least trusted by people in general.

Trust in web search tools and internet-based life stages has diminished in numerous nations, with the steepest decrease in the US Tech organizations' security rehearses, especially Apple, Google, and Amazon have been the fundamental driver of declining trust. A review directed by Fortune magazine seen Facebook as the least trusted of significant tech organizations with regards to shielding client information.

Edelman's 2018 Trust in Technology report found that rising advancements are the least trusted by the overall population with blockchain trusted by marginally under 50%, self-driving vehicles at 50% and man-made consciousness at 56%.

Around half of US grown-ups might want innovation organizations to be all the more intensely controlled, as per an overview by Pew Research Center. Americans are erasing or changing the manner in which they use Facebook, and a few brands (P&G and Mars) are slicing computerized advertisement spends because of information wellbeing concerns.

3.2.2. Simulated Intelligence for Good

Artificial Intelligence (AI) is set to change businesses over each area and can possibly quicken endeavors to handle the world's greatest cultural and ecological difficulties. The test for tech organizations will be to guarantee innovative work constructs frameworks which have value, security, and morals at their center. Accenture gages that AI could twofold financial development rates in 2035 by changing the idea of work and could expand work profitability by up to 40%.

Studies gage that somewhere in the range of 14 to 54% of US laborers have a high likelihood of seeing their occupations mechanized throughout the following 20 years. The yearly estimation of AI is required to be most elevated in the gadgets, customer bundled products, and retail parts, as indicated by the McKinsey examination. Overall spending on subjective and man-made brainpower frameworks is relied upon to reach $57.6 billion out of 2021.Organizations are taking activities to demonstrate that AI advances can be utilized for good –, for example, Microsoft AI for Earth which intends to make AI-based arrangements over farming, water, biodiversity, and environmental change.

Studies have featured how AI can fortify race and sex inclinations due to innovation being created by groups overwhelmed by white men (Figure 3.2).

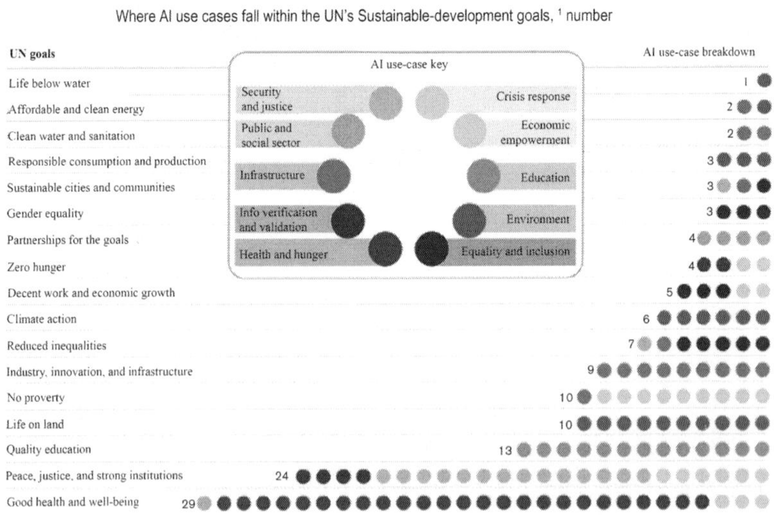

Figure 3.2. AI potential.

Source: *McKinsey Global Institute.*

3.2.3. Battling Waste with Reuse

Before it restricted e-waste imports, China was taking in 70% of the world's electronic waste. Since the boycott, Thailand, Laos, and Cambodia have gotten top goals for e-waste from North America and the EU. Therefore, these Asian nations are currently confronting basic degrees of natural contamination from e-waste reusing. Looked with developing worry about waste and store network impacts, a developing number of innovation organizations are receiving inventive round economy arrangements so as to diminish dependence on limited materials, recoup important minerals and arrive at new clients and markets.

Mac has uncovered its new MacBooks made with 100% reused aluminum. The organization as of late reported an aspiring objective of moving to a shut circle store network where items are constructed utilizing just sustainable assets or reused materials.

Dell has been an industry head-on reusing and has as of late helped discovered the next wave plastics alliance, which expects to make a worldwide system of supply chains intended for gathering and reusing plastics.

An ongoing report found that numerous buyer items produced using reused electronic waste contain harmful synthetics and approaches the EU to characterize e-waste as dangerous.

Innovation organizations are confronting developing reaction for arranged outdated nature of their items, and right to repair bills are being set up for 2019 crosswise over numerous US states as force develops to slow the measure of new equipment available.

3.2.4. Future Expectations

2019 will probably be another unstable year for the tech division. We will see innovation organizations face more noteworthy doubt and investigation from governments, representatives, and more extensive society. An expanding number of organizations will follow in the strides of Amazon, who as of late propelled its Sustainability Data Initiative, as they try to secure their ways of life as great corporate residents. Built up tech organizations will work to reinforce corporate informing with respect to the social and natural estimation of items and administrations, yet this methodology will probably crash and burn with educated partners except if it is supported by significant activity and expanded straightforwardness.

1. **Grasp Straightforwardness:** Absence of straightforwardness is probably the best hindrance to confide in right now confronting the tech segment. From sharing moral structures administering the advancement, what's more, arrangement of new innovations, to tolerating tax assessment in the nations in which they work, tech organizations need to grasp straightforwardness and a sense of metro obligation.
2. **Grasp Development:** Tech organizations have a task to carry out in building up the abilities of developments, yet accomplishing the capability of innovation can't be practiced by this segment alone. Organizations in different segments assume a critical job in interfacing mechanical aptitude with basic human needs. Just through this joint effort can the advantages of innovation be appropriated as broadly and as equally as could be expected under the circumstances.
3. **Comprehend Your Lifecycle Impacts:** The full lifecycle of numerous innovation applications and items is yet to be comprehended. Organizations must contribute to comprehend the impacts of advances – from advancement through to application. Just by doing so can these effects begin to be tended to.

3.2.5. Healthcare and Pharma

"Society can spend only so much money on healthcare, so we have to spend it wisely. It's important that we spend it on things that are actually creating value and having an impact."—Kenneth Frazier, CEO, Merck & Co. From air contamination, to antimicrobial resistance, the soundness of people, animals, and the biosphere are inseparably connected.

The human services division faces concurrent difficulties and openings – from the dangers of antimicrobial resistance and atmosphere empowered pandemics, to the progressing customer-driven move to health and all-encompassing disease avoidance. Like never before, nourishment makers, retailers, pharmaceutical organizations and approach producers are being compelled to cooperate to discover answers for interconnected worldwide wellbeing challenges.

3.2.6. Lopsided Access

While financial and innovative advances are extending social insurance, it is spreading at a lopsided rate far and wide. Pharmaceutical and human services administrations organizations have the opportunity to help social insurance extension through joint efforts, development, promotion, and the mix of innovation into their existing plans of action to help United Health Care (UHC). Be that as it may, the industry likewise faces dangers of more tightly guidelines, tested development, and needs to discover its way in a world understanding the intensity of anticipation and progressively all-encompassing consideration.

China has stretched out essential wellbeing inclusion to in excess of 90% of the populace. The quantity of individuals ready to get key wellbeing administrations including vaccination, family arranging, and bed nets has expanded in the 21st century. However, over a portion of the total populace still can't acquire basic human services, regularly pushed into destitution because of paying for social insurance costs.

The biopharmaceutical business is participating in more multi-sectoral associations to help the development of UHC around the globe. For example, cell phones and video gushing administrations are as of now being utilized for remote specialist discussions furthermore, remedies.

The medicinal services segment is viewed as the area with the potential most noteworthy generally speaking effect on the achievement of the sustainable development goals (SDGs).

The ascent of constant diseases and a maturing populace will keep on moving human services organizations and governments towards more prominent interest in preventive medication, wellbeing, and an entire wellbeing approach (Figure 3.3).

Figure 3.3. Mobilizing capital will be one of the key success factors.

Source: *WHO.*

3.2.7. Sound Biosphere, Healthy Humans

From biodiversity to air contamination and environmental change to malady transmission and the development of antimicrobial opposition, our physical condition, imparted to animals, is inseparably connected to human wellbeing and the other way around. Biodiversity misfortune and environment harm—by the two people and a changing atmosphere—assumes a significant job in the spread of irresistible ailments and pandemics. As of late episodes of SARS, Ebola, flu, and intestinal sickness have been credited to human effects on biodiversity, untamed life exchange, or unsustainable land use.

The conservation of biodiversity is additionally essentially connected to sub-atomic decent variety and fruitful medication improvement. The mass annihilation of plant and creature species will have untold negative effects on human wellbeing.

The One Health idea perceives that the wellbeing of individuals is associated with the wellbeing of animals and the earth and has been progressively developing in conspicuousness among policymakers, industry, and different partners.

The financial estimation of products and ventures, including direct medical advantages, given by environments is evaluated at $33 trillion every year.

WHO evaluates that all-around in excess of 91% of the total populace are presented to air quality levels that surpass safe breaking points.

Because of expanding utilization of anti-microbials for people and animals and untrustworthy rehearses, anti-microbial resistance is turning into an undeniably earnest issue. Levels of medication safe contaminations are anticipated to cost the world $100 trillion in lost yield between now and 2050, which is more than the current worldwide economy.

Most of all anti-infection agents delivered are given to domesticated animals—about a portion of all anti-infection agents in the UK, 66% in the EU, and 70% in the US.

The US Food and Drug Administration has endorsed just nine anti-infection agents in the decade ago, and pharmaceutical organizations including Novartis and Sanofi have relentlessly stripped from their anti-toxins research to organize the advancement of progressively productive medications for incessant sicknesses.

3.2.8. Pandemic: Vigilance or Preparedness?

The worldwide network isn't doing what's needed to get ready for the following pandemic—with nations more powerless than any other time in recent memory because of changing populace socioeconomics, globalization, anti-toxin resistance, and environmental change. One hundred years on from the deadliest pandemic ever, Spanish influenza, gages have indicated that if a comparative occasion was to happen today, the loss of life could be as high as 147 million individuals around the world.

The global pharmaceutical market merits an expected $1 trillion; however, antibodies speak to just 3%. Vulnerability about when and where scourges will develop implies there is minimal money-related motivator for pharmaceutical organizations to put up genuinely necessary antibodies for sale to the public.

The world at present gives little to pandemic readiness, with Bill Gates cautioning it is the one zone where the world isn't gaining enough ground.

The US Center for Disease Control and Prevention has reported it will scale back its pestilence counteractive action exercises.

The UK as of late reported its first Vaccine Manufacturing Innovation Center to empower the fast advancement of prescriptions in case of the UK or worldwide plague.

Illness observation stays one of the most useful assets to help foresee, watch also, limit the damage brought about by flare-ups and expands information about what prompts pandemic episodes.

3.2.9. Future Expectations

Biopharmaceutical organizations will keep on concentrating on wellbeing advancement and aversion through advancements in item and administration advances which empower progressively customized, all-encompassing consideration. One Health will increase further noticeable quality, with various divisions, businesses, and partners imparting and cooperating to accomplish better general wellbeing results. Framework-wide ways to deal with handle anti-infection opposition will likewise develop in reach and significance in 2019, with more noteworthy joint effort between domesticated animals ranchers, nourishment makers, nourishment retailers, pharmaceutical organizations what's more, approach producers at neighborhood, territorial, national, and worldwide levels.

1. **Bolster Universal Health Coverage Endeavors:** Innovative work for future medications will stay critical for biopharmaceutical organizations and remain the biggest commitment they can make to UHC—through new medications as well as antibodies and other avoidance related administrations. All organizations can ensure the advantages to their workers and all through their worth chains get us closer to UHC.
2. **Go About as One Health:** The Interagency Coordination Group on AMR met by the UN will share suggestions in 2019, which will control governments and industry on the bunch issues identified with antimicrobial resistance (AMR), including devices like guideline. Ahead of time of that, life sciences organizations ought to think about joining the AMR Industry Alliance.
3. **Backer for Pandemic Readiness:** Governments are integral to planning for the following pandemic, yet business can likewise contribute arrangements including by supporting for more prominent impetuses required for interest in immunizations and associating patients and care suppliers with general wellbeing laborers through versatile media communications to identify and act against contamination episodes.

3.3. ENERGY AND UTILITIES

The energy segment has arrived at a point of change. Jolt is picking up force: from decentralized sustainable power source to electric vehicles (EVs), the upset has started.

The lines between oil and gas organizations and electric utilities are starting to obscure as conventional non-renewable energy source organizations put resources into the low-carbon change. Urban areas are on the forefront of progress—driving on savvy lattices, energy stockpiling, and EV foundation and digitized energy and carbon exchanges. Difficulties in regards to issues like foundation financing and fair access to reasonable clean energy stay focal.

3.3.1. Urban Energy Revolution

Urban areas are at the main edge of low-carbon developments and endeavors to turn away worldwide warming. Huge information and IoT keep on offering energy productivity gains for structures and transportation. Electric and self-sufficient vehicle innovation is prompting progresses in matrix stockpiling and decrease in emissions. Energy change is being demonstrated in urban areas, with exercises for locales and countries. Energy organizations will become accomplice at the city level to progress more brilliant, cleaner energy.

Worldwide spending on keen urban areas innovation is relied upon to practically twofold from $80 billion every year in 2018 to $158 billion out of 2021.

Chairmen have vowed that new structures in 19 urban communities, including London, Los Angeles, New York City, Tokyo, Paris, and Sydney, will have zero discharges by 2030, with existing structures getting zero by 2050.

Brilliant lattice advances could help cut ozone-depleting substance emissions by 3.9% by 2030.

Organizations including California utilities Pacific Gas and Electric (PG&E) and Southern California Edison are starting to address a "simply progress" – the evenhanded change to sustainable power sources and EVs.

EV possession is relied upon to arrive at 125 million by 2030, prodded by approaches that support drivers, armadas, and regions to buy zero discharges vehicles (Figure 3.4).

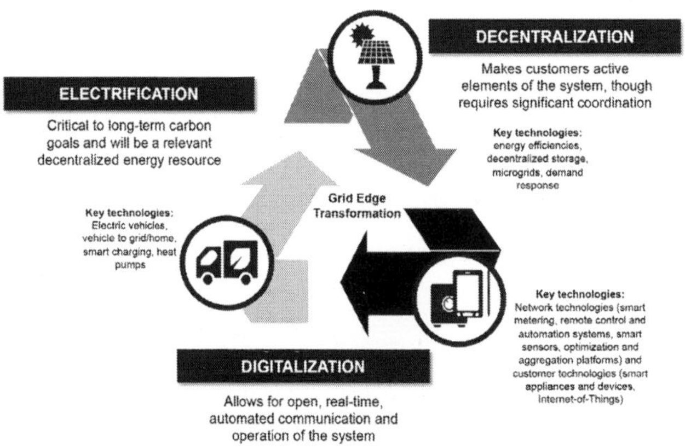

Figure 3.4. Electrification, decentralization, and digitalization.

Source: *World Economic Forum.*

3.3.2. Digitized and Decentralized Energy Trading

Jolt won't occur rapidly, yet its rising currently appears to be inescapable. Developing advances are constraining oil and gas organizations to change their plans of action to stay focused. Utilities will keep on moving ceaselessly from coal to renewables. These changes will require progressing and profound commitment with external partners, for example, financial specialists, government, and nearby networks.

Statoil (presently Equinor) and DONG energy (presently Orsted) have both experienced ongoing name changes that mirror their days of work away from petroleum derivatives and developing interest in sustainable power source.

Shell has been quickly putting resources into the power and EV space, with various acquisitions in the course of the most recent two years. The organization has focused on burning through $1–2 billion every year until 2020 on low carbon arrangements.

French energy mammoth Total is planning to turn into an aggressive gas and electric supplier in Europe with its takeover of power retailer Direct Energy and overwhelming interest in sustainable power source and gaseous petrol.

Significant financial specialists, for example, BlackRock and State Street are starting to put open pressure on organizations to evaluate atmosphere dangers.

For electric utilities to stay aggressive, administrative advancement and change, such as rate change and Performance-based Regulation (which give a structure to interface objectives, targets, and measures to utility execution or official remuneration) will be fundamental.

Charge won't occur rapidly, yet its climb presently appears to be unavoidable. Developing innovations are driving oil and gas organizations to change their plans of action to stay aggressive.

Tech new companies, utilities, and governments are exploring different avenues regarding blockchain innovation to reform keen framework the executives and encourage shared energy exchanging.

Blockchain can empower little makers of energy to give Renewable Energy Credits (RECs) that would then be able to be followed and offered to organizations hoping to diminish their carbon impression. Blockchain empowered exchanging pilots are right now in progress in Thailand, Singapore, South Korea, Europe, the United States, Canada, and Australia.

The innovation will keep on being applied as our energy frameworks move to a more disseminated model. A developing number of battery organizations, including Californian battery new companies Sunverge and Stem, Panasonic, and German energy organization Sonnen bunch are utilizing blockchain to empower virtual distributed energy sharing systems that use home batteries and EVs to balance out lattice energy utilization.

Japan's TAKE Energy Corporation is offering clients a sun-based and capacity bundle which will enable distributed power deals through blockchain. The nation's second-biggest energy organization, Kepco, is sticking to this same pattern.

SP Group, the power lattice administrator in Singapore, is permitting little scale sun-based and wind tasks to issue blockchain-produced RECs.

In the UK, a consortium of energy organizations is supporting the advancement of a blockchain-empowered adaptable exchanging stage for energy conveyance.

Ben and Jerry's is utilizing blockchain innovation to break carbon credits—that balance GHG discharges of an organization's tasks—into small-scale exchanges that empower customers to purchase a carbon credit for each scoop of dessert bought.

3.4. FINANCIAL SERVICES

"CEOs will see in the tone of our questions that we are geared towards long-term performance—both from a shareholder perspective, but also from the perspectives of their stakeholder needs and their organizational resilience."—Matt Christensen, Global Head of Responsible Investment at AXA IM.

The money-related administrations area is at last paying attention to ESG also, not thinking back. Expanding consciousness of natural, social, and administration (ESG) issues, joined with the money part's developing comprehension of the effect of ESG on corporate execution, is driving banks, resource administrators and financial specialists to incorporate sustainability information into basic leadership at extraordinary levels.

ESG information has developed to where it has been grasped by the fund area as a key method to recognize the organizations situated to succeed, and those that may fail to meet expectations or fizzle. A larger part of ESG records outflanked their non-ESG partners in 2018. Feasible, mindful, and sway contributing resources under the executives additionally rose to $12 trillion in the US in 2018, up 38% from $8.7 trillion of every 2016. In 2019, expanding coordinated effort over the fund part will keep driving activity on themes like comprehensive free enterprise, environmental change, firearm viciousness, and assorted variety.

3.4.1. New Devices, Measurements, Alliances

From expanded interest in SDG-adjusted activities to new partnerships and alliances, monetary administrations organizations are awakening to the opportunity's introduced by a progressively practical economy. This year will probably observe more prominent investigation with respect to estimation of ESG and SDG-centered fund items. Elevated Level Expert Group on Sustainable Finance set up by the EU has distributed its proposals for a money-related framework that supports feasible ventures. In light of these proposals, the Commission is currently concluding a multi-year procedure on economical funds in the EU. The Embankment Project for Inclusive Capitalism (EPIC) has united CEOs from more than 30 organizations, resource administrators (like BlackRock, Fidelity, Vanguard, and State Street) and resource proprietors to recognize and make new measurements to quantify and show long term an incentive to money related markets. UNEP FI and 28 banks propelled the Principles for Responsible Banking to characterize the financial business' job and duties in molding a manageable future. A dominant part of ESG lists outflanked their non-ESG partners in 2018 as indicated by information from MSCI. Specialists anticipate that ESG records will keep on outflank a greater part of non-ESG during the worldwide financial downturn gage for 2019–2020.

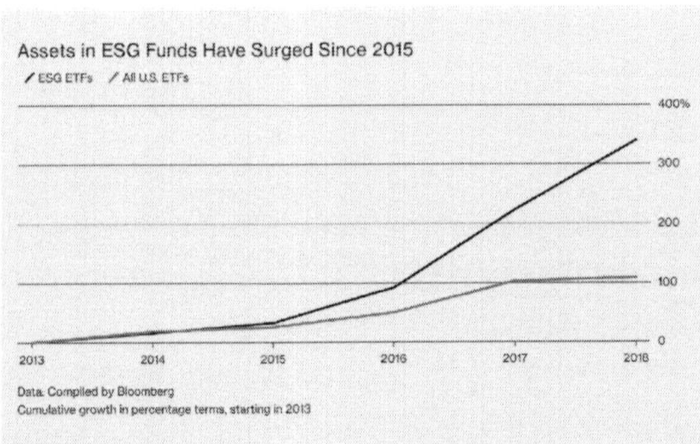

Figure 3.5. Climate risk and disclosure.

Source: *Bloomberg.*

New items and instruments proliferate from Just Capital and Goldman Sach's ETF and Blackrock's ESG ETFs to the World Benchmarking Alliance SDG benchmarking; be that as it may, the effect of new venture items specifically is not yet clear (Figure 3.5).

3.4.2. Atmosphere Risk and Exposure

Driving banks and financial specialists are progressively incorporating atmosphere opportunity in their activities furthermore, are progressing from estimation to the executives.

Banks and financial specialists are progressively working together to create measurements, draw in with organizations and request more prominent government activity on atmosphere.

UNEP finance initiative and 16 of the world's driving banks met up to pilot usage of proposals by the taskforce on climate-related exposures (TCFD) and create situations, models, and measurements to empower evaluation and revelation of atmosphere-related dangers and openings.

An ongoing report on organizations' readiness for TCFD proposals found that in the US, just 64% of money-related firms have board-level oversight of environmental change, contrasted with all organizations in the UK and 82% in Canada.

As it were, 50% of organizations' environmental change opportunity administration systems expand further than six years out.

Around 415 financial specialists with a joined $32 trillion in resources have requested government's increment activity to handle environmental change, marking an explanation that asks governments to fortify their nationally determined contributions (NDCs) to meet the objectives of the Paris agreement.

The five-year Climate Action 100+ activity, presently supported by 310 financial specialists with more than $32bn in resources under administration, drives signatories to draw in with fundamentally significant ozone harming substance producers and organizations approaching them to improve administration on environmental change, control emissions and fortify climate-related budgetary exposures.

Portfolio decarbonization is getting a move on as increasingly institutional financial specialists seek after methodologies to dispense with stocks with high carbon risks.

3.4.3. Rising Shareholder Activism for Sustainability

Driven by more prominent attention to ESG dangers and openings, also rising desires from society and a more youthful age of financial specialists, resource chiefs, and banks are feeling the warmth and making more noteworthy moves on ESG issues. Prominent points like weapon brutality, assorted variety, environmental change, and narcotics are seeing the most activity among banks and speculation firms, driven by investor activism and progressively modern ESG risk examination. Resource directors are currently cooperating to support better rehearses among portfolio organizations on issues like sexual orientation assorted variety.

Goldman Sachs inquire about found that Twitter posts on ESG account themes have risen 19x since 2010. For the most part determined by exchanges identified with environmental change, venture-related terms (ESG, feasible contributing, sway contributing, and so forth.)

Florida Parkland secondary school shooting lobbyist David Hogg made a generally plugged call to blacklist BlackRock and Vanguard prior to 2018 because of each organization's interests in firearm makers and retailers. While the blacklist was ineffective, BlackRock, and state street both vowed to draw in firearm makers in discussions on expanding firearm security. BlackRock additionally propelled two new firearm free ETF files and bolstered lobbyist investor proposition requiring firearm security exposure, more – 33x in 2017 from 2010 levels.

As you sow and CODEPINK discharged Weapon Free Funds, another device from to assist financial specialists with evaluating their record and shared reserve ventures for property in military temporary workers and weapon producers and retailers.

Further reacting to wild weapon savagery in the US in 2018, the CEO of speculation firm Calvert Research and Management, John Streuer, effectively constrained Kroger to quit selling guns.

Twenty-seven organizations (£10.5 trillion resources under administration) have now marked an announcement of purpose, composed by the 30% Club, to advance more ladies to the senior administration and sheets of the British organizations where they contribute.

BlackRock, state street, and vanguard are increasing weight on organizations to increment assorted variety and are starting to foundationally cast a ballot against male-just sheets.

Barclays set another open arrangement expressing it won't finance extends in World Heritage destinations or Ramsar Wetlands.

This year will bring activity, commitment, and results from solid alliances; for example, EPIC, the Principles for Responsible Banking, and the US Alliance for Sustainable Money—that framed in 2018. Budgetary administrations organizations that are not part of these collisions are probably going to be feeling the squeeze to join these organizations.

Banks will step-by-step start actualizing TCFD as they figure out how to survey and unveil atmosphere opportunity, while resource supervisors, financial specialists, and banks will keep on connect with portfolio organizations on need subjects like atmosphere and sexual orientation.

We moreover expect a further deluge of ESG items and more prominent investigation with respect to the effects of those items.

1. **Work with Peers:** It is basic for money-related administrations to work and stand together to send an assembled sign to governments that ESG issues are basic to long term productivity also, budgetary achievement. Financial specialists and portfolio directors must beginning inquiring vital ESG inquiries during organization profit calls and roadshows.
2. **Know Where You Stand:** With developing examination on corporate activities, banks, resource supervisors and speculators must be sure about their qualities and the moves they are making to genuinely epitomize their qualities.
3. **Put Resources into ESG Examination:** From human cash flow to AI and enormous information, having the aptitude and capacity to break down and assess ESG impacts, including atmosphere risk and opportunity, will turn into an upper hand for banks and resources chiefs.

Chapter 4

Strategic Macrotrends and Disruptions Shaping 2020–2030

CONTENTS

In 2010, the World Business Council for Sustainable Development (WBCSD) delivered Vision 2050, a milestone piece of work that spread out a pathway to a world in which nine billion individuals can live well, inside planetary limits, by mid-century. In 2019, WBCSD chose to return to its Vision 2050 work – 10 years on, there has not been as much advancement made along the Vision 2050 pathway as required. WBCSD is cooperating with 40 part organizations to refresh the pathway to mirror a portion of the incredible changes that have unfurled, to align the pathway with the Sustainable Development Goals (SDGs), and to focus on the basic moves that business can make to open the advancement needed for the sorts for changes that our Vision 2050 requests. From the second we chose to refresh Vision 2050, we realized we expected to consider what the following 10 years may toss at business. Not simply as far as sustainability challenges: we needed to research what the world would resemble, and consider what that would mean for business' capacity to work effectively (so they can likewise work economically). Our aggregate capacity to follow through on Vision 2050 (9+ billion individuals living great, inside planetary limits) is subject to our capacity to comprehend and explore a powerful working climate. This implies contemplating every one of the pressing factors that shape the world we live in, and that business works in, from socioeconomics and financial aspects, to innovation and legislative issues. WBCSD cooperated with Volans to research the world that lies in front of us.

The WBCSD research reports offer the proof behind our endeavor here to sum up the macrotrends and potential disturbances liable to shape that working climate throughout the decade ahead. This issue brief, and the exploration behind it, is anything but a bunch of gages, expectations or situations. We are making an effort not to put a specific twist – positive or negative – on the investigation. The fact is to take an unmistakable perspective on what the 2020s may have coming up, with the goal that we can foster more successful systems for how to react and gain ground on Vision 2050. We will require procedures that bridle the energy made by patterns that can go about as tailwinds, and we will require systems that are versatile despite unavoidable headwinds. One such headwind is the COVID-19 pandemic.

Very much like most different conjectures of ongoing years, we had distinguished a pandemic as something that the world would be unfit to manage were it to happen, also something that was quite liable to happen. But, we also wind up staggered by the appearance of the COVID-19 worldwide general wellbeing emergency in the primary long stretches of the decade. It is intensely exhibiting the significant, wide-running – and, usually, durable – outcomes that such disturbances can have. Coronavirus has set off numerous troublesome stuns and sped up large numbers of the macrotrends that we had recognized. It has made certain things more probable and others more uncertain. With both the general wellbeing emergency and the connected financial disturbance actually unfurling, there stays a significant degree of vulnerability about what the full implications of COVID-19 will be for the decade ahead. In any case, the macrotrends and disturbances canvassed in this synopsis have not disappeared. As a rule, COVID-19 may serve simply to speed up or strengthen them. It is hence fundamental that we keep on thinking about the master plan simultaneously as arranging the reactions and inevitable recuperation from the current emergency. WBCSD provides a different research paper that glances in more prominent profundity at the ramifications of the COVID-19 pandemic, both as far as the macrotrends and disturbances spread out in this book and all the more comprehensively as to exercises gained from past recuperations and subsequently how business ought to react to this emergency.

4.1. MACROTRENDS

4.1.1. Demographics

The worldwide populace is developing, maturing, and urbanizing. By 2030, two-thirds of us will live in urban areas – and a developing number, especially in Africa and Asia, in megacities (however, megacities are relied upon to represent under 10% of the absolute metropolitan populace). Movement – both inside and between nations – is likewise expanding.

1. **Generational Handover: from Baby Boomers to Millennials and Gen Z:** Around the world, those brought into the world after 1980 now dwarf those conceived before. A generational handover of political, social, and financial force is as of now in progress and will proceed all through the 2020s. Progressively, pressures between the various ages are probably going to rise to the surface. These mirror the distinctive developmental encounters of various companions. For instance, the individuals who grew up around 2007–2008 will in general be significantly more doubtful of unregulated economy private enterprise than their archetypes who grew up during the Cold War. The nations with the biggest Millennial companions are all in Asia, the Middle East and Africa:

India alone has 385 million millennials. Conversely, the nations with the biggest baby boomer associates are in Europe, North America and Oceania: by 2030, generally 30% of the number of inhabitants in Europe will be more than 60 years old.

2. **Population Growth in Asia and Africa:** The populaces of numerous African and Asian nations are anticipated to keep rising quicker than the worldwide normal during the 2020s, adding to a continuous shift of international and monetary force toward these landmasses – and, maybe particularly, the developing number of megacities they contain. This will likewise put extra strain on regular assets, prominently water: four of the five most weak focal points for potential "water wars" are in Africa or Asia. The blend of rising flourishing and the rising recurrence and seriousness of environmental debacles is probably going to likewise make the quickly developing populaces of Asia and Africa altogether more versatile. Paces of relocation both inside and between nations are set to rise consistently. Thus, this is probably going to significantly affect legislative issues – both in nations that see undeniable degrees of displacement and in those that see significant degrees of migration.

4.1.2. Environment

As we enter the 2020s, human culture is as of now dealing with numerous planetary limits. Our monetary, social, political, and wellbeing frameworks all have an undeniable degree of interdependency with the climate. There is proof to propose that the blend of deforestation, biodiversity misfortune and environmental change add to an expanded danger of zoonotic pandemics. More slow movement natural emergencies, for example, soil corruption and pollinator misfortune, are sabotaging biological system administrations, diminishing the financial efficiency of key areas, like horticulture. As these different, interlinked emergencies extend, so the political and social craving for change develops. Public mindfulness and worry about sea plastics and environmental change flooded in the last part of the 2010s. Over the course of the decade ahead, we can hope to see more citizens and shoppers focusing on natural issues – especially where there is a solid, direct connection to their own wellbeing, similarly as with air quality.

1. **Worsening Climate Impacts:** As the planet keeps on warming, outrageous climate events will turn out to be more continuous

and more extreme. This will cause enduring and relocation. It will likewise force monetary expenses – harming property, subverting jobs and decreasing the efficiency of both land and work, with those in lower-income nations liable to endure lopsidedly. The probability of contention in districts that are antagonistically affected by environmental change will increment. Given this consistent drumbeat of awful news, tension on governments and organizations to convey significant environmental activity is sure to develop. Thusly, this will build the size of change dangers (and openings) confronting a few enterprises, as governments behind schedule receive more grounded environment arrangements. Furthermore, it's not just green legislators who will procure a political profit: so too will patriot strongmen who flourish with the sort of dread and precariousness that the environment emergency produces.

2. **Local Pollution, Degradation and Scarcity Create Impetus for Innovation**: In spite of the fact that environmental change will without a doubt be the greatest natural story of the decade, other, more limited, ecological difficulties will likewise have critical ramifications for both business and society. Soil and land debasement will substantially affect horticulture in numerous districts. Air quality will be worrying in numerous urban communities – particularly the quickly developing megacities of Asia and Africa – with extreme ramifications for general wellbeing. 66% of the total populace could be living in water-scarcity nations by 2025. Like environment, these different biological difficulties will cause enduring, removal, precariousness, and financial expenses. In any case, they ought to, without a doubt should, likewise go about as an impetus for development – to accomplish more with less – and fuel requests on governments and organizations to oversee characteristic assets all the more capably.

4.1.3. Economics

COVID-19 has transformed the short-term economic outlook, but the longer-term trajectory of the global economy remains deeply uncertain. Given the weaknesses the global economy was carrying before COVID-19 hit (for instance, under-investment, high debt and inequality, slow productivity growth, stranded asset risk), the opportunities of a swift recovery are slim.

But the crisis also creates an opportunity for a political reset that could unlock a wave of sustainable and inclusive growth if policymakers rise to the challenge.

Coronavirus has changed the momentary economic viewpoint, yet the more drawn out term direction of the worldwide economy remains profoundly unsure. Given the shortcomings the worldwide economy was conveying before COVID-19 hit (for example, under-venture, high obligation and disparity, moderate efficiency development, abandoned resource risk), the odds of a quick recuperation are thin. In any case, the emergency additionally sets out a freedom for a political reset that could open a rush of manageable and comprehensive development if policymakers meet people's high expectations.

1. **Transient Crisis; Long-Term Slowdown**: The COVID-19 pandemic, joined with an oil value battle among Russia and Saudi Arabia has set off what appears to be the most noticeably awful economic crisis since the Great Depression. Estimates from March 2020 recommend that world GDP may fall by 4% or more this year – fundamentally more than the last worldwide downturn in 2009. Even before the pandemic hit, worldwide development was easing back and obligation levels were high. A few long term factors, like low usefulness, high disparity and the danger of abandoned resources, made a log jam during the 2020s almost certain. Governments, organizations, and families are on the whole prone to rise up out of the pandemic with seriously debilitated accounting reports and expanded obligations, which could imply that there is a long monetary headache from COVID-19. The pandemic has additionally changed the political condition in numerous nations. Enormous monetary upgrade bundles are presently on the table in each country that can manage the cost of them. In the event that all around focused, state intercession to launch monetary recuperation could trigger another flood of maintainable development as speculation is directed towards decarbonization and other long term cultural objectives. In any case, it could likewise trigger a delayed time of something likened to 1970s-style stagflation. Also, there is a danger that pieces of the creating scene get abandoned, in light of the fact that they are essentially unfit to rescue themselves from the financial emergency.

2. **Pinnacle Globalization and the Rise of Asia**: The worldwide economy's focal point of gravity is moving conclusively towards Asia – and in a roundabout way to nations and districts that Asia (especially China) favors. A lot of worldwide GDP is figure to surpass half right on time during the 2020s and keep on ascending consistently. Right on time during the 2020s, Asia will likewise get home to half of the world's working class. With this comes a critical change in the locus of worldwide demand. Trade pressures will probably stay a component of the international scene all through the 2020s, prodding fracture, a shortening of supply chains and a reestablished center around public independence – may be sped up by the effect of COVID-19. Asset patriotism and rivalry between states for control of crucial crude materials are probably going to turn into an inexorably significant factor in global relations.

4.1.4. Technology

Coronavirus has sped up – and will keep on speeding up – the organization of a wide scope of existing advancements. Web-based business, distant working, internet learning and telemedicine have all gotten a lift that will just halfway disseminate after the emergency passes. The competition to foster an immunization is supercharging mechanical development in the drugs area. Robotization of creation and dissemination measures is speeding up as a method of limiting the spread of the infection temporarily – and to make supply binds stronger to the sort of stun a pandemic makes in the more extended term (however, amusingly, this may build weakness to various types of dangers, for example, cyberattacks). In the meantime, key advancements in various regions – from biotech to environmentally friendly power – are creating along remarkable pathways that could prompt financial tipping focuses during the 2020s. An essential inquiry is the way evenhandedly the additions of mechanical advancement will be shared. Numerous computerized advances made by developed nations brings home all the glory elements, which, without countervailing intercessions from government, will in general increment both market focus and disparity. There are a few signals that administrations may venture upon this issue during the 2020s: the EU's way to deal with antitrust requirement and the OECD/G20's work on corruption aversion are promising in such manner, however considerably more will be required if innovative advancement is to fuel comprehensive development as opposed to worsen disparities.

1. **Mechanization Impacts Every Industry and Country:** The spread of mechanization in each industry – from assembling to funding – will speed up, driven by the development of a wide scope of innovations like man-made brainpower, mechanical technology, and 3D printing. These can possibly empower more brilliant and more reasonable utilization of assets – and to fuel future development. Computerization will likewise cause disturbance for some specialists and put further strain on the connection among work and monetary security in numerous spots. One tradition of COVID-19 might be a reinforcing of social security nets, which would help alleviate the effect of robotization on specialists. However, assuming, then again, COVID-19 attendants in another period of starkness, there is a high danger that robotization will prompt rising disparity inside nations, filling outrage and disappointment, and fanning the flames of populism. Customary reskilling will turn into a prerequisite for most. Supply chains, as well, will be reshaped – and, as a rule, abbreviated – as admittance to leading-edge advancements turns out to be more basic for both assembling and administrations than admittance to a modest, talented labor force.
2. **Datafication: Smarter, More Efficient and More Surveilled:** For better or worse, business, money, and government will all turn out to be substantially more data-driven. This should empower enormous asset and work usefulness gains across enterprises – especially in regions like assembling, food creation and co-ordinations – that can possibly make riches and lessen natural effect. The money area will progressively saddle the influence of Big Data and AI to evaluate possible advances and speculations: if these are utilized to help survey sustainability impacts, this could help trigger a reorientation of economic streams on the side of practical turn of events. Also, we will definitely see new degrees of observation and control in assistance of the two benefits and force: 'Reconnaissance Capitalism' just as the Surveillance State. Without a cultural and administrative "techlash" that prompts substantially more tough implementation of antitrust and information security/proprietorship rules, Big Tech will keep on storing up residents' information and transform it into megaprofits. Without administrative changes, the advanced countries will retain all the glory market elements are probably going to fuel

disparity and smother contest. Algorithmic inclination could intensify the scenario by sustaining and demolishing disparities. Obviously COVID-19 has sped up the organization of observation innovations in a few nations – from China to Israel. There is each opportunity that crisis estimates will become perpetual post-emergency.

4.1.5. Politics

There is not a single clear finish to be seen to the increment in polarization, populism, and patriotism that has been a characterizing normal for the second half of the 2010s. The underlying reaction to COVID-19 all throughout the planet has regularly featured the strength of patriotism and the shortcoming of multilateralism. There will be openings, in the outcome of the current emergency, to revamp a more powerful worldwide request, however at present it shows up almost certain that administrations will turn their consideration internal, zeroing in on cultivating recuperation at a public level. Relations between states are probably going to turn out to be more value-based and, sometimes, more unfriendly. On a more sure note, the slow handover of political capacity to an age whose political perspectives have been fashioned in our current reality where the environment emergency and disparity are main concerns may prompt a lot more prominent prioritization of these issues by governments as the 2020s progress.

1. **Polarization and Radicalism on the Rise**: The social, environmental, and economic disruptions that lie ahead will lead to a world that is more polarized and a politics that is more radical. Levels of dissatisfaction with political and economic elites are high – and have been for some time: a 2017 survey of 18,000+ people across 23 countries found that 71% of people agreed with the statement "my government does not prioritize the interests of people like me." This will drive defenders of the status quo to embrace ever more reactionary positions. Meanwhile, those with less to lose will be increasingly open to radical alternatives. Just as the 1930s produced both the Third Reich and the New Deal, the 2020s will likely offer up a combination of resurgent populist nationalism and Green New Dealism.
2. **Geopolitical Instability:** The ascent of egalitarian patriotism all throughout the planet has essentially debilitated multilateralism as patriot pioneers will in general be antagonistic towards

worldwide foundations and deals. They likewise will in general overlook the intricacy of the advanced world and possess little energy for protecting the interests of partners or putting away cash and lives to look after security. Electorates in certain nations may rebuff egalitarian pioneers at the surveys for their absence of capability notwithstanding a general wellbeing crisis, however somewhere else COVID-19 has plainly sped up a float towards patriot dictatorship. Also, COVID-19 is giving libertarian systems and organizations a pardon to twofold down on existing plans that were probably going to diminish worldwide strength (for example, the monetary and ecological liberation that we see occurring). While US-China contention rules features, there are numerous other likely wellsprings of insecurity: from Russia and North Korea to Iran and Venezuela. Countries in relative decay and those whose long-term possibilities are compromised by monetary, social, and natural change have less motivation to stick to the worldwide guidelines and standards that support dependability.

4.1.6. Culture

Social change will be generally molded by shifts in different regions. For instance, urbanization (and the expanded versatility of populaces inside and between urban areas) ought to speed up a change in social inclinations from possession to sharing. Coronavirus, in uncovering society's reliance, may make a few social orders become less individualistic and spotlight more on aggregate rights and obligations, especially according to wellbeing, cleanliness, and security. As the environment and biodiversity emergencies deteriorate, especially as far as their effect on lives and jobs, environmentalism, and natural equity's social and political clout is set to rise. In spite of the fact that in no way, shape or form widespread, this will change perspectives to what and how we burn through for a huge minority of the worldwide populace and may trigger at any rate a halfway shutting of the hole between what buyers say about sustainability and how they act.

Rising degrees of movement (coming about because of environmental change or different variables) may likewise fuel political disunity, since migration is frequently a central point of interest for libertarian patriots, regardless of whether against foreigner legislative issues regularly has little to do with real migration numbers.

1. **Materialism and Post-Materialism:** Attitudes and Lifestyles Diverge: The manners by which people measure their status and achievement fluctuate significantly across nations. 70% of Chinese say they measure their prosperity by the things they own. Just 21% of Swedes and Spaniards agree. In created economies, and especially among more youthful age partners, more individuals are beginning to esteem encounters and access over responsibility for products. Ways of life are adjusting to a developing cognizance of planetary limits – at any rate among some segment gatherings. Interest in wellbeing, good dieting, personal satisfaction and personal development is on the ascent, and a portion of the working class practices of mass isolates all throughout the planet will acquire ubiquity. The consumerist way of life holds a solid allure in numerous places where individuals have not yet gotten an opportunity to appreciate it, in any case. Financial aspects isn't the sole determinant of this disparity: in Peru, only 30% of individuals measure their prosperity by what they own, which is generally identical to the levels in Germany (31%) and Australia (29%) – nations whose per capita GDP is just about multiple times higher than Peru's.
2. **Culture Wars Escalate**: Qualities divisions are developing and hardening inside numerous countries all throughout the planet. Polarizing occasions – from the Brexit vote in the UK to new Citizenship Laws in India – are both a manifestation and reason for these partitions. A spellbound and divided (web-based) media scene additionally intensifies the pattern. There is no single issue that characterizes the new culture wars: they are about mentalities to race, religion, movement, sex, sexuality, place, globalism, nationhood, and that's just the beginning. These social parts map defectively onto segment partitions: in numerous nations, there is a metropolitan rustic as well as old-youthful measurement to these culture wars; frequently schooling level is a solid indicator of individuals' social perspectives. The way of life wars add to political polarization and thusly feed off it. Given this supporting input circle, there is a danger that conflicts over personality will increase in the decade ahead.

4.1.7. Significant Level Ramifications of the Macrotrends

How might these macro trends affect Vision 2050? Unquestionably, some can possibly brush us off base if not very much oversaw. Yet, others could practically be outfit to speed up progress. Here we research six of the patterns (grouped into three themes) that are general as far as their ramifications and which bring up significant vital issues for the Vision 2050 plan.

4.1.7.1. The Politics of Generational Handover

The rise and fall of distribution ages is a steady in human culture, so what makes the generational handover that will unfurl during the 2020s prominent? Old and youthful consistently see the world in an unexpected way, yet, in some significant ways, the interests and assessments of the present old and youthful are further separated – and possibly in more prominent pressure with each other – than in earlier many years. For millennials and Gen Z, their early stages have been overwhelmed by the aftermath from the 2007–2008 crisis – and now the COVID-19 pandemic. They have grown up with the mindfulness that environment mayhem in the course of their lives is almost certain except if revolutionary changes to the worldwide economy are executed. This setting has brought about numerous millennials and Gen Z being profoundly embittered with the state of affairs (counting with 'private enterprise') – however, there are special cases for this, outstandingly in quickly developing economies like Indonesia. While all ages will in general get more moderate with age, there is a decent possibility this pattern will be less articulated among those at present under 40, exactly on the grounds that they have been financially pressed and realize that, on current directions, they will experience their advanced age in a world seriously disturbed by environmental change and biodiversity misfortune. The political results of this specific generational handover could along these lines be significant – however, it isn't sure how this will work out during the 2020s. There are three conceivable situations:

1. Recent college grads and Gen Z neglect to enlist as a huge political power during the decade – in light of the fact that they "conform," don't turn out at decisions dependably enough and additionally in light of the fact that they are excessively divided. In this situation, the 2020s are overwhelmed by the undeniably moderate governmental issues of the children of post-war America. Another variety of this situation includes millennials specifically being "skipped," as boomers keep on sticking to

control from one side of the planet to the other. This could prompt a quick ascent in the impact and force of Gen Z, as they assemble to try not to be abandoned similarly as the recent college grads before them.

2. Twenty to thirty-year-olds and Gen Z are a destabilizing power because of significant degrees of estrangement with business as usual. In this situation, their impact makes governmental issues more limited and energized; bargain, alliance building and multilateralism all become harder.

3. Twenty to thirty-year-olds and Gen Z become the appointive bedrock of viable reformist governments, which focus on issues like financial change and tending to environmental change. In this situation, they channel their disappointment into promotion for administrative intercessions that location social imbalance and natural harm. From the viewpoint of Vision 2050, situation 3 is obviously the most ideal. Vitally, however, it requires the two organizations and governments to exhibit that a valid reformist elective exists.

4.1.7.2. Automation, Jobs, and the Economy

In numerous nations, the connection between work and financial success has been debilitating for an age, with a thin monetary first-class catching an outsized portion of the new abundance made by usefulness gains. A mix of powers – mechanical change, globalization, the declining force of worker's organizations and a persevering spotlight on investor esteem among numerous organizations – has prompted stale wages and progressively unstable types of work for some specialists. From gig economy laborers in the US to traveler workers in India, the financial effect of COVID-19 is hitting a considerable lot of these equivalent individuals hardest. Innovation and exchange may make social orders more well off in total, yet, without viable rearrangement, they aggravate a few people off – either in outright terms or comparative with different districts and financial classes. This has been an essential factor in the ascent of populism, patriotism, and the dismissal of globalization – prominently in the US, yet in addition somewhere else. Lamentably, the monetary arrangements being sought after by egalitarian pioneers all throughout the planet today are probably not going to change this – and, in certain occasions, will compound the situation. Exchange wars will dispense monetary damage on the individuals who have profited by globalization (in both created and non-industrial nations), without essentially improving life for the individuals who have not. Elective ways are conceivable. Computerization will keep on making interruption occupations, yet organizations and governments could act to alleviate the unfavorable cultural effects of this pattern by building more grounded social wellbeing nets, reallocating riches and moving to a more partner situated type of free enterprise. Coronavirus has set off a brief reinforcing of social security nets in certain nations. Governments have carried on of need and a considerable lot of the crisis estimates embraced in the early long stretches of 2020 are not monetarily practical over the long haul. Yet, by making the already inconceivable inescapable, COVID-19 may have improved the probability that laborers, bosses, and governments will discover better approaches to share the dangers and prizes related with mechanization all the more fairly.

4.1.7.3. Nationalism and Globalism

The resurgence of political and social patriotism that has happened throughout the most recent decade gives no indication of blurring. This has debilitated multilateralism – and will very likely keep on doing as such. Having libertarian patriots in power builds the danger of war breaking out among countries, and it makes a setting where rough fanatics inside society feel encouraged. Customary way of thinking would recommend that this is terrible information for the Vision 2050 plan – and without a doubt from numerous points of view it is. Sustainability issues (especially environmental change) have to a limited degree speed in the way of life wars that are seething in numerous nations. Supporters of sustainable improvement are frequently seen (without anyone else just as by others) as globalists – individuals who esteem their way of life as "residents of the world" profoundly; who are prouder to be "woke" than to be energetic. There are, be that as it may, openings just as dangers for the Vision 2050 plan in this, especially if the accomplishment of reasonable improvement needs can be hitched to sensations of public personality and pride among residents, and to political goals of public safety and intensity. Parts of the Vision 2050 plan will in any case require multilateralism and business should attempt to reinforce multilateral cycles and foundations where it can. Yet, a significant part of the groundbreaking change required can occur at a public or even sub-public level, and keeping in mind that this may make intricacy for worldwide organizations that work across various wards, it might likewise set out open doors for quicker advancement in numerous spaces.

4.2 DISRUPTIONS

Not everything on this rundown will happen during the 2020s, yet all are conceivable enough that they warrant pondering and, to the degree conceivable, planning for. Not all are terrible – and, even those that are can possibly catalyze positive changes, similarly as past emergencies have. As with the macro trends, there are numerous potential interlinkages between these interruptions.

Cascading types of influence – where one disturbance triggers others – are one opportunity. For instance, we are as of now living through a worldwide pandemic that may yet trigger a monetary emergency, mass unemployment, and a significant clash as well as famous uprisings that lead to shift in power. In the marginally longer-term, COVID-19 may likewise have improved the probability of a tipping point for the worldwide energy change showing up during the 2020s (surely a few examiners currently accept that petroleum derivative interest may have crested in 2019), which could thus trigger an unexpected rectification in the manner finance business sectors value environment risk. The way that the tech monsters will more likely than not rise up out of the current financial emergency in a much more grounded position comparative with (potential) contenders may build the credibility of an administrative kickback later in the decade.

In the interim, expanded familiarity with the connections between agribusiness, deforestation, biodiversity misfortune and the danger of zoonotic pandemics like COVID-19 could give an after wind to the biotech business, speeding up the change in food creation from land to lab.

At long last, while COVID-19 may in the present moment have occupied worldwide pioneers from managing environmental change, it might likewise have created an enduring change in residents' assumptions regarding the job of government in reacting to emergencies and interceding in monetary life to guarantee results that advantage society. Joined with the requirement for significant public venture to invigorate monetary recuperation, this could make the conditions for something like a Global Green (New) Deal to arise during the 2020s. To put it plainly, while none of this is ensured, the COVID-19 pandemic could yet go about as a trigger for each and every other interruption on this rundown during the decade ahead. Kindly note, we have given a different Vision 2050 research paper investigating the drawn out results of COVID-19 in more profundity.

4.2.1. Financial Crisis

The joined impact of nations going into lockdown to moderate the spread of COVID-19 and an oil value battle among Russia and Saudi Arabia has hastened one of the quickest, most profound financial exchange crashes ever – and that is simply Q1 2020. Dissimilar to in 2007–8, when money related arrangement (e.g., quantitative facilitating and financing cost cuts) for the most part took the strain of restoring the worldwide economy, governments have effectively needed to carry out uncommon monetary measures in light of the Covid prompted crash – and there will be substantially more boost to come. A great deal is riding on how very much focused on government bailouts and boost bundles are – including how versatile the economy is the point at which the following accident comes, as it definitely will.

4.2.2. Global Pandemic

At the hour of composing, the quantity of affirmed instances of COVID-19 keeps on rising dramatically in numerous nations all throughout the planet. It is probably going to keep making death toll and interruption social orders and economies for quite a long time – if not years – to come. Furthermore, COVID-19 didn't appear unexpectedly. The previous 20 years have seen five possible pandemics – SARS, H1N1, Zika, Ebola, and MERS – which were all just a single hereditary change away from being pretty much as troublesome as COVID-19. We may yet see further pandemics in the decade ahead, with similar potential to overpower medical services frameworks, disturb supply anchors and shut economies and social orders for a while. Obviously there are exercises to be discovered that could improve versatility notwithstanding the following pandemic. Regardless of whether governments and organizations notice those exercises stays not yet clear.

4.2.3. Major Conflict

The opportunity of a genuine struggle between at least two countries with incredible militaries and abundant resources can't be precluded. Were such a contention to break out, all things considered, digital assaults on basic framework would highlight vigorously in the strategies of the fighting countries (in fact, ostensibly, there are now numerous cyberwars seething all throughout the planet). During a time of developing digital reliance, this could cause extremely critical damage and death toll among customary residents. So too could the organization of atomic, natural or compound weapons. As occurred in the Second World War, such a contention would probably trigger a full preparation of society and the economy in help of public conflict points in those nations included – and would create a feeling of social fortitude inside and between countries unheard of since the 1940s.

4.2.4. An "Economic Singularity" Leading to Mass Unemployment

Assessments about the effect of computerization and man-made brainpower on the quantity of occupations in the worldwide economy shift so uncontrollably that it's ideal to take any figure with a huge touch of salt. However, imagine a scenario in which those determining an inevitable breakdown in the absolute number of occupations – here and there alluded to as a financial peculiarity – are correct. Regardless of whether, over the long haul, innovation creates many new positions as it annihilates, the danger of certain locales and areas enduring a delayed time of extreme unemployment is high. Also, as the COVID-19 emergency illustrates, mechanization isn't the solitary factor that can trigger a time of mass unemployment. The danger of a delayed time of mass unemployment – regardless of whether because of computerization, a pandemic or another factor – has huge ramifications for political strength: governments will probably battle to adapt to the aftermath and this could fan the flares of revolutionary legislative issues and populism of both left and right.

4.2.5. "Techlash"

In the 20 years since the dot-com bubble burst, the tech area has had a simple ride. Social orders have accepted new advancements with insignificant dithering, and controllers have tossed moderately couple of barricades in the method of tech organizations doing what they need. That may now be evolving. There is rising disappointment and disappointment in numerous nations with the manner in which computerized innovations are being utilized to serve the interests of a limited monetary as well as political tip top. Customers are more mindful of the adverse consequences of innovation on wellbeing and prosperity. Worries about protection and information possession are on the ascent, however governments are not generally as worried about security as their residents are. Contest requirement has become an undeniably hotly debated issue in the EU and the US. New principles about the lawful status of "gig economy" laborers and the duties of web-based media organizations for the substance they host could subvert the reasonability of stage plans of action. And afterward, there's the effect of international contention: the furore over Huawei could be a preview of what might be on the horizon, with governments boycotting unfamiliar firms and unions stressed because of picking sides.

4.2.6. Popular Revolts Leading to Regime Change

Rising disparity inside nations and an apparent absence of responsiveness from political elites is powering an assorted arrangement of (generally peaceful) fight developments all throughout the planet. Given that the hidden reasons for these well-known uprisings look set to deteriorate during the 2020s, almost certainly, both the recurrence and seriousness of fights against business as usual will rise. The crucial obscure is the way viable they will be: the 2010s saw a sensational decrease in the achievement paces of peaceful missions requesting foundational political change. But there is no assurance that this pattern will proceed: as residents become angrier and more estranged, we could see apparently stable political systems across the world either brought down or compelled to act considerably more unequivocally in light of residents' requests.

4.2.7. A Climate "Minsky Moment"

Throughout the 2020s, there is little uncertainty that finance business sectors will improve at estimating both progress and actual environment risks into resource valuations. Other natural, social, and administration issues are additionally progressively on the finance business' radar, yet environment is the issue destined to prompt a quick and emotional repricing of resources soon. There is a decent possibility environment-related monetary revelations will get compulsory at some stage in the main portion of the decade. Innovations that empower more prominent straightforwardness into resource level information are likewise growing quick. As the nature of data accessible improves and the expected misfortunes to financial backers become both bigger and more inescapable, a significant – and possibly abrupt – reorientation of economic streams turns out to be progressively likely. This could trigger a purported environment "Minsky Moment": an unexpected descending amendment of resource valuations in carbon-concentrated areas.

4.2.8. Energy Transition Reaches a Tipping Point

Energy progress watchers are isolated into two camps: those that expect continuous change and those that anticipate a significantly more fast innovation as well as policy-driven disturbance over the coming decade(s). If the last gathering is correct, at that point, we can hope to see interest for petroleum derivatives pinnacle and start to fall during the 2020s, which would have significant ramifications for the energy business, financial backers and, obviously, environmental change. The speed and size of cost decreases in the sustainable power area in the course of the most recent decade have reliably surpassed assumptions, and renewables are presently at or near cost intensity with non-renewable energy sources in numerous pieces of the world. Depending on how rapidly those expense decrease bends base out, a financial tipping point might be nearer than most experts might suspect. This doesn't imply that the switch will occur incidentally: it will in any case set aside some effort to work out limit and foundation, and governments and organizations that keep on putting resources into petroleum derivative limit today (for instance, China's financing of coal power creation) will attempt to try not to record abandoned resources as long as they can.

4.2.9. Biotech Boom

Engineered science can possibly change food creation, medication, and materials production. In a portion of these spaces, we may see nonlinear improvement during the 2020s as costs decay dramatically. For instance, one ongoing report on the food business anticipated that meat created in a lab, utilizing a cycle called 'exactness maturation,' will get cost cutthroat with conventional hamburger from cows in the mid-2020s and could be really much significant for the farming business, just as for human wellbeing and the climate. Huge parcels of agrarian land could be opened up for different employments. In the meantime, in the wellbeing area, engineered science is being utilized to foster quality treatments and customized prescriptions, while the plastics business is progressively putting resources into bio-based other options.

4.2.10. Global Green (NEW) Deal

Actually like the 2000s, the 2010s got done with a disillusioning arrangement of environment talks (COP15 in Copenhagen in 2009; COP25 in Madrid in 2019). In any case, there is a critical possibility that the 2020s will see a leap forward in worldwide environment strategy activity – however, whether this will occur through the systems of the Paris Agreement or not remaining parts an open inquiry. From the EU's Green Deal to South Korea's declaration of a net-zero objective, energy is working in huge economies across the world.

This is notwithstanding negative political changes in some key nations (e.g., US, Brazil, Australia) since the Paris Agreement, and the proceeded with opposition of states like Russia and Saudi Arabia. While the last are probably going to stay impervious to environment strategy activity for a long time to come, there is each opportunity that, post-trump, the US will venture (once more) into a position of authority on worldwide environment activity during the 2020s. Across the globe, resident activism is probably going to be a critical driver of political activity – and the consistent drumbeat of outrageous climate occasions will keep environmental change high in open cognizance and on the political plan for most governments.

Chapter 5

Creating Resilient Strategies

CONTENTS

5.1. STRATEGY CREATION

At the point when organization CEOs are pulled before administrators or researched by the press to clarify their duty issues, work rehearses or ecological calamities, something has plainly turned out badly. Additionally defective are the organizations that pass up new business sectors since they neglect to see the potential in web-based media, natural insurance or developing business sectors' thriving working class. The chiefs of such organizations have neglected to foster procedures that are adequately far-located and vigorous to adapt to a quick changing working setting. Albeit barely any hit the features as fantastically as Starbucks, Apple or BP, many organizations have been similarly blinkered about urgent changes on the planet that influence their systems. We accept that essential reasoning is commonly too thin, caught in ordinary investigation and incognizant in regards to troublesome changes in individuals' needs and standards. Firms work in an intricate, unique setting – including monetary, social, political, innovative, social and ecological cooperations. They need to completely comprehend the idea of this unique situation, tolerating that organizations need to deal with a progression between associations with other key entertainers in the public arena. They are a necessary piece of this greater picture. Fostering this more extensive viewpoint, extending skylines and time periods to spot openings for development that will support long-term achievement is what we have called Resilient Growth. A few organizations are aware of quick monetary movements and conceivably troublesome innovations in their businesses, yet few appear to be prepared to search for long-term problematic patterns. As of late, the innovation area has created instances of development with a capable outlook and versatility. Organizations, for example, Patagonia base their constitution on various qualities and aspirations. Be that as it may, most settled organizations are battling to re-set the conventional plan of action and vital setting. Accordingly, essential deduction inside many organizations botches fundamental freedoms for development.

The risks of botched freedoms and powerful dangers are more prominent now than at any other time. These are unpredictable occasions. Organizations need to foster techniques with regards to extraordinary vulnerability about what's to come. Organizations must be adequately prepared to respond to advancements, while as yet seeking after a system that guides dynamic towards long-term objectives inside a structure of crucial qualities. Vital reasoning is planned to deliver an incorporated viewpoint of the business, however on the off chance that it overlooks the amazing powers influencing an organization and its business sectors, it can't satisfactorily distinguish the heading where the association should move. We accept strong procedures are expected to give the more profound bits of knowledge that will bring long-term achievement.

5.1.1. How Ready Are Organizations To Key Nearsightedness?

Accepting that there is a requirement for a major change in the manner organizations advance to guarantee a long haul, reasonable future, we explored how and why a few organizations have started to foster strong techniques.

1. Is an organization's business procedure advancement educated by the monetary, social, political, innovative and ecological setting where it works?
2. How does the organization endeavor to recognize problematic turns of events and keep away from the snare of straight reasoning?
3. How does the business endeavor to comprehend its interrelationships with numerous partners and handle clashing requests?
4. What makes for progress or disappointment in essential reasoning? We trust this exploration will incite banter about the significance and importance of the more extensive cultural setting in creating effective techniques?

5.1.2. Instability and Vulnerability

The beginning stage for our request was to address how organizations can predict possible dangers and opportunities that should impact their essential bearing and arranging measures. Business experts realize they can't anticipate the future yet they should endeavor to get ready for what lies ahead. This is more troublesome as the world is changing in a heap of ways at a frantic speed, for certain principal changes lying outside the ordinary extent of corporate aptitude. Corporate Citizenship has outlined four megatrends that organizations need to get ready for.

Understanding advancements, for example, moving force structures, new friendly connections and incredible new needs is imperative for organizations to foster fruitful methodologies. However, our exploration proposes that even organizations among the CSR pioneers are attempting to coordinate these elements in their endeavors to adapt to the dubious future.

Figure 5.1. Social threats and opportunities.

5.1.3. How to Adapt to Vulnerability?

There are no straightforward responses to the difficulties of vulnerability, instability and vagueness about the future business, social, political, and social climate. Notwithstanding the troubles in any case, organizations that fall into the snare of extrapolating from ongoing experience hazard experiencing huge shocks whenever startling occasions or openings arise. Indeed, even all that laid plans can't expect the 'obscure questions,' however tacticians need to consider a wide scope of improvements and follow up on those that are the most critical and material to the organization. Our exploration discovered proof of such a wide-based skyline examining among a few of the organizations we met. In 0the most complete model, one organization has made an exploring bunch that counsels a wide scope of assessment formers and specialists in a few disciplines not straightforwardly identified with the business. The point is to accumulate insight on the key social and logical movements that will shape the eventual fate of the business. Another organization has a Strategic Foresight Team which inspects the worldwide patterns that may affect the business over the more drawn out term, educated by a course of internal commitment with chiefs. Chief administration is tested to reevaluate their major perspectives on how the world and the cutthroat climate are developing. The methodology interaction centers around individual themes and thinks about situations for conceivably problematic powers. Situation practices are utilized in different organizations, with an essential suspicion that there will be huge changes. In one case, the senior authority group programs conversation of long-term advancements at its yearly gathering. While such activities help to recognize dangers and openings, one interviewee remarked that, at last, there would consistently be vulnerabilities, and it is important to accept that the central methodology of the business will support achievement. We additionally discovered proof of less deft practices. In a few organizations the methodology cycle has all the earmarks of being fairly unthinking and tied near more quick business drivers. Interviewees enlightened us regarding brand insurance work, statistical surveying and quick issues in their business sectors, however not with regards to more extensive and less prompt angles. Some expressed that they have a drawn-out point of view; however they couldn't well-spoken what this has really meant for the business system. Others remarked that the CSR groups know about significant long-term patterns, yet these don't show up in the danger register and openings network that advises key reasoning. In one case, the CEO has encouraged his groups to search for troublesome impacts; however there is all things considered a solid accentuation on investor esteem in arranging and a period skyline of only three years.

5.1.4. How Wide Is the Viewpoint?

Organizations that are modern in their way to deal with vulnerability and non-direct reasoning may by the by have a genuinely thin spotlight on regular business drivers. For instance, innovation organizations realize that interruption is common in their area, however, even their all around created innovation filtering may in any case miss key cultural patterns. A solid beginning stage for a more extensive way to deal with methodology is vision and qualities which perceive the significance of cultural connections. We noticed this methodology in a few organizations we addressed. In two organizations the qualities were set somewhere near the author/proprietors and are unmistakable in all major decision-making. One current CEO demands that all ventures should stick to the establishing esteems while one more discussions about "another mechanical upset" and the "associated world" the organization is important for. Another tells representatives that in spite of monetary pressing factors, think about the organization "filling a more significant need" which is reflected in upsides of reasonableness, uprightness and straightforwardness. The vision is a beginning stage, yet it should animate reasoning that accepts society past the limits of monetary measurements and the momentary requests of the market. At the end of the day, it should be a live, significant thought instead of only an assortment of fine trademarks. It should drive chiefs to draw in with the more extensive setting of financial, social, political, mechanical social and ecological connections. The vast majority of these organizations endeavor to comprehend cultural patterns through their customary associations, in some cases including formal partner commitment. Clients, particularly those with high-profile buyer openness, are a significant wellspring of qualities arranged contributions for one organization.

However, while a few organizations effectively examine for such turns of events, some seem to depend on routine statistical surveying, which is regularly limited to standard business issues and buyer perspectives, conceivably missing significant turns of events. One interviewee portrayed searching explicitly for joins between friendly conduct and innovation and the organization's items. Be that as it may, one more said the organization depends on the corporate danger work, which was accepted to have excessively restricted of a viewpoint.

5.1.5. Broadband Reasoning

Attempting to expect what's to come is the beginning stage. The everyday the truth is that this interaction needs to squeeze into an authoritative construction. The organizations remembered for our examination revealed to us how to make the suitable administration detailing lines that help the advancement of long-term thinking on business system. We were especially intrigued by how they coordinate cultural viewpoints into methodology, with or without the investment of CSR experts and specialists.

5.1.6. Who Is Mindful?

Extreme obligation regarding technique in each business lies with the CEO and leader group. In a large portion of the organizations we addressed, procedure advancement is designated to others outside this chief group, however in one case ranking directors structure a Strategy Council that meets monthly to audit the vital parts of the business climate. Most organizations in our example have devoted system or business improvement groups who lead on technique advancement, however we discovered improvements both away from and towards this model. One organization has as of late delegated a Director of Strategy to foster a more noteworthy vital core interest.

For another situation, the committed corporate procedure work has been disbanded as it was viewed as having an "ivory tower" approach. All things being equal, each significant capacity in this organization currently has key liability regarding its own subject matter. In different organizations, every business division is answerable for its methodology, with the middle having a co-ordinating and evaluating capacity.

5.1.7. What Sort of Hierarchical Core Interest?

Organizations can embrace various ways to deal with system improvement, creating methodology for the whole organization or procedure for a specialty unit. Most organizations we met revealed to us that they foster technique in both the corporate and specialty unit setting. In one case, be that as it may, a group has been made to zero in explicitly on a significant new essential drive at a more miniature level. The unit is treated as a smaller than normal beginning up inside the business, answering to the technique group. This Insight Team is entrusted with investigating new market openings, understanding mechanical turns of events and making imaginative items and administrations that will fulfill expected shopper needs in 10–15 years' time. The thought is to make a solid spotlight on explicit goals, liberated from large numbers of the standard corporate limitations, to accomplish outstandingly quick advancement. This Insight Team is tied in with making a move to foster new ideas (in this specific case planning a drastically new item), not just distinguishing future difficulties or market requests. Note that this methodology is distinctive to the Strategic Foresight Team at another organization which focuses thinking on future patterns.

5.1.8. What Is the Time Skyline?

We tracked down a wide scope of ways to deal with the broadness and profundity of vital reasoning. A few have long timescales and expansive skylines, however others seem to consider procedure as minimal more than medium-term arranging. Five-year timescales are average. Three organizations are from the utilities sector so their methodology is normally determined by the administrative structure and timescale. Generally, this envelops a five-year plan as well as a prerequisite for a 25-year key vision. In the innovation area, skylines can be long-term (consider Google Glass and Amazon drones), but simultaneously can be likewise compacted by the speed of mechanical change and the generally short lifecycles of items and administrations. Two organizations have a 20-year viewpoint and two others expressly request that chiefs think ten years ahead. In one model, a ten-year procedure was presented a couple of years prior on the grounds that the CEO saw the need to consider factors past the quick, transient issues that engross ranking directors. Outside of these models, nonetheless, there were nearly as many organizations where it is uncommon to look forward over five years

5.1.9. What Sort of Information Sources?

Outside inputs assist chiefs with acquiring a more extensive viewpoint. Technique counseling firms were regularly referenced as suppliers of external ability and knowledge. Industry bodies additionally give area explicit data sources and a few organizations utilize free statistical surveying and financial examination. Just one organization approaches an outside counseling organization to get CSR skills and a more extensive cultural setting to the technique advancement measure. One method of social event various perspectives is through a conventional board or warning board. One organization has such a gathering comprising of senior leaders from different ventures, the scholarly community, non-governmental associations (NGOs) and different specialists. It meets double a year with ranking directors. Another has made a leading body of specialists on water assets – the key regular asset pertinent to the organization's area. The specialists assist ranking directors with understanding the basic external improvements to which they need to react. Another organization teams up with a scholarly establishment that spotlights on wide issues for the fate of the area.

5.1.10. Is There An Association Between CSR and Procedure Groups?

While the corporate vision oftentimes consolidates cultural aspirations – expressly in a few cases – this isn't really reflected in a nearby association between the CSR group and the procedure interaction. In something like three cases the head of CSR plays a significant part in procedure advancement. Nonetheless, in many organizations, the job of the CSR chief is more roundabout. Their perspectives and mastery are frequently separated through one of the senior chiefs, who goes about as a CSR champion, or senior leaders might consolidate cultural thoroughly considering their enrollment in a CSR Council or Committee. One interviewee disclosed to us that CSR and vital arranging had been completed autonomously previously yet there were presently moves to adjust the two. Any oversight of this more extensive logical deduction in the system advancement measure is twofold edged. It implies that CSR experts are not adequately drawn in with corporate methodology, just as the business may possibly neglect to assess key cultural advancements for their potential benefit.

5.1.11. Business and Society Connections

The third region our request considered was the manner by which the methodology improvement measure is educated by external viewpoints. We consider this to be an imperative component in making a strong system that assesses the megatrends recently recognized. We examined further to find how organizations endeavor to comprehend the business/society relationship. The ease and quick-changing nature of the scene rolls out this improvement hard to nail down and monitor. Many organizations react with explicit commitment of partners and following components, and we discovered a few models. It is intriguing to take note of that partner commitment isn't a panacea – there were blended perspectives on its adequacy. The organized partner commitment measure in one organization is driven by the CSR group's understanding that others' issues present business openings.

The cycle is connected to a materiality practice that covers the whole worth chain and distinguishes partners who give the best chances and who the organization needs to see better. By and large, be that as it may, commitment seems, by all accounts, to be strategic – worried about prompt issues as opposed to more generous patterns with vital importance. For sure, one interviewee remarked that partners frequently have exceptionally brief time frame skylines and are not keen on examining issues past the following several years. The commitment interaction can likewise under convey by restricting the sort of associations addressed. One member has done a considerable discussion, yet a large portion of the partners were from the business or were industry-trained professionals. Barely any friendly vested parties or customers were incorporated, gambling rather thin ends. In two cases, NGOs are unmistakably seen as having little to add to key reasoning. Albeit fundamental as accomplices in conveying explicit projects, they are viewed as having a limited viewpoint dependent on the issue they support. In that capacity, one organization trusts it is hard to separate helpful insight based on what are viewed as doomsayer messages.

Another embraces an inactive, protective stance, avoiding the chance to connect with as this would incite analysis. Others acknowledge that some commitment can be useful, yet there is a component of experimentation in discovering the gatherings that can assist organizations with understanding the evolving setting.

Acquiring key bits of knowledge is especially hard for organizations working in various nations (the greater part of those in this exploration). One organization coordinates commitment from the middle yet it is completed locally by every nation activity. Solidifying these conversations might make an abstract of nearby concerns instead of educating a wide-running vital agreement. To enhance partner inputs, a few organizations look to formal exploration and tap the assets of research organizations, including some that emphasis explicitly on CSR. One organization commissions research on expected patterns, especially in business sectors where it isn't all around addressed and consequently has less understanding than in its home market

5.1.12. How Broad Is Mindfulness Inside the Organization?

As business procedure is the obligation of the chief initiative and the most senior administration, it is fundamental that cultural experiences acquired through the cycles we have depicted are perceived by all experts that help create or execute system. An internal commitment measure is essential for the essential importance of any experiences to be completely perceived. The exchange between the leader group, procedure experts and CSR experts requires shared agreement. It is about the business utilizing every one of the assets available to its (the two partners across the association with various focal points for survey the world just as outside partners) to comprehend the business setting. Such shared agreement is important to recognize patterns that probably won't be the most significant on a worldwide scale yet have most pertinence for the organization's procedure – as well as the other way around, megatrends that are less pertinent in the organization's particular area and conditions. In a portion of the organizations this shared arrangement is obviously illustrated.

One methodology proficient disclosed to us that senior administration become more keen on CSR themes the more they see the connection to business achievement. One more said the climate bunch looks five years ahead, attaches its intuition to the strategies and makes mindfulness through programs that connect to business targets. A few organizations have formal board councils or chief gatherings committed to CSR-related points. Be that as it may, it is hard to pass judgment on the degree to which such bodies really draw in with vital issues.

Our examination provides reason to feel ambiguous about some whether shared comprehension inside organizations is far reaching. For instance, interviewees advised us:

- As long as exercises are legitimate, ranking directors consider any to be as specialty issues.
- CSR centers around citizenship programs, instead of worldwide issues like security and tax collection.
- Some of the senior supervisory crew comprehend the significance of cultural issues, however not all.

- There is a craving among senior chiefs to take a gander at things in an unexpected way, however it is curbed.

5.1.13. Fruitful Strategising

Characterizing fruitful procedure improvement is famously troublesome. Appropriately, our interviewees didn't offer any single answer to tackle every one of the difficulties. To be sure, some remarked that achievement can never be ensured and disappointment ought normal. Disappointment is in the idea of hazard taking – as Einstein's greatly cited saying has it: "Anybody, who never committed an attempted, had a go at nothing new." One superseding prerequisite for progress is the requirement for savvy instinct. Judgment, in view of clear qualities and convictions, is the center element for sound system. It can't counter every one of the dangers in another endeavor, however misguided thinking will subvert in any case solid cycles. The best essential reasoning won't convey achievement in the event that it prompts some unacceptable ends.

Be that as it may, while practical insight is fundamental, and could be supposed to be the substance of administrative dynamic, it is truly challenging to control or record for. The accompanying system presents judgment, close by different rules perceived in this exploration, to outline the critical components in a tough methodology and the connections between them.

1. Process Refers to the methodologies an organization has set up to foster its business technique. While we start with this component, perceive that this cycle is indispensable to how an organization makes culture and performs commitment. The cycle component envelops authoritative constructions, jobs and obligations, and the degree to which a business utilizes outside consultants to plan the instruments for system advancement. In pondering fitting cycles, an organization needs to respond to three key inquiries:
    a. Who is liable for what – should key reasoning be a cross-utilitarian or expert movement?
    b. How far do we depend on specialists all the while and content of system advancement?
    c. What is the best construction for guiding technique to move from intuition to activity?
2. Commitment Concerns the organization's inclination to construct further relations with a more extensive gathering of external consultants, specialists and assessment formers. To be successful,

this will include a skyline filtering measure that joins a more all encompassing perspective on the setting wherein the business works. It isn't sufficiently just to comprehend future patterns according to numerous viewpoints – the sign of a genuinely tough business is one that can draw out the linkages among various (and now and then contending) perspectives on the world. Key inquiries to pose include:

a. Is the organization willing to draw in with pundits of the business, just as the individuals who are steady of our exercises?
b. Where are the genuine wellsprings of motivation and edification that can assist us with understanding what's to come?
c. How would we guarantee the voices of specialists from nontraditional foundations both talk with power and are treated in a serious way?

5.1.13.1. Culture

Relates to the association's capacity to accept change and advance development. Somewhat, this can be affected by the cycles portrayed above – authoritative designs can help or prevent key development. Essentially, culture is emphatically affected by the judgment of the initiative group who regularly set the upsides of the business (talked about underneath). Senior administration can do a lot to advance a culture that moves individuals to think deliberately. In this regard, the chief group of an organization needs to resolve such inquiries as:

- Is our business driven by long term contemplations of benefit advancement, or transient worries of benefit augmentation?
- Is vital deduction coordinated towards hazard relief, or would we say we are worried about setting out open doors?
- Do we emphatically advance distinction and creativity among our representatives, or do we esteem and award individuals that think the same way as us?

5.1.13.2. Judgment

The last component of the essential arranging measure concerns the convictions and judgment of senior pioneers. Not at all like the other three components of this model, this center fixing is harder to control, yet it stays conceivable to impact senior administration thinking. It gets to the core of the point of view of the singular individuals from the chief group – where do they think society is going; what will be the effect of the megatrends like populace development and environmental change: what will be the job of business in the public eye in 2025? The Director of Strategy and the Chief CSR Officer can't anticipate changing these basic perspectives and decisions, however they can surface them by posing such inquiries as:

- What are the standards illuminating the chief's intuition on key choices?
- What were the purposes behind deciding NOT to seek after certain business openings?
- What are the implicit convictions of individual Executive colleagues that drive their vision of the working climate?

5.1.13.3. Reality Strategy

The interaction between procedures, culture, commitment and judgment is what enables an organization to foster a triumphant strategy that will convey results over the long haul. Be that as it may, success can never be ensured. We generally return to the problem that Einstein alluded to – perceiving that any essential advancement carries with it the expected danger of disappointment. Be that as it may, there is a significant contrast between a fruitless procedure and helpless technique improvement. A helpless procedure with minimal likelihood of coming out on top is probably going to rise up out of a deficient methodology approach. That is a reprehensible mistake that organizations should keep away from. With regards to our exploration, it is the inability to assess cultural improvements for development and effect. An ineffective system is unique.

A technique with savvy instinct, strong cycles, and the entirety of different components portrayed above, may fall flat as a result of unforeseeable conditions, misreading of patterns, innovative vulnerabilities or different questions. Be that as it may, the system approach was the right one. The right system approach, one that outcomes in a versatile methodology – a procedure that will situate the organization for long term achievement – has a lot more noteworthy likelihood of coming out on top. A strong technique depends on a comprehension all through the organization of the potential for progress coming from the cultural setting wherein the business collaborates and works. This thusly will foster the experiences and motivation that lead to development and versatile development

5.1.14. Reasonable Guidance on Strategy Development

We accept that to foster a strong procedure, organizations should be able to do:

- Looking comprehensively at the cultural setting to perceive interdependencies.
- Collaborating to accomplish new, productive bits of knowledge.
- Articulating the central qualities that characterize the job of business in the public arena and its commitment past the thin bounds of the accounting report.

In view of our exploration, we give these helpful bits of knowledge into making a versatile procedure:

- Corporate qualities ought to be unmistakable and significant, empowering proactive conduct and giving individuals certainty to make decisions and get things going.
- Success requires thorough examination of a wide scope of variables.
- The business should take on a forward-looking viewpoint on the grounds that as patterns develop, the organization will be very much situated to take administration.
- Success relies upon understanding the requirements of a wide scope of partners, keeping an open exchange with various gatherings and acclimating to evolving requests.
- To install a methodology all through the organization it should be invigorating and sound appealing to the people who should get it going.
- It is important to constantly survey and adjust – presumptions might not be right however you can in any case make ventures pay by reacting quickly and fittingly to the new setting.
- An organization ought to consider the drawn out CSR of the business as a central reason for the methodology improvement measure, instead of just an empowering influence.

We add a few components for effectively coordinating cultural variables in system advancement:

- The corporate vision ought to expressly include the business/society relationship – clarifying both the business and social reason for the organization and drawing out the linkages between the two.

- Horizon checking necessities to look past the traditional business drivers to comprehend, expect and profit by a more extensive arrangement of long term issues.
- The CSR group should be completely incorporated into the procedure advancement measure, instead of working in a vacuum without association with the corporate methodology.

5.2. BENCHMARKING

The business world is driven by information. In the economy and society, we use numbers to get what has occurred previously, and estimate what may happen later on. Speculation choices are directed by monetary information. Buyer buying decisions are educated by data on cost and quality. Indeed, even the medications that specialists can endorse have been the subject of definite calculating to set the cost of the medication and evaluate drug viability. In the realm of corporate obligation (CR) and sustainability, information is pivotal to understanding and further developing organization execution. Disclose to partners how the organization analyzes as far as top tier execution and different measures. Issues range from seeing how your organization adds to work across the worth chain to estimating the effect of local area venture programs. The cutting edge CR specialist basically couldn't manage their work without superior grade, solid information. Be that as it may, information in separation is inane. We need to contrast that information with something. Past execution in your own association sets a benchmark which is fundamental for checking progress. Yet, genuine worth stems from examinations with the more extensive world. Is your exhibition top notch? Is it true that you are falling behind the bunch of friends and best practice organizations on a specific issue? Contrasting CR and sustainability measurements and a more extensive arrangement of organizations is key to comprehension your present exhibition in setting, yet in addition your future potential. Furthermore, an organization's monetary, social and ecological presentation should be thought about in contrast to standards, laws and principles set by society. They go about as the external benchmark by which an organization's conduct is judged.

Benchmarking is a goal assessment, in view of clear definitions and measurements, that analyzes execution against a particular standard, standards or gathering of organizations. It is generally famous as a method for appraisal to survey an organization's exhibition with regards to friends and best-practice organizations. Inside, this can drive enhancements, make a feeling of contest and move new thoughts. For instance, if a contender has gained huge headway to dispense major struggles from minerals acquisition from its production network, they may be utilizing a clever methodology from which you could learn. Remotely, it can show partners how the organization contrasts and others and what progress it is making to resolve an issue. In the event that your own corporate obligation technique is elite, your external acknowledgment through evaluations, norms, and grants should contrast well and direct contenders just as a more extensive arrangement of best-practice organizations. There are incalculable various sorts of benchmarking: monetary benchmarking analyzes the monetary competitiveness of organizations; measure benchmarking surveys how business methods are completed; benchmarking against a standard sets a base exhibition level to be met. Execution benchmarking evaluates how an organization oversees or resolves a specific issue in contrast with a bunch of organizations or principles. This can be quantitative, for example, contrasting the measure of water utilized with make a unit of item, or subjective, for example, looking at provider sourcing plans. The capacity to benchmark in the field of CR has been enormously helped by the expanding number, and normalization of, sustainability detailing. Around 95% of the Global 250 issue sustainability reports and associations like Global Reporting Initiative and Sustainability Accounting Standards Board have been attempting to normalize revealed information. These standards not just communicate/informs external partners what's going on inside the organization's sustainability procedure, yet in addition permits organizations to think about execution in a similar way within different parts of the business.

Most importantly, benchmarking permits organizations to gain from each other and settle on more astute choices. By considering execution in contrast to peers or a norm, organizations can drive gradual upgrades across the business and increment usefulness. Spearheaded by quality administration master W. Edwards Deming, ongoing exploration has shown that quality benchmarking further develops execution in fields as different as assembling measures, corporate administration, wellbeing and security, variety and inventory network integrity.

Critical investigation and analysis of information accumulated can likewise highlight future patterns and assist organizations with keeping up to date with and even advance beyond peers. For instance, organizations with enormous stock chains in agricultural nations progressively need to show that their crude materials and fabricated items are delivered with trustworthiness. These organizations have thought that it is basic to benchmark provider work rehearses, like the option to worker's guild participation and the end of kid and constrained work, against worldwide principles just as neighborhood laws and standards. The UN Universal Declaration of Human Rights has given a norm against which business conduct can be judged.

Benchmarking evaluations can be of specific worth to CR and sustainability leaders working in organizations. Seeing how you look at on a specific issue can advise dynamic and reinforce correspondence channels with inside and outside partners. There are two fundamental benefits for the CR professional to acquire from a powerful benchmark:

1. The case can be made that the organization needs to do more to accomplish best practice norms in a specific region. For instance, in the event that it very well may be shown that your provider set of principles is feeling the loss of a few components saw as best practice by inventory network specialists, the case can perfectly be developed that it could be an ideal opportunity to refresh your implicit rules to line up with best practice.
2. Furthermore, precise benchmarked information can back up cases of authority. This is especially valuable in cases we have seen where the organization either needs to make a case of predominance, or when execution in enduring an onslaught from outside partners. For instance, if the extent of organization enrollment in your business is essentially higher than the public normal in each nation of activity, the information may uphold the argument against allegations of being antiorganised work.

The benchmarking has its constraints:

While great benchmarking is about execution and best practice, terrible benchmarking can prompt unremarkableness. Awful benchmarking is utilizing information to legitimize normal execution, instead of testing and driving upgrades. This typically comes from choosing some unacceptable correlation bunch. Just in light of the fact that others are performing at a specific level, doesn't mean this is the level at which you ought to perform. In the event that your whole industry doesn't resolve the issue of a living pay, this doesn't imply that your pay theory is fundamentally a decent one. As well as advocating unremarkable execution, awful benchmarking can smother advancement. While you might have a set friend correlation bunch inside your area, individual organizations and ventures dominate in various regions. Organizations that acquire the most worth from a benchmark frequently consider some fresh possibilities and hope to get thoughts from other areas by asking who is awesome at a specific issue and what are they doing another way? For instance, Southwest Airlines looked to further develop its on time execution. Rather than benchmarking against different carriers, the organization looked to NASCAR where pit groups rapidly and effectively get their race vehicles back on the track as wellspring of development. Benchmarking can offer a new interpretation of an issue and yield basic experiences to improve execution. In any case, prior to plunging into nitty-gritty information investigation, set out what you need to accomplish. Here are five expected points:

1. Identify a position in the peer group: To understand overall performance, take stock of how you compare. How does my performance compare on my priority areas? Is my recent drop in performance still within typical industry practices?

2. Inform strategy development: To recognise areas of strength, opportunities to differentiate, key vulnerabilities and potential performance gaps. In which areas do I lag behind my peers? Where can I distinguish myself as a leader?

3. Determine best practice elements and set targets: To set sustainability targets and inspire action, examine the actions of best in class companies, the performance of innovative leaders, and the highest standards within an industry and across industries. How does my performance compare to world-class standards? To what degree have leading companies outside of my sector improved their performance?

4. Understand trends over time: To track how the market is moving on a key issue, review available data over the past years and analyse for trends. Has the variation among companies decreased? Has overall sector performance improved? Has an improvement programme been successful?

5. Communicate performance to external stakeholders: To build a constructive dialogue with allies, partners and even critics, make the findings from a benchmark public. A narrative should accompany any benchmark that sets performance in context.

Figure 5.2. 5 Steps to benchmarking.

A clear process is needed to identify the right metrics and to transform the available data into valuable insights. We recommend using a five-step process:

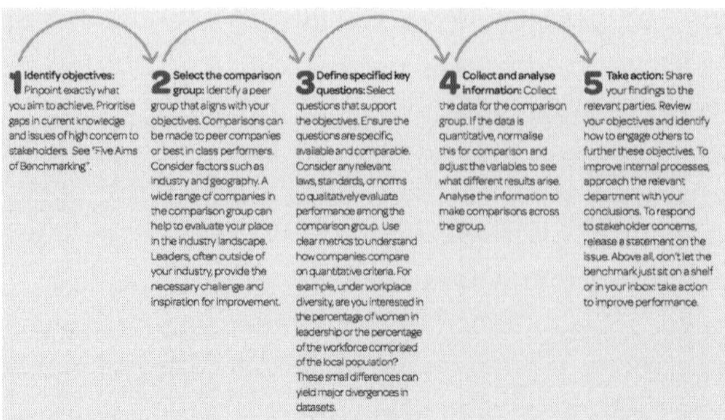

Figure 5.3. 5 steps process to benchmarking.

The end goal of benchmarking is not a benchmark. The real benefit stems from understanding the market and identifying how to improve performance and develop new ideas. Benchmarking can have its limitations. It cannot provide all the answers. There is often the temptation to look for a single right answer – the underlying explanation for performance differences can sometimes be complex. Most data only makes sense when understood in context, for example, where aggressive target-setting has driven superior performance for an organization. For this reason, benchmarking is best thought of as a first step. After interpreting the data, it's the action that follows that really differentiates companies. An illustrative quantitative benchmarking criteria is given in Figure 5.4.

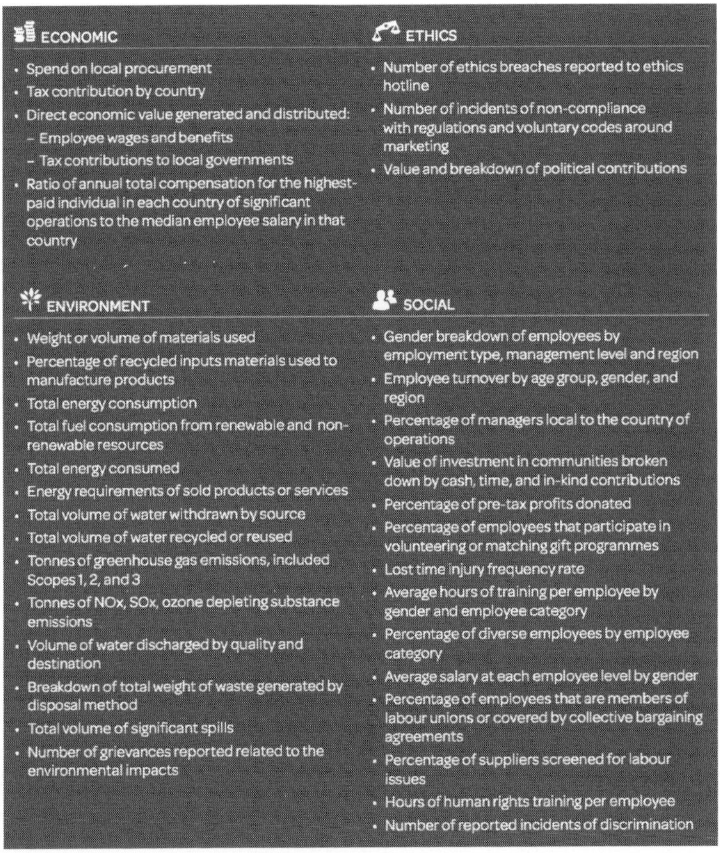

Figure 5.4. Illustrative quantitative benchmarking criteria.

5.3. MASTERING RESILIENT GROWTH

Key arranging by organizations needs to change. Numerous organizations are confronting intense difficulties, including how to: develop incomes in a quick evolving world; expect the up and coming age of client needs; forward-plan in a questionable economy; and keep up with discipline on costs. However, such a large number of organizations take on a foolish and restricted way to deal with key administration. They center around beating their rivals by coordinating with their exercises, creating comparable items through steady upgrades and conveying esteem through the normal, worn out plans of action. They need to utilize the old models however make them work more enthusiastically. The drawn out achievement of organizations today is at this point not ensured. To be sure, the actual presence of numerous organizations is under danger. The normal life expectancy of a S&P 500 organization has contracted from 61 years in 1958 to only 18 years today.

History is full of companies that failed because they neglected to adjust sufficiently quick to new market elements, like Blockbuster video, Pan American Airlines and Polaroid cameras. An extreme reexamining is required. The way in to what's to come is getting what we call the unique circumstance – the patterns, effects and connections between a business and the more extensive world. Examining the setting of any business can uncover incredible bits of knowledge for advancement. This can support execution as long as possible. A tough procedure is one that is in sync with an organization's more extensive setting, permitting the business to flourish for quite a long time to come.

Business doesn't exist in a vacuum. Setting alludes to the financial, social, political, mechanical and natural issues that set out business open doors and dangers. These variables have customarily been considered as a feature of a restricted danger evaluation by most organizations. In any case, there is a greater chance. An examination of applicable connections, effects and patterns can give new bits of knowledge. When drawn closer deliberately and comprehensively, Corporate Citizenship's Resilient Growth approach can assist with enduring the hardships and reveal the chances from startling guidelines, changing client designs and more extensive financial variances. This section sets out how any ground breaking business can comprehend its specific circumstance, examine the opportunities, open new experiences and advance for long term development. It provides insights into the tools that business can use to foster an effective and coherent methodology in a fast-changing world.

5.3.1. Planning the Unique Situation

No business is an island. Imperceptible bonds shape the firm through a complicated communication of financial, social, political, mechanical and natural patterns. Organizations that need to be situated for long term achievement need to acquire a comprehensive comprehension of the connections that shape their unique circumstance. This should comprise of:

1. Understanding the organization's mind boggling connections in its many business sectors, and with its numerous partners.
2. Dissecting the sorts of market influences and impacts that can possibly affect business achievement today and later on.
3. Distinguishing how to coordinate this speculation into business procedure and intending to catch the most esteem and guarantee long-term achievement.

There is a two-way communication between the business and its unique situation. Society makes expenses and an incentive for organizations and business makes worth and expenses for society. A more profound examination of these connections can give a springboard to advancement.

5.3.2. Future Change

The setting is dynamic, not static. A billion new buyers are added to the world each fifteen years. Around 4.2 billion individuals utilize a cell phone to get to web-based media today. Some progressions can be astonishing. Who might have conjecture in 1990 that interest for natural food would detonate by 3,000% to turn into a $30 billion market – 4.2% of all food deals in the United States today? Regulation can be emotional as well: in 2008, China restricted super flimsy plastic packs while Denmark presented an assessment on food sources high in soaked fat. A few organizations react by keeping the principles. This might be vital on account of laws, and alluring on account of standards, however it isn't adequate to acquire upper hand. Others go further and look to recognize the chances for "mutual benefits" where they can profit from a change. These covering interests can make examples of overcoming adversity in select regions. The most nimble organizations embrace change and use it for their potential benefit. Dominating Resilient Growth is a foundational reaction: expecting change, appreciating the associations, bridling new bits of knowledge, molding the actual setting and making genuine upper hand that can be supported for quite a long time to come.

5.3.3. Advancement With a Wide-Point Focal Point

Advancement is fundamental to open the chances for Resilient Growth. The business setting ought to be surveyed comprehensively with a 'wide point focal point's that ganders at an expansive scope of elements throughout different time scales, including 10, 20 and 30 years ahead. By extending this edge of vision, organizations can recognize suffering freedoms that can be supported for long term achievement. Breaking down the setting can reveal insight into new plots for organizations to improve all the more inventively, diminish dangers and fabricate more prominent flexibility. At its heart, this interaction is tied in with recognizing and reacting to beforehand unidentified, implied or neglected necessities through new items, administrations and plans of action. These regularly come from an examination of patterns and effects, and how the interdependencies between them could shape startling results later on.

5.3.4. What Sorts of Progress Can Arise?

- New items and administrations that meet a formerly neglected need (for example minimal expense energy; safe food and drinking water; further developed schooling and wellbeing; upgraded foundations and framework)
- New plans of action that further develop efficiencies and yet again use items in a shut circle model that makes additional worth from less sources of info
- Employment and occupation creation in the store network that might include disregarded gatherings (for example smallholder ranchers; ladies; the jobless)
- New proprietorship structures that offer rewards in an unexpected way (for example cooperatives)
- New coordinated efforts with providers, joint endeavor accomplices, clients and non-benefits that meet common objectives

5.3.5. What Are the Possible Business Benefits?

- Top line development from new item and administration advancement
- Lower cost of merchandise from further developed efficiencies
- Faster reaction to new guidelines than contenders

- Improved discernibility in the production network
- Reduced dangers and expanded flexibility of business tasks
- Improved wellbeing and security record
- Reduced exchange costs from more significant levels of trust (for example with clients)
- Enhanced standing and brand value
- Improved worker inspiration and efficiency
- Increased innovativeness and thought age
- Attraction of better ability and decreased staff turnover
- New collusions and more beneficial coordinated efforts through shared objectives
- Lower cost of capital from a lower hazard profile

The chances are interesting to each organization. They will rely upon the particular setting and friends aspirations. No two cooperations are something similar and these issues change from one organization to another, just as landmass to mainland. The unique idea of the setting implies that new issues are continually arising.

Forward-looking organizations should try to catch the rising worth before contenders do. However, driving organizations don't simply respond to patterns; they effectively attempt to shape them for their potential benefit. Organizations needing to reclassify their business sectors don't simply acknowledge the future, they try to change the standards of the game and change frameworks and individuals for their potential benefit.

5.3.6. Long Term Value Optimization

Business adventures should be beneficial over the long haul. Canny business pioneers realize that this doesn't generally mean the goal ought to be momentary benefit augmentation. There are no proper standards about the timescale over which worth should be made. It is society's pressing factors – from nearsighted predispositions to securities exchange assumptions – that regularly oblige organizations. Throughout the next few years, we hope for something else and more organizations to discuss a shift away from momentary benefit amplification to long term esteem advancement. Tough Growth recognizes new advertisement helps that can support benefits and investor esteem over the long haul.

5.3.7. How Resilient Growth Makes an Incentive for Organizations

A few organizations are now exploiting these kinds of bits of knowledge. An anecdotal contextual analysis shows how the cycles can be applied. It depends on our experience of working with organizations on these issues. ABC Pharmaceuticals has experience a lack of development, declining net revenues and a pipeline which financial backers see as unsuitable. Representative confidence is low, innovativeness is missing and a progression of issues have escalated into adverse media remarks. An essential audit utilizing the Mastering Resilient Growth approach would start by understanding the association's most noteworthy impacts on society and how value is created for the business from society.

Likewise, benchmarking recognizes a bunch of new medium to longterm dangers and openings. From an extensive rundown of likely thoughts, another knowledge is distinguished to offer a groundbreaking wholesome item at a lower cost to a lot more individuals. This significant change has so far been undiscovered. A creative new plan of action is needed to understand the aspiration and guarantee it conveys inside asset and spending limitations. Close by offering the food, the organization gives a free nearby wellbeing check to buyers. An association with limited scope merchants empowers the help to make back the initial investment and arrive at scale all the more rapidly. This opens up new courses to advertise that were beforehand undiscovered, and permits more items to be sold. In the interim, functional and store network capacities set out on a program of improved detectability for the item and a more slender creation measure. This conveys a lower cost of merchandise, a greater item and a stronger inventory network. Following quite a while, the endeavor is productive after fast volume development that was unrealistic under the old plan of action. Close by top-line development and rising net revenues, new ability is drawn to the organization. Worker assurance and imagination rise. As a feature of the business turnaround, the more drawn out term pipeline improves. The financial exchange invites the outcomes and an expanded trust in administration is confirmed through a lower cost of capital. More grounded associations with partners – like clients, controllers, and the media – make a more grounded brand, more elevated levels of trust and support rising overall revenues into what's to come. Obviously, this anecdotal model sounds unrealistic. However, it's not a long way from the kinds of new items that organizations like Danone (Shakti Doi yogurt), Vodafone (M-Pesa cash move), Unilever (Pureit water purifier) and Cemex (moderate lodging in Mexico) have brought to showcase. Truly, the excursion is rarely direct and there are set-backs en route. In any case, the proof shows that these kinds of approaches are conceivable and can be beneficial.

5.3.8. Methods of Working As Long As Possible

Powerful system expects organizations to get and support upper hand. Tough Growth is a perspective that can open worth through taking a gander at the world recently. In the midst of progress, it can give the new bits of knowledge expected to take off another contender, increment incomes and support development into what's to come. It gives another dialect and new speculation for business.

Two better approaches for believing are needed to completely understand the advantages of Resilient Growth. Right off the bat, interdependencies should be truly perceived. No business is an island, yet in addition no issue exists all alone.

Patterns in the setting interface and shape each other. How should purchaser assumptions shape guideline? How is it possible that a would new innovation impact the inventory network? The most beneficial experiences frequently come from looking comprehensively, not at single issues in seclusion. Also, better approaches for working through coordinated effort can achieve greater advantages for all. Coordinated effort starts through conversation with the rest of the world at the Insights stage.

Organizations frequently don't concoct extraordinary thoughts all alone. Association can likewise stretch out to connecting up with the right provider, joint endeavor accomplice or non-benefit at the execution stage. This is on the grounds that viable organization can give new bits of knowledge, decrease expenses for the business, scale a drive all the more quickly and increment the size of the pie for all. Applying the thoughts by and by is no simple undertaking. Dynamic requires information however not all things can be precisely estimated. Directors should be open to managing vulnerability. Compromises might be required. No arrangement can be awesome and here and there five stages forward requires three back. This implies that the director's outlook might have to change for Resilient Growth methodologies to be viable. Strong Growth implies an associated and commonly useful connection between the organization and society. The prize is a business that is more inventive and ground breaking than the opposition; a firm that expects new client needs, and encounters less astonishments on the lookout.

However, in particular, Resilient Growth guarantees that the organization can support its exhibition a seemingly endless amount of many years. By calibrating the business to be in a state of harmony with the rest of the world, the organization can flourish for quite a long time to come.

5.3.9. The Glad Side-Effects of a Tough Technique

By being more on top of the world and its assumptions, organizations advantage their partners, society and the climate en route. Business can be an incredible power for social great by applying their assets deliberately in order to guarantee long-term productivity that is in sync with society. We find that "being seen" to be "doing acceptable" just for reputational reasons is normally less productive than distinguishing the smart activities that can assist the business with prevailing in the long haul. We tell our customers that social advantages and more grounded notorieties ought not be considered as the objectives of such a methodology, however a supporting side-act, the cheerful result of a supported spotlight on business achievement.

5.4. ENHANCING BOARD COMMITMENT

Corporate sustainability is best when sponsored by convincing help from senior decision-makers. Capable strategic approaches are as of now not the protect of one office. They should slice across issues and groups to acknowledge genuine incentive for the business and society. While many organizations guarantee that sustainability is significant, scarcely any sheets methodically think about the issues. The way to conquering this hole is to interpret corporate obligation from a specialty, specialized issue into a language that resounds with sheets. That implies clarifying how mindful strategic approaches support the drawn out benefit of the firm. Directors looking to get purchase in for sustainability need to comprehend the center abilities of the board. Viewpoints; abilities and information shift, and organizations wind up at various phases of the sustainability venture. A bunch of nine ways to deal with welcoming the board 'on board' can help slice through the commotion and improve on sustainability for senior leaders.

Powerful corporate sustainability requires great corporate administration. Firms should guarantee that senior chiefs comprehend and can react to the difficulties and chances of economic turn of events. This is especially obvious today in light of the fact that corporate sustainability traverses assorted issues, from new item developments to burden arrangements. However, sustainability directors every now and again experience hindrances to connecting with leaders. This paper sees how to comprehend the board and their differing skills. It recognizes the most proper devices to get purchase in to sustainability drives. It is planned for public organizations with a Board of Directors, yet the experiences will apply similarly to various degrees of the executives and different sorts of association Responsible strategic approaches have developed in ongoing a long time from impromptu, altruistic action to key, expansive drives that adjust the social, natural and financial effects of a firm with business achievement. Chiefs entrusted with executing these projects should guarantee senior-level purchase in to concur the degree of desire; arrange drives across various specialty units; and convey programs that advantage the entire organization. To understand the benefits for the firm and society, switches should be pulled from the top. An examination ready for the World Economic Forum tracked down that empowering sheets to more readily comprehend the all out ecological effects of an organization's items and administrations would be the single most prominent supporter of a stage change in sustainability around the world.

Despite the fact that CEOs and friends chiefs say that sustainability is a need, not many sheets give the issues a lot of unmistakable quality. All things being equal, the board's essential consideration frequently just spotlights on a narrowly defined set of monetary controls. Non-monetary effects get passing notice – or neglect to make the plan by any means. Yet, there is a reasonable acknowledgment of a requirement for more noteworthy obligation to sustainability from organization chiefs. As indicated by a United Nations study, 93% of CEOs say that sustainability is essential to their organization's future success. The Companies Act in the UK expresses that chiefs should have "respect to the effect of the organization's procedure on the local area and the climate." Sarbanes-Oxley in the United States forces to distinguish and unveil material issues. However, dynamic board commitment in dependable strategic approaches remains low. Indeed, when gotten some information about their needs for the year ahead, only 2% of organization chiefs everywhere American firms refer to "CSR." All things being equal, "key arranging" positions highest. The clear hole among "CSR" and "vital arranging" is the key motivation behind why scarcely any sheets offer unmistakable quality to corporate sustainability. To defeat this, administrators need to break corporate obligation out of its storehouse and clarify it in a language that reverberates with the board. Great corporate administration expects chiefs to have the foreknowledge to guide an organization through unchartered waters.

That implies an oversight of: long term system; changing business sector elements; hazard controls; financial backer viewpoints; administrative consistency; and notoriety the board. These issues are central to present day corporate sustainability. Large numbers of our customers have revealed to us that their greatest boundary to inside purchase in is getting time on the load up's bustling plan. Be that as it may, time is just a large portion of the story – what issues is the load up being approached to consider? While some may turn off at the notice of energy the executives or worker chipping in, similar individuals sit up while talking about the drawn out dangers and openings confronting the organization. Mindful strategic approaches ought to be converted into a language that presents them as deliberately important to the drawn out benefit of the firm.

A bunch of instruments to assist with articulating the connection between sustainability and business achievement are researched later. Prior to drawing in with board chiefs, comprehend a singular's beginning stage. Not all board chiefs are something similar. The basic capabilities of the board can be separated into points of view, abilities and information. It is fundamental to comprehend these distinctions to adequately connect with the two people, on a one-to one premise, just as a board aggregately. Points of view are the mentalities and upsides of people. They identify with good and close to home needs, like genuineness, uprightness, esteem decisions, encounters and even predispositions. Viewpoints are profound situated individual characteristics that advance gradually over the long run. Points of view are hard to change, however a few chiefs depict an 'revelation second' that has done precisely that.

Abilities contrast according to points of view in that they are values-unbiased and useful. They incorporate aptitude, for example, in partner relations and organization working, just as bits of knowledge, like the capacity to think about various perspectives. In contrast to points of view, abilities are agreeable to being instructed and created. Information alludes to the data that is accessible for dynamic. Handy loads up need to approach the right data, at the ideal opportunity, to settle on compelling choices. Information might come from related knowledge (which influences viewpoints), or another source. Streams of information can be expanded. For instance, board individuals can be advised on new information on non-monetary issues, like changing cultural assumptions, natural freedoms, representative inspirations and long term industry elements.

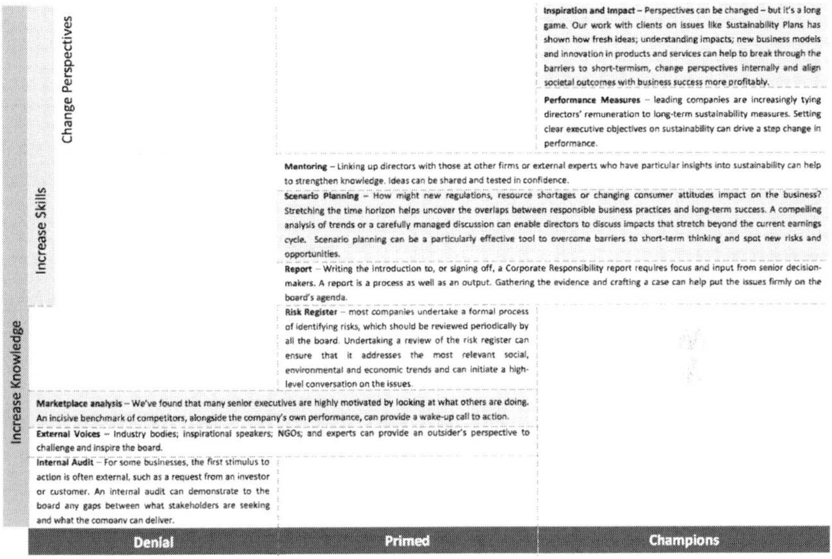

Figure 5.5. Board engagement strategies.

For the sustainability expert, the central questions to consider are:

1. Where is your board on the sustainability venture?
2. Except if you are extremely near the CEO, and exceptionally persuasive, you are probably not going to have the option to change their profound situated points of view. Yet, you can open the board to new data and urge them to foster new abilities.
3. Give motivation and groundbreaking thoughts.

New data sources are expected to spruce up an organization's way to deal with corporate sustainability and assist chiefs with recognizing the advantages. Understanding these three elements of decision-making will assist you with choosing the proper methodology to draw in the board. The board ought to be asked to think about an inquiry: where does sustainability "fit" on the organization's plan in the short and long haul? Is it part of the corporate vision? Or then again lined up with inventory network and hazard work? Explaining the degree of desire, just as the space that sustainability sits inside, is fundamental to viably following through on a program.

Without this knowledge, progress will be testing. Putting sustainability at the core of senior dynamic is a drawn out game. It requires better approaches for deduction, new thoughts and approaches that are custom-fitted to every interesting setting. Successful commitment of the directorate should prompt a more grounded obligation to corporate sustainability. However, the genuine prize will come from an exhibition to the board that, in the long haul, business achievement can go inseparably with more prominent advantages to society.

Chapter 6

Overall Sustainability Implementation Process

CONTENTS

6.1. IMPLEMENTING AND ASSESSING SUSTAINABILITY

6.1.1. Defining the Strategy

How to start off implementing Sustainability? It is often daunting to start because there are a series of unclear points:

- How do we start?
- Who do we include?
- How shall we carry it out?

Step 1: Establish the PDCA Methodology (Figure 6.1):

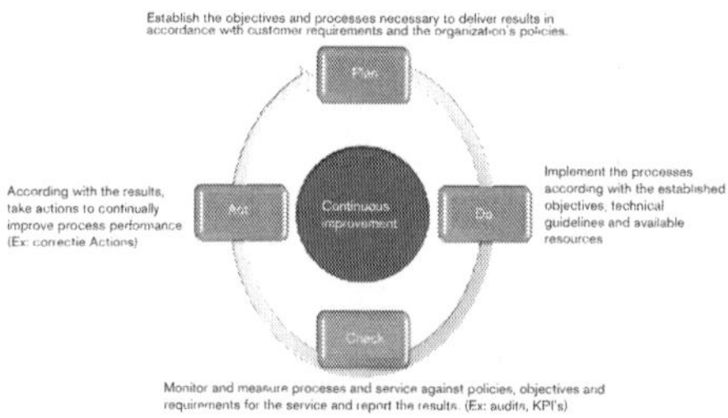

Figure 6.1. Continuous improvement cycle.

Step 2: Design the Implementation Phases (Table 6.1):

Table 6.1. Sustainability Implementation Process

When	How
Plan	· Assemble a leadership team; · Develop a working definition of Sustainability and Responsibility; · Identify legal requirements; · Review corporate documents, processes, and activities, and internal capacity; and · Identify and engage key stakeholders.
	· Build support with involved decision-makers; · Research what others are doing, and assess the value of recognized sustainability instruments; · Prepare a matrix of proposed sustainability actions; · Develop ideas for proceeding and the project case for them; and · Decide on direction, approach, boundaries, and focus areas.

Do	· Do a scan of sustainability commitments; · Hold discussions with major stakeholders; · Create a working group to develop the commitments; · Prepare a preliminary draft; and · Consult with affected stakeholders.
	· Develop an integrated sustainability decision-making structure; · Prepare and implement a sustainable business plan; · Set measurable targets and identify performance measures; · Engage employees, collaborators, partner, family, and others to whom sustainability commitments apply; · Design and conduct sustainability training; and awareness; · Create internal and external communications plans; and · Make commitments public.
Check	· Measure and assure performance; · Engage stakeholders; and · Report on performance, internally, and externally.
Im-prove	· Evaluate performance; · Identify opportunities for improvement; and · Engage stakeholders.
Repeat	· Return to plan and start the next cycle.

6.2. CONDUCT A SUSTAINABILITY ASSESSMENT

6.2.1. Amass a Sustainability Administration Group

A sustainability procedure needs both state administration vision and support, and purchase at all levels of the organization. Thus, a sustainability authority group would incorporate agents from the top managerial staff and top administration or proprietors, and in addition, volunteers from different units inside the firm that are influenced by or included in sustainability issues.

6.2.2. Build Up a Working Meaning of Sustainability

The primary task of the authority group is to build up a working meaning of sustainability for the project. This will end up being the reason for whatever remains of the evaluation. The definition for sustainability ought to be something very broad.

6.2.3. Illustrations

i. Sustainability is the company's practices and approaches that add to the prosperity of the earth, economy, and society. They address the necessities of clients, providers, shareholders, and representatives, and additionally those of government, the overall population, and the groups where the firm works, without trading off the capacity of future eras to address their particular issues.

ii. Sustainability is the way the organization coordinates financial, natural, and social targets while, in the meantime, tending to partner desires and supporting or improving shareholder esteem.

6.2.4. Recognize Legitimate Necessities

A sustainability approach is not a consistency-based action. It is all above intentional decisions a firm makes to enhance its execution and the way it identifies with society. In this specific situation, a fundamental stride is to guarantee that the business as of now regards existing laws, regardless of whether in connection to such things as administration, tax collection, pay off, work, or condition. A decent sustainability procedure—and the company's notoriety—can be immediately harmed if it is observed to be in break of essential laws.

6.2.5. Survey Corporate Archives, Procedures, and Exercises

With a working sustainability definition and an underlying comprehension of the inspirations driving the company's enthusiasm for sustainability, the group ought to then review key corporate archives, procedures, and exercises for real and potential sustainability suggestions.

Examples:

- Sustainability policy, code of conduct, the procedure for the specific activity, impact assessment, analysis;
- Recognize and connect with key partners.

Although the work of the administration group ought to uncover imperative social duty patterns, issues, and chances to follow up on, the group may all things considered miss vital issues that are clearer to those outside the firm. Thus, the group may wish to have dialogs with key external partners about sustainability. Mapping the interests and worries of partners against those of the firm can uncover both opportunities and potential issues.

Without a doubt, many successful firms now observe partner engagement as fundamental to the undertaking of distinguishing the issues that are most material to them (Table 6.2).

Table 6.2. Description of Action Lines for Sustainability Implementation

Engagement strategy	Set vision and level of ambition of future engagement and review past actions
Stakeholder mapping	Define criteria for identifying and prioritizing stakeholders and select an engagement mechanism
Preparation	Focus on short- and long-term goals, determine logistics for the engagement, and set the rules
Engagement	Conduct the engagement itself, ensuring equitable stakeholder contribution and mitigating tension while remaining focused on the issues
Action plan	identify opportunities from feedback and determine actions, revisit goals, and plan next steps for follow-up and future engagement

6.2.6. Partner Identification

From the beginning, you ought to know who your partners are and characterize what they require and what they anticipate from you. This examination and collaboration with them will empower you to recognize dangers and opportunities at an early stage and ensure you are tending to them effectively before it is past the point of no return. Right, and exhaustive partner recognizable proof will empower you to concentrate necessities that will ensure and empower a reasonable and enabling undertaking on the short and long haul.

Partner definition: A man, gathering, or association that has interest or worry in the venture. Partners can likewise be the individuals who might be influenced by or have an impact on the venture.

Sorts of partners, described by their relationship to the exertion being referred to:

1. **Primary Partners:** These are the general population or gatherings that remain to be straightforwardly influenced, either decidedly or adversely, by the venture. Cases: client, suppliers, and employees.
2. **Secondary Partners:** These are individuals or gatherings that are in a roundabout way influenced, either emphatically or contrarily, by the venture. Illustrations: community, shareholders, and government.
3. **Key Partners:** These who may have a place with either or neither of the initial two gatherings, are the individuals who can have a positive or negative impact on the venture, or who are imperative inside or to an association, office, or establishment occupied with the venture. Illustrations: United Nations (International Organizations), Lobby associations.

The chief of an association may be a conspicuous key partner, however, so may the line staff-the individuals who work specifically with employees-who complete the work of the exertion. If they do not have confidence in what they are doing or do not do it well, it should not have started. Different cases of key partners may be funders, chosen or selected government authorities, heads of organizations, or pastorate and other group figures who employ a lot of impacts.

6.2.7. Step by Step Instructions to Distinguish Partners

1. Brainstorm: Get together with individuals in your association, authorities, and others effectively included in or educated about the venture and begin getting out groups and names. Some portion of the purpose of conceptualizing is to come up with anything that rings a bell, regardless of the possibility that it appears to be senseless. On reflection, the senseless thoughts can end up being among the best, so be as far-going as you can. Following 10 or 15 minutes, stop, and talk about every proposal, maybe distinguishing each as an essential, auxiliary, and additionally key partner.
2. Collect classifications and names from sources in the group (on the off chance that they are not accessible to be part of a meeting

to generate new ideas), especially individuals from a populace or occupants of a geographic territory of concern.

3. Consult with associations that either are or have been included in comparative endeavors or that work with the populace or in the zone of concern.
4. Get more thoughts from partners as you recognize them.

Keep in mind: Stakeholders are for the most part:

- Concerned in any capacity with the venture;
- Located in the area;
- Hold a compelling position;
- It may be influenced by the issues tended to in the venture.

5. As a reference the basic stakeholders are usually:

- Clients;
- Suppliers;
- Community;
- Government;
- Employees.

6.2.8. Stakeholder Contact

In this section we will define the best ways to interact with them and how will you ensure a long-term relationship.

Benefits of including stakeholders (Table 6.3).

Table 6.3. Stakeholder Engagement Benefits

Benefits	Explanation
It puts more ideas on the table.	More ideas than would be the case if the development and implementation of the effort were confined to a single organization or a small group of like-minded people.
It includes varied perspectives from all sectors and elements of the community affected.	Giving a clearer picture of the community context and potential pitfalls and assets.

It gains buy-in and support for the project.	By making them an integral part of its development, planning, implementation, and evaluation. It becomes their effort, and they will do their best to make it work.
It is fair to everyone.	All stakeholders can have a say in the development of an effort that may seriously affect them.
It saves you from being blindsided by concerns you did not know about.	If everyone has a seat at the table, concerns can be aired and resolved before they become stumbling blocks. Even if they cannot be resolved, they will not come as surprises that derail the effort just when you thought everything was going well.
It strengthens your position if there's opposition.	Having all stakeholders on board makes a huge difference in terms of political and moral clout.
It creates bridging social capital for the community.	Social capital is the web of acquaintances, friendships, family ties, favors, obligations, and other social currency that can be used to cement relationships and strengthen community. Bridging social capital, which creates connections among diverse groups that might not otherwise interact, is perhaps the most valuable kind. It makes possible a community without barriers of class or economics, where people from all walks of life can know and value one another.
It increases the credibility of your organization.	Involving and attending to the concerns of all stakeholders establishes your organization as fair, ethical, and transparent, and makes it more likely that others will work with you in other circumstances.
It increases the chances of the success of your effort.	For all of the above reasons, identifying stakeholders and responding to their concerns makes it far more likely that your effort will have both the community support it needs and the appropriate focus to be effective

When you have your partners recognized you need to set up contact. List the individual contact for every partner, on account of a gathering, it might be a few people. Illuminate them on the venture and gather their thoughts and concerns.

The primary objective is to extract from them the imperative data for your venture and to decide whether they are occupied with taking an interest in any capacity. What are their needs and desires and the additional esteem that the venture will bring them?

For the situation where the venture negatively affects the partner, attempt to concentrate data that will empower you to limit that effect.

The most effective method to get the contact data for those gatherings of partner you do not have contact:

- Search online for any contact.
- Contact somebody that you think may know.
- Contact another partner for this data: case: you deal with a venture with United Nations and do not have the contact of the group pioneer Ask your United Nations Contact on the off chance that he has any contact in the group or if nothing else data of what association to contact.

Remember that real exertion in getting contacts will be required to start with, however, you will, as of now have these contacts for future undertakings.

Ways you can establish contact:

- Email;
- Videoconference;
- Physical meeting if possible;
- Phone call.

If you contact a partner and they are not interested, this is not an issue. You will not think of them as given that they have no interest they will not influence your venture. On the off chance that you distinguish an essential partner and cannot acquire the contact data or they are not accessible, you will attempt to join another partner that may have the same view. On the off chance that it is inconceivable, you will not think of them as.

6.2.9. Partner Analysis and Mapping

Presently you have recognized the partners and reached them, you comprehend what truly matters to them and what desires they have on the venture. You have a considerable measure of data sources and significant data to incorporate into your plan stage. Now and then it is exceptionally hard to deal with the majority of the data, particularly if a few information sources are contradicting. This is the reason we have the examination and mapping step. Partner examination (partner mapping) is a method for figuring out who among partners can have the best or negative impact on the venture, and how you ought to work with partners with various levels of intrigue and impact.

Most strategies for partner investigation or mapping isolate partners into one of four gatherings, each possessing one space in a four-space network (Figure 6.2).

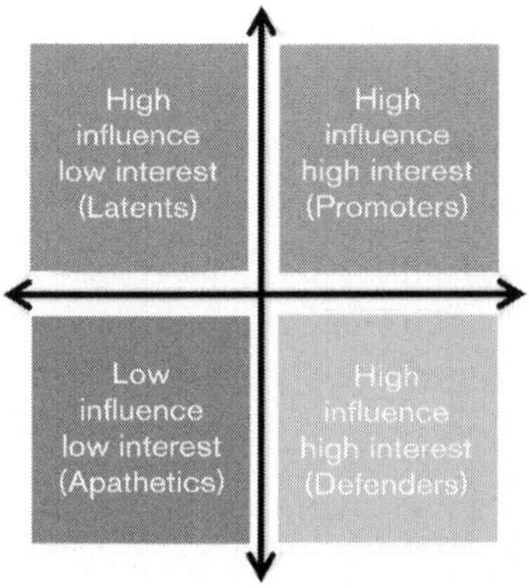

Figure 6.2. Stakeholder mapping and analysis grid.

As you can see, low to high influence over the effort runs along a line from the bottom to the top of the grid, and low to high interest in the effort runs along a line from left to right. Both influence and interest can be either positive or negative, depending on the perspectives of the stakeholders in question. The lines describing them are continuous, meaning that people can have any degree of interest from none to as high as possible, including any of the points in between.

Decide what stakeholder falls into each box and you already have a priority list for the integration of criteria provided by them.

6.2.10. Stakeholder Engagement Matrix

According to the categorization made earlier, your communication and integration plan has been prepared for all stakeholders. Corresponding to the same boxes identified before this is the type of relationship to maintain (Figure 6.3).

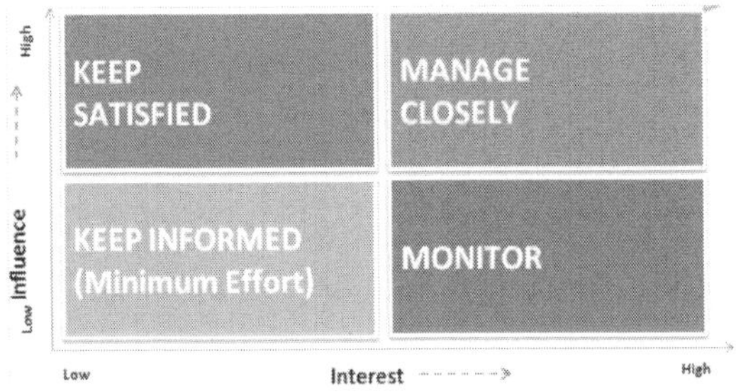

Figure 6.3. Stakeholder communication strategy matrix.

6.2.11. Important Stakeholder Trends

1. **The Culmination of Weaker Control is More Noteworthy Stakeholder Engagement:** The new U.S. government as of now has flagged that it might want to debilitate or disassemble control in key areas. However, this is probably not going to ease working conditions for business, as any debilitating control at the national level will be joined by an expansion in stakeholder engagement, intensified by the quarrelsome political atmosphere.
   Organizations must figure out how to proactively create trust through ethical systems that go past mere legislation requirements. Many organizations are setting up ethical frameworks that collaborate with, yet are separate from, consistent systems. Others are investigating cooperative energies including the review, consistency, and sustainability capacities to best advance their qualities.
2. **Neighborhood Clashes can Increase Worldwide Differences:** Hyper-straightforwardness implies that group questions can be intensified to win overall noticeable quality. For instance, indigenous rights groups in Latin America are joining forces with worldwide support associations to attract regard for their agenda.
   In horticulture, organizations that long have separated between venture-level group engagement and corporate notoriety administration are discovering this qualification progressively hard to keep up.
   Different organizations that customarily have considered partner engagement as a yearly exercise are attempting to characterize and comprehend their partners all the more profoundly, which is a perplexing activity when it is not characterized by the geographic concentration of a venture.

3. **Political and Social Hazard is Focalizing:** Artificial Intelligence and robotization are changing the work market and putting social administrations under outstanding weight.
   In the Global South, the development of the white-collar class has expanded individual and aggregate strengthening, while at the same time changing the progression of political and social risks. Open restriction to government and business is blending around a typical dialect of ecological equity, hostile to debasement and human rights. At the point when protestors voice their frustration towards non-efficient administrations, nearby elites move with fluctuating degrees of achievement to release their energy. Organizations no longer can isolate social and political hazard contemplations, which implies understanding the association among partners — not exactly how partners draw in with organizations.
4. **Understanding Your Effects is no Longer Discretionary:** The field of business and human rights has become an adult, highlighting the need to stretch out a risk assessment to understanding effects. The dispatch of the sustainable development goals (SDGs) in September 2015, as well, is urging organizations to create vigorous structures to gauge the outcomes of their exercises.

Human rights specialists have appropriately distinguished oversight of worldwide supply chains as a key corporate weakness. It has turned out to be clear to all that debasement whenever it is encouraged by worldwide money transactions is not ethically implemented.

Neither legitimate consistency nor standard hazard administration apparatuses are adequate for organizations who wish to survive and flourish in the new time. Or maybe, versatile organizations will concentrate on center qualities, authority, and a more comprehensive way to deal with business.

6.3. DEVELOP A SUSTAINABILITY STRATEGY

6.3.1. Define a Mission, a Vision, and Your Values

Take your time through this step. It is a difficult exercise and you will need time to figure out all three. What will they bring you? They are the essence of your business. They will let the world know what you do, the purpose of it, and where you are going. They will help you create an organizational culture, attract, and engage talent, define effective strategies, and keep you on track (Figure 6.4).

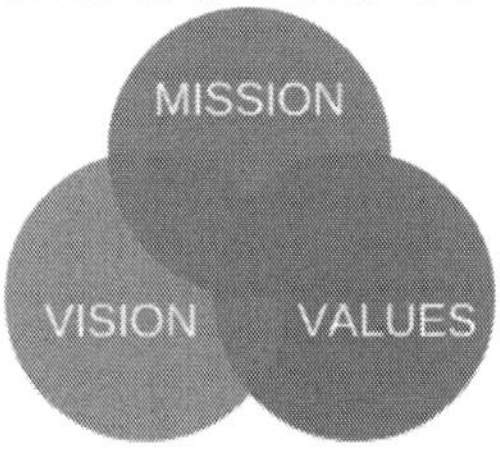

Figure 6.4. Venn diagram on mission, vision, and values.

The difference between them is simple: your mission is your current state, your vision of what the future will be and your values are your personalities.

Your mission will let the world know, what you do, who you do it for, and how you do it. Keep it simple, you do not need to have a long mission statement that no one will be able to understand. The most effective mission statements are direct, use easy language and people can relate and remember them. Do not leave it so general that it applies to many businesses; it should describe your business.

Your vision will state, where you are going, how you want to be, and what your purpose is. Keep it optimistic, highlight the possibilities that are awaiting, show you are the leader and an important change agent.

Your values will form the personality of your business; they will guide your employees, your actions, and strategies and define the type of relationship that you want with your stakeholders. Values keep everybody in the same boat and bring security and trust. Keep it realistic, when defining values, identify what you are already doing, what you give most importance to, and what you would appreciate as a client.

6.4. DEVELOP SUSTAINABILITY COMMITMENTS

6.4.1. What Are Sustainability Duties?

Sustainability duties are arrangements or instruments a firm creates or signs on to that demonstrate what the firm plans to do to address its social and natural effects. Sustainability duties spill out of the Sustainability appraisal and procedure and are produced right when a firm moves from wanting to do:

- They guarantee that the company's corporate culture is reliable with sustainability values;

- They help adjust and coordinate the company's business methodology, targets, and objectives;
- They give direction to representatives about how they ought to act; and
- They convey the association's sustainable way to deal with business accomplices, providers, groups, governments, the overall population, and others.

Before creating sustainability duties, firms must comprehend the scope of accessible responsibilities and the qualifications between them. A key qualification is amongst optimistic and prescriptive responsibilities.

Optimistic duties have a tendency to verbalize the long-haul objectives of a firm and are typically composed when all is said and done dialect, while prescriptive responsibilities, for example, sets of accepted rules, stipulate more particular practices to which the firm unequivocally consents to go along. Optimistic duties regularly appear as vision, mission, qualities, and morals articulations, or contracts.

As a rule, firms may as of now have optimistic and prescriptive responsibilities set up that can be changed in accordance with completely coordinated sustainability. Optimistic responsibilities shape the background for particular and prescriptive sets of accepted rules and guidelines, which are generally intended to benchmark or specifically control conduct.

The primary goal of optimistic responsibilities is to explain an abnormal state and regular comprehension of what a firm stands for and how it might want to be respected. For sustainability to be incorporated into qualities, basic leadership, and exercises, an association's optimistic responsibilities should completely mirror its social and ecological positions.

Without sustainability optimistic duties, there is a hazard that different parts of the association will set out on sustainability usage exercises experiencing some miscommunication. The probability is diminished when work starts with a mutual perspective of what the firm stands for and where it is heading. An assortment of firms the world over has created optimistic duties, which frame some portion of their business and correspondences technique.

6.5. IMPLEMENT SUSTAINABILITY COMMITMENTS

6.5.1. Build Up a Coordinated Sustainability Basic Leadership Structure

Albeit each firm is distinctive, each has a basic leadership structure set up to guarantee that it can meet its duties and client needs. The key thing to ask here is, "given the company's current mission, measure, division, culture, a method for sorting out its undertakings, operations, and hazard zones—and given its sustainability methodology and responsibilities—what is the best and effective sustainability basic leadership structure to set up?" It is basic that the firm adjusts and incorporates its sustainability objectives and basic leadership with its general objectives and methodologies so that considering sustainability contemplations incorporate basic leadership moves toward becoming as normal as considering client points of view.

A few firms will incline toward a unified sustainability basic leadership structure, others a de-brought together one, while still others will need a half and half, contingent upon their working components and administration style. There is no single method for sorting out a company's sustainability basic leadership.

6.5.2. Get Ready and Actualize a Sustainability Marketable Strategy

The basic leadership structure recognizes who is in charge of sustainability basic leadership and activity inside the firm. These individuals assume their roles in creating and actualizing the sustainability marketable strategy, which ought to spill out of the sustainability system and responsibilities.

The sustainability marketable strategy might be independently portrayed or included as a component of the association's current general marketable strategy. With the methodology, duties, and basic leadership structures set up, the sustainability strategy for success guarantees that the words are changed into powerful activity. An amazing method for doing this is to figure out what human, money-related, and different assets and exercises will be required to complete the sustainability methodology and responsibilities.

6.5.3. Set Quantifiable Targets and Recognize Execution Measures

Similarly, as with whatever other part of business execution, viable sustainability usage requires the setting of quantifiable objectives aligned with the responsibilities. In such a manner, firms carry on independently of the team. Competitors may set individual objectives, for example, "win an Olympic decoration," however they as often as possible set more achievable, middle of the road targets, for example, "run the 100 m sprint in under x seconds," "decrease my weight to y kilograms" and "be in the main five at the trials next November."

Generally, these moderate targets are guideposts en-route to a definitive objective, giving a gage of advancement and opportunities for re-assessment, training, or asset needs. Whenever accomplished, targets may likewise be a wellspring of festivity in their own particular right. In this sense, they can help fabricate motivating force and energy.

An association's way to deal with setting quantifiable ecological, monetary, and social targets and following accomplishments in meeting them is in a general sense the same as the competitor's way to deal with winning an Olympic award. A broadly utilized way to deal with measuring achievement is to distinguish the targets set for the sustainability responsibilities, create key performance indicators (KPIs), work out the estimation strategy and afterward measure the outcomes. Regardless of the exact approach taken, it should follow the "SMART" guidelines:

- Simple;
- Measurable;
- Achievable;
- Reliable; and
- Time-bound.

6.6. ASSURE AND REPORT ON PROGRESS AND EVALUATE AND IMPROVE

6.6.1. Sustainability Assessment and Communications

The assessment and communication of sustainability expand upon the adage that 'what gets measured gets overseen.' Subsequently, with a specific end goal to enhance execution along with different partner measurements sustainability practices must be assessed to distinguish and organize areas for improvement.

The assessment of sustainability can be completed along the five measurements recognized by Dahlsrud (2008), i.e., natural, monetary, social, partner, and intentionality.

All the more particularly, this can be encouraged through the improvement of quantifiable indicators along with the recognized measurements of sustainability. Various indicators for tracking these measurements have been accounted for in academic writing.

The most generally referred to as an arrangement of indicators is the Global Reporting Initiative (GRI) standards (GRI, 2006). The standards recognize 79 indicators along social, natural, and financial measurements. The GRI system likewise incorporates 15-part supplements, including extra indicators, to provide inputs for the one-of-a-kind needs of individual departments.

There are, in any case, some inborn shortcomings in the GRI detailing structure. Goel (2005), for example, takes note of that:

- It is not an administration apparatus;
- It is excessively broad;
- There are numerous indicators; and
- The business case for actualizing the GRI rules is not yet clear.

Different commentators say that it might be a valuable beginning stage, however sums to minimal more than box-ticking; or more awful, it can give a cover to poor execution (Economist, 2008). Faultfinders likewise contend that it might strengthen 'the same old thing' and a more prominent level of unsustainability (Smith and Lenssen, 2009). On the positive side, the rundown of indicators in the GRI system furnishes associations with a critical beginning stage for their sustainability activities. It makes sustainability assessment and reporting more methodical and makes it conceivable to think about various associations along with a given arrangement of indicators.

The GRI has additionally brought issues to light of the significance of corporate sustainability reporting. Regardless, the GRI system remains generally utilized as a part of sustainability assessment and communications (Moneva et al., 2006; Smith and Lenssen, 2009). The impediments intrinsic in institutionalized arrangements of indicators, for example, the GRI, highlight the requirement for setting particular indicators. Subsequently, while associations can depend on existing institutionalized indicators as a source of perspective point, they likewise need to create indicators that suit their particular business necessities and all the more precisely speak to the far-reaching internal and external effect of their business forms. With a couple of exemptions, for example, Keeble et al. (2003); Lohman et al. (2004); and Searcy et al. (2007), there is a shortage of writing on partner association in the advancement of indicators.

The improvement of business-particular indicators requires an efficient partner investigation approach whereby the association cooperates with partners to distinguish their key desires and territories of concern. They can then be changed over into indicators utilizing the logical standards of lessening and reflection and lined up with hierarchical assets and needs, as required.

This implies unstructured sustainability-related prerequisites got from conceptualizing and broad collaboration with partners are grouped around sustainability measurements and formed into quantifiable indicators. For subtle elements on the way toward growing new indicators the intrigued per user has alluded to Keeble et al. (2003); Lohman et al. (2004); and Searcy et al. (2007). The following stage in the wake of measuring sustainability execution is to report the outcomes (inside and remotely). The transparency of sustainability activities is essential for various reasons. To start with, sustainability detailing might be required by controllers or other intense partners, for example, significant clients. Second, the detailing of sustainability presents a chance to build up a capable picture for the organization (Ziek, 2009). At last, covering sustainability is likewise essential for legitimation reasons (DiMaggio and Powell, 1983). As we realize that most associations are reliant on their partners for a proceeded with a supply of assets (for instance money related, skill, or even human); to guarantee the proceeded with a supply of such assets, administrators need to convey the consequences of their drives to partners keeping in mind the end goal to make goodwill. Another driver for authoritative senior administration is to reassess their systems in light of the examination and discoveries from sustainability activities.

While the GRI detailing system remains an essential alternative, as specified prior associations could likewise utilize different means for conveying sustainability activities, including the yearly report, the yearly shareholder letter, nonfinancial reports, and site pages (Figure 6.5) (Holder-Webb et al., 2009; Ziek, 2009).

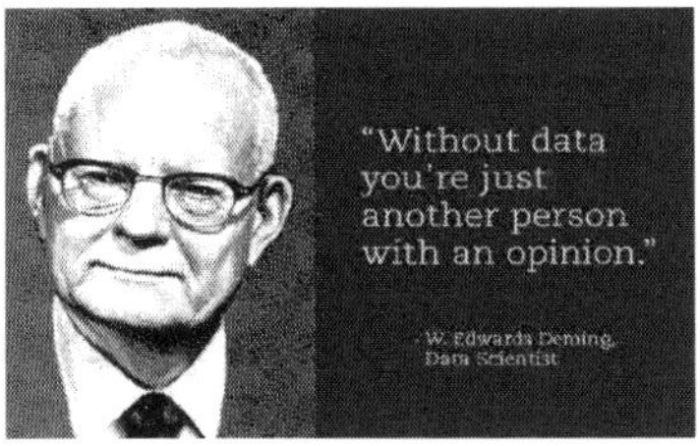

Figure 6.5. Edwards Deming, data scientists quote.

6.7. RETURN TO PLANNING AND START THE NEXT CYCLE

6.7.1. Means to Kick Off Innovation

When posing disruptive questions to employees, some leaders prefer to start a meeting immediately with one to set the tone, while others hold back until a brainstorm sputters and stalls. Milder approaches include emailing questions to participants in advance of a meeting or creating an online questionnaire where anonymity is assured. And among the hundreds of provocative questions I have heard, the following queries have been known to kick the status quo out of any room:

- If you could only work on one project for a year to transform the business, what would it be and why?
- What is the shortest path to the customer? How could we get there in 6 months?
- What suffers more breakdowns: our products, our processes, or our people? How could we fix this?
- It's 2025 and we are the best company to work for in the world: What two things did we do to earn this award?
- Which parts of your job would you like to kill or eliminate?
- What would our dream testimonial from a customer say?
- What can we offer for free that no one else does?
- You have just written a tell-all book about this company: Which secrets does it reveal?
- How can our services be turned into physical products? How can our products be turned into a service?

- If we could hire five more people, what unconventional skills would they have and why?

This type of questioning possesses the power to transform brands and entire industries. When you apply provocative inquiry to every corner of your business, there will be a collective ripple of unease. Embrace it: this is how status-quo busting happens, and what an innovation opportunity looks and sounds like.

6.7.2. Culture

Culture is an output, not an input of your leadership, and there are three pillars for creating a startup or innovative culture, regardless of your organization size:

1. **Speed of Execution:** The number one reason why startups succeed is speed. Successful startups are those that can simply maneuver, iterate, or build faster than their competitors.
2. **Empowerment of People:** I am often asked what I do as a CEO, my response is "I enable people to make decisions until they can't, and then step in so they can." Empowerment is about giving ownership of a problem, the resources they require to solve that problem, and a share in the reward that comes from solving that problem.
3. **Tolerance of Failure:** Being innovative means you are going to break things. Tolerance of failure means that rather than rewarding the success, you reward the attempt. Tolerance of failure means you openly discuss when things go wrong, and collectively work out how to prevent it, and then empower the people to ensure it does not happen again.

Chapter 7

The Stakeholder Perspective

CONTENTS

7.1. GOVERNMENT

In creating and developed nations, governments are updating strategies in light of key sustainability issues, including ozone-depleting substance discharges, dangerous chemicals, water utilization, work, and human rights.

In the United States, there is restored enthusiasm for growing more compelling oversight of and responsibility for corporate exercises that effect society and the earth. Specifically, the eagerly awaited control of carbon outflows will give a more level playing field for bring down producers. However, these measures are very much dependent on the elections of 2017.

7.2. INVESTORS

More investors are currently requesting that organizations detail and measure sustainability dangers and opportunities in their monetary divulgences. As organization proprietors, they look to sustainability execution as an indicator of solid administration and long term considering future development potential. Long-term speculators compensate organizations that coordinate sustainability into key objectives. Sustainability-based stock files benchmark corporate execution against peer organizations and place weight on organizations to meet expanding desires.

7.3. WORKER'S UNIONS

Unions anticipate that organizations will address issues that influence employees, regardless of whether they are financial issues, for example, wages, and social insurance, or natural issues, for example, wellbeing, and environmental change. They effectively activate and speak to their individuals through formal arrangements, engagement on open approach, and coordinated effort with different businesses that help basic positions.

7.4. COMMON SOCIETY

NGOs and group bunches anticipate that organizations will address their ecological and social effects. Offering voice to planetary concerns and who and what is to come, and additionally those affected by corporate activity today, these gatherings weight organizations through legitimate activity, open crusades and cooperation to address a full scope of sustainability issues.

7.5. BUSINESS PARTNERS AND SUPPLIERS

Organizations expect that those they work with will take after similar principles that they improve the situation incorporating sustainability into their business. Business-to-business connections in this manner progressively consolidate sustainability models and criteria reflected through changes in Request for Proposals (RFP), and acquisition rules. As clients, organizations are themselves pushing sustainability crosswise over areas and the esteem chain. Gatherings of organizations in the car, clothing, electric utility, hardware, and pharmaceutical areas are among those working together to raise sustainability guidelines over their whole industry supply chains.

7.6. CONSUMERS

A developing section of individual customers are putting their cash where their qualities are, requesting a comprehension of the sustainability effects of the items and administrations that they purchase. Purchaser concerns incorporate the conditions under which items are made, the materials utilized, and post-utilize recyclability. An expanding enthusiasm for dependable sustainability data goes with this pattern, including at the purpose of procurement. The monetary emergency has not dulled buyer sense of duty regarding nature, with 78% of U.S. buyers in a 2009 Cone review showing that they are as likely or more inclined to purchase ecologically dependable items as they were before the emergency.

One of the most grounded powers requesting change originates from inside. Current employees and skilled employment competitors look for work that is important and of verifiable incentive to society, and they are set up to get a lower pay in return for work at a socially capable organization. They search out bosses that have an unmistakable vision for their commitment to an economical worldwide economy, and once inside, hope to impact the heading of corporate sustainability and drive upgrades through their particular obligations.

Similarly, as with the current crumple of the monetary markets – originating from an absence of controls, disappointment of responsibility, and deficient exposure of dangers that speculators were expecting – sustainability and environmental change additionally exhibit broad concealed dangers to which the money related industry needs to give careful consideration.

Progressively, speculators are perceiving and making a move on administration issues, including natural and social issues that posture material business dangers and that can possibly specifically influence long term monetary execution. On the other hand, they see significant advantages to be picked up by financing organizations that are proactive on these issues.

The Investor Network on Climate Risk (INCR) is centered around the monetary effects of environmental change. The gathering was built up in 2003 with an enrollment of twelve financial specialists speaking to $600 billion in aggregate resources, and now incorporates more than 80 speculators with $8 trillion in aggregate resources. INCR has been exceptionally dynamic, calling for solid national and worldwide atmosphere strategies, asking the U.S. Securities and Exchange Commission for institutionalized revelation of sustainability dangers, specifically captivating organizations, recording investor resolutions, and making critical interests in clean innovation.

We have seen a blast of sustainability and particularly atmosphere-centered research and speculation items in a previous couple of years, quite a bit of it occurring amidst one of our most noteworthy financial moderate downs. We have additionally observed the number of money-related records that address sustainability widen and extend.

A considerable lot of these records are being overseen by "standard" money-related houses, including the S&P/IFCI Carbon Efficient Index, HSBC Climate Index, Prudential Green Commodities Index, FTSE4Good, and NASDAQ's Global Sustainability 50 Index. Also, speculators are seeing the outcomes. For instance, KLD Research and Analytics (now part of Risk Metrics) propelled a Global Climate 100 Index and posted a 57% return (17% annualized) since its dispatch in 2006.

Notwithstanding remain solitary sustainability lists, money-related businesses are incorporating sustainability into center basic leadership. Various banks, including Citi, Morgan Stanley, and Credit Suisse, have set up a carbon-centered due ingenuity process for any future loaning for coal-let go control and other carbon concentrated undertakings. Bank of America has likewise indicated initiative by setting a particular focus to diminish the rate of ozone-depleting substance outflows in its loaning to the utility business, and by transparency openly that it is utilizing a $20 to $40 per ton cost of carbon in assessing credits.

Socially dependable contributing has advanced from being a "boutique" issue, to developing at a quicker pace than the universe of all venture resources under expert administration – growing 18% in the vicinity of 2005 and 2007 – while professionally oversaw resources became under 3%. A report by Robeco Investment Management and Booz and Company anticipates that dependable contributing will develop to as much as 20% of aggregate resources under administration by 2015.

The budgetary emergency has additionally brought about an expanded concentrate on the hazard administration forms at money-related organizations, with a push for more noteworthy straightforwardness, all-encompassing danger distinguishing proof and a more drawn out term center. The 658 signatories to the Principles for Responsible Investment, which all in all speak to over $18 trillion of advantages, trust it is in the long-term enthusiasm of their recipients to figure sustainability speculation basic leadership.

A 2009 Report by the Asset Management working gathering of the UNEP Financial Initiative declares that speculators have a guardian obligation to think about sustainability segments and those that don't may confront genuine hazard by opening themselves up to lawful liabilities.

The primary concern for business is this: financial specialists are compensating organizations that see how sustainability issues affect their business and that are executing procedures and activities that will empower them to flourish in a sustainable worldwide economy.

Chapter 8

The Eight Key Expectations

CONTENTS

8.1. GOVERNANCE FOR SUSTAINABILITY

1. **Board Oversight:** The Board of Directors will provide oversight and accountability for corporate sustainability strategy and performance. A committee of the board will assume specific responsibility for sustainability oversight within its charter.
2. **Management Accountability:** The CEO and company management–from C-Suite executives to business unit and functional heads–will be responsible for achieving sustainability goals.
3. **Executive Compensation:** Sustainability performance results are a core component of compensation packages and incentive plans for all executives.
4. **Corporate Policies and System:** Companies will embed sustainability considerations into corporate policies and risk management systems to guide day-to-day decision-making.
5. **Public Policy:** Companies will clearly state their position on relevant sustainability public policy issues. Any lobbying will be done transparently and in a manner consistent with sustainability commitments and strategies.

8.2. STAKEHOLDER ENGAGEMENT

1. **Focus Engagement Activities:** Companies will systematically identify a diverse group of stakeholders and regularly engage with them on sustainability risks and opportunities, including materiality analysis.
2. **Stakeholder Dialogue:** Companies will engage stakeholders in a manner that is ongoing, in-depth, timely, and involves all appropriate parts of the business. Companies will disclose how they are incorporating stakeholder input into corporate strategy and business decision-making.
3. **Investor Engagement:** Companies will address specific sustainability risks and opportunities during annual meetings, analyst calls, and other investor communications.
4. **C Level Engagement:** Senior executives will participate in stakeholder engagement processes to inform strategy, risk management and enterprise-wide decision-making.

8.3. DISCLOSURE

1. **Standards for Disclosure:** Companies will disclose all relevant sustainability information using the Global Reporting Initiative (GRI) Guidelines as well as additional sector-relevant indicators.
2. **Disclose in Financial Findings:** Companies will disclose material sustainability issues in financial filings.
3. **Scope and Content:** Companies will regularly disclose significant performance data and targets relating to their global direct operations, subsidiaries, joint ventures, products, and supply chain. Disclosure will be balanced, covering challenges as well as positive impacts.
4. **Vehicles for Disclosure:** Companies will release sustainability information through a range of disclosure vehicles, including stand-alone reports, annual reports, financial filings, websites, and social media.
5. **Product Transparency:** Companies will provide verified and standardized sustainability performance information about their products at the point of sale and through other publicly available channels.
6. **Verification and Assurance:** Companies will verify key sustainability performance data to ensure valid results and will have their disclosures reviewed by an independent, credible third party.

8.4. PERFORMANCE

1. **Operations:** Companies will invest the necessary resources to achieve environmental neutrality and to demonstrate respect for human rights in their operations. Companies will measure and improve performance related to GHG emissions, energy efficiency, facilities, and buildings, water, waste, and human rights.

a. *Greenhouse Gas Emissions and Energy Efficiency:* Companies will reduce greenhouse gas emissions by 25% from their 2005 baseline by 2020: Improving energy efficiency of operations by at least 50%. Reducing electricity demand by at least 15%. Obtaining at least 30% of energy from renewable sources.

b. *Facilities and Buildings:* Companies will ensure that at least 50% of their owned or leased facilities, and all new construction, will meet rigorous green buildings standards. When setting up facilities, companies will follow best practices that incorporate sustainable land-use and smart growth considerations.

c. *Water Management:* Companies will assess water-related impacts and risks and will set targets to improve water use and wastewater discharge, with priority given to operations in water-stressed regions.

d. *Eliminate Waste:* Companies will design (or redesign, as appropriate) manufacturing and business processes as closed-loop systems, reducing toxic air emissions and hazardous and non-hazardous waste to zero.

e. *Human Rights:* Companies will regularly assess key risks related to human rights throughout their entire operations, and will employ management systems that are aligned with internal policies and support the implementation of universal standards.

8.5. SUPPLY CHAIN

Companies will require their suppliers to meet the same environmental and social standards as the company has established for itself. Companies will establish sustainable procurement criteria, catalyze improved supplier performance, and facilitate disclosure of suppliers' sustainability information.

1. **Policies and Codes:** Companies will set supply chain policies and codes aligned with overall social and environmental standards.
2. **Align Procurement Practices:** Companies will address sustainability performance in procurement criteria and contracting.
3. **Engaging Suppliers:** Companies will ensure that at least 75% of the company's Tier 1 and Tier 2 suppliers and 50% of Tier 3 suppliers meet the company's standards for sustainability performance.
4. **Measurement and Disclosure:** Companies will disclose a list of their Tier 1 and 2 suppliers and measure and disclose suppliers' sustainability performance.

8.6. TRANSPORT AND LOGISTICS

Companies will systematically minimize their sustainability impact by enhancing the resiliency of their logistics. Companies will prioritize low impact transportation systems and modes, and address business travel and commuting.

1. **Transportation Management:** Companies will develop transportation criteria that incorporate distance requirements from site to market and establish decentralized and localized distribution networks.
2. **Transportation Modes:** Companies will review logistics to prioritize low-impact transportation modes.
3. **Business Travel and Commuting:** Companies will decrease greenhouse gas emissions from business travel and employee commuting by 50% from a baseline of 2005.

8.7. PRODUCTS AND SERVICES

Companies will design and deliver products and services that are aligned with sustainability goals by innovating business models, allocating R&D spend, designing for sustainability, communicating the impacts of products and services, reviewing marketing practices and advancing strategic collaborations.

1. **Business Model Innovation:** Companies will innovate business models to reduce material inputs and prioritize a transition to sustainable products and services.
2. **R&D and Capital Investment:** Companies will use sustainability as a primary filter through which all R&D and capital investments are made. 50% of the R&D investment will be focused on developing sustainability solutions.
3. **Design for Sustainability:** Companies will approach all product development and product management decisions with full consideration of the social and environmental impacts of the product throughout its lifecycle.
4. **Marketing Practices:** Companies will align their marketing practices and product revenue targets with their sustainability goals, and will market their designed-for-sustainability products and services with at least the same effort as their marketing of other products.

5. **Strategic Collaborations:** Companies will collaborate within and across sectors to innovate and scale sustainable products and services, and contribute to the development of open source solutions.

8.8. EMPLOYEES

Companies will make sustainability considerations a core part of recruitment, compensation, and training, and will encourage sustainable lifestyle choices.

1. **Recruitment and Retention:** Companies will incorporate sustainability criteria into recruitment protocols, employee performance processes, compensation, and incentives.
2. **Training and Support:** Companies will develop and implement formal training on key sustainability issues for all executives and employees, and facilitate coaching, mentoring, and networks for sustainability knowledge sharing.
3. **Promoting Sustainable Lifestyles:** Companies will promote sustainable lifestyle choices across their community of employees through education and innovative employee benefits options.

Chapter 9

Strategic Competencies

CONTENTS

9.1. INTRODUCTION

Filled by globalization, innovative change, population development, and moving socioeconomics, sustainability superpowers will influence the capacity of business to succeed and flourish throughout the following 30 years. With the worldwide population anticipated that would increment from 7 to 9 billion individuals by 2050, organizations should rehash themselves to secure their entrance to assets and the social permit to work and develop. On the WGAP, mankind is as of now devouring 1.5 times the assets that can be restored in a year. Similarly, as concerning, the pay imbalance gap keeps on broadening, additionally undermining social attachment. Organizations that foresee, anticipate, and help lighten these patterns will not just form their upper hand, they will add to building a suitable society for all.

For the business to succeed in this new worldwide setting, present, and future leaders will require a large group of new abilities and capabilities. Driving organizations will retool their ability administration frameworks to mirror the new competency objectives to position their organizations for future achievement. They will characterize the mission-basic ranges of abilities and outlooks leaders need to make and secure future incentives for the organization and society and install these in their authoritative competency models.

9.2. UNDERSTANDING COMPETENCY MODELS

Competency models are a key instrument to recognize, create, and convey top ability to drive superior and acknowledge business results. They characterize the execution and behavioral desires-the aptitudes and information-which add to business achievement. Driving organizations utilize competency Profiles to illuminate their ability administration techniques, including:

- Recruitment and determination;
- Onboarding;
- Training and improvement;
- Career improvement arranging;
- Job depictions;
- Performance administration;
- Compensation;
- Succession arranging.

Organizational competency models are basic devices for the determination and enrollment of up-and-coming leaders or high possibilities. Indicating the key aptitudes and learning pertinent to authoritative achievement enables leaders to comprehend what is required keeping in mind the end goal to enhance execution levels. By imparting reliable, detectable, and quantifiable execution gages, competency models give a guide to professional success. They additionally uncover opportunities for advancement mediations to upgrade individual and group competency levels. In addition, as businesses progressively remunerate directors not only for their outcomes but rather for how they accomplish these outcomes, sustainability skills shed light on the attractive properties that legitimacy motivator pay.

Well-established organizations overhaul their competency profiles because of mergers, an adjustment in the plan of action, or another essential move. Similarly, the changing business condition requires a competency display refreshment. Previously, businesses worked inside a genuinely unsurprising, stable framework. Conversely, the present businesses work inside huge and complex reliant systems, expecting them to work all the more remotely and receive a more forward-looking methodology. With a specific end goal to encourage compelling basic leadership in this new business reality, customary administration abilities, for example, examination, relationship-building, and change initiative should be taken to another level. Business leaders will require more noteworthy capability in overseeing complex foundational change and hierarchical change. They will likewise require further developed psychological, social, and passionate limits.

9.3. ADDRESSING THE COMPETENCY GAP

Many management directors accept there is a sustainability aptitude and learning execution gap in their businesses, as uncovered by the Ash ridge Business School in a 2008 worldwide review directed with 194 business leaders. More than 75% think creating sustainability aptitudes and learning in their association is vital, while less than 10% trust their association is doing this well. They likewise trust that business colleges and expert enrollment bodies ought to convey sustainability instruction and training, yet few are doing this effectively. Tending to this begins with recognizing the sustainability skills that will be expected of future leaders. While much has been composed about this competency gap, there is an absence of direction on the most proficient method to address it through authoritative competency models. The present examination arranges the key abilities distinguished in the sustainability and administration writing esteemed essential to drive high sustainability and, in this way, authoritative execution and composes it into a competency display system. More than 30 articles, research papers, and books distributed in recent years by HR and corporate sustainability consultancies, sustainability business systems, administration specialists, scholastic organizations, and others were checked on. From this, the best-prescribed abilities which are viewed as fundamental for business leaders to guide their businesses through the dynamic sustainability landscape of the coming decades were distinguished. The underlying discoveries were imparted to specialists in the different abilities for approval and refinement.

9.4. SUSTAINABILITY TALENT MANAGEMENT

The literature review reveals there are five sustainability competencies-three skills and two knowledge areas-which companies should add to their existing leadership competency models to position the firm for future success. These include:

- Systems thinking;
- External collaboration;
- Social innovation;
- Sustainability literacy; and
- Active values.

While the sustainability superpowers are new and their full impacts are not liable to be felt for at least 10 years, groundbreaking organizations would be astute to consider incorporating these five abilities in their authority profiles. The business advantages of doing as such include:

- Better capacity to foresee and oversee dangers;
- Increased advancement and opportunity distinguishing proof;
- Early access to new markets with economical products and administrations;
- Enhanced critical thinking and more successful basic leadership;
- Greater capacity to react to changing monetary conditions; and
- Improved employee fascination, maintenance, and engagement.

Organizations that reskill their authority positions to prevail later in the economy will discover early arrangements and understand an upper hand while enhancing the social setting for their worker and client families and groups.

9.6. FIVE SUSTAINABILITY LEADERSHIP COMPETENCIES

For what reason does it make a difference?

Fundamental super patterns will influence the suitability of business and society and create expansive scale issues requiring all-encompassing, not reductionist, arrangements. Prompt difficulties are frequently profoundly installed in frameworks and must be tended to at the root through changing foundational co-operations, standards, or asset streams. A framework thinking viewpoint helps leaders all the more completely comprehend the issues they confront, which thus encourages them to recognize and use their focuses to cultivate change. Numerous points of view increment experiences and alternatives to enhance hierarchical flexibility and deftness. They are the best way to completely comprehend complex issues and may permit win-win answers for managing struggle and rivalry. Frameworks to upgrade the capacity of leaders to watch and distinguish behavioral subtle elements in the exercises of clients, providers, contenders, and others to cultivate and enhance advancement. This reasoning enhances the ability to anticipate conceivable bounce back impacts-where improvements are made in one region with fallback in others.

9.6.1. Systems Thinking

What is it? It is the capacity to see and comprehend interconnections and association between performers (partners, connections, and so forth.) and areas (social, financial, ecological), crosswise over time (past, present to future) and scales (neighborhood to worldwide) to reframe and address difficulties and opportunities for business and societal advance. What capabilities does it expand upon? Critical thinking, analytical thinking, and strategic planning.

9.6.1.1. Foundational

Applies frameworks thinking to issues and choices:

- Sees the master plan, takes a long term to see and comprehends the expansive setting while tending to an issue or challenge.
- Takes a comprehensive way to deal with the investigation that spotlights in transit a framework's constituent parts interrelate and how frameworks function after some time and inside the setting of bigger frameworks-can move from reality-based administration to design-based administration as needed.

- Demonstrates "entire framework mindfulness" which is the ability to switch between alternate points of view, scales, and perspectives to see the master plan and interconnections and interdependencies inside the framework at all levels, including having the capacity to downsize to little subtle elements.
- Frames issues as far as long-term patterns and underlying drivers as opposed to quick concerns.
- Construct's framework maps that find a test, association, or strategy in connection to different performers, trends, organizations, and so on that have made the present circumstance.
- Perceives the bigger framework and web of connections-businesses, supply chains, enterprises, urban areas, districts, and eco-frameworks-of which the association is a section, instead of concentrating on the detail of a specific piece.
- Understands the interconnectedness and part of every on-screen character in the public eye (government, business, common society) and how they interface with each other.
- Understands the businesses between issues at a nearby, provincial, biological system, national or worldwide level, and creates business arrangements in connection to the scale and nature of the test.
- Pays regard for interrelationships, examples, and progression to search for interconnections, underlying drivers, and various causalities and to characterize and take care of issues.
- Takes a sweeping, 'superior' perspective of an issue or challenge and keeps away from discontinuity of subjects and over-rearrangements of issues as basically right/wrong or genuine/false.
- Sees businesses between expansive, divergent assortments of information.

9.6.1.2. Advanced

Applies frameworks thinking in joint efforts with a specific end goal to progress hierarchical and fundamental change:

- Works in inside and outside coordinated efforts to examine complex frameworks crosswise over industry segments, esteem chains, product life-cycles, and geographic scales (neighborhood to worldwide) to see immediate and aberrant effects, exchange offs, falling impacts, inactivity, criticism circles, time delays, and unintended outcomes of individual, hierarchical, and aggregate activities to outline sustainable products and strong and versatile businesses and frameworks.

- Recognizes how changes to parts of the framework influence the entire utilization and comprehension of how components of a framework relate and forms inside an entire associate to outline dangers and opportunities, distinguish conceivable use focuses or activities, upgrade them for a coveted result, make arrangements and advance the wellbeing of frameworks.
- Creates helpful change in money-related markets, customer conduct, hierarchical change, open strategy, innovation, and other substantial frameworks.
- Demonstrates consciousness of complex framework practices, for example, rise, causation, inactivity, and tipping focuses and the way they join to deliver unforeseen, non-straight, and sudden change.
- Has aptitude in standards of frameworks administration, for example, flexibility, and overseeing for the rise.
- Applies multi-disciplinary and tri-segment (government, business, common society) points of view to framework change.
- Has huge multi-disciplinary experience, incorporating capability in at least two zones, for example, engineering, and promoting, human sciences and modern outline, engineering, and brain research.
- Uses framework thinking devices, for example, causal circle graphs, stock, and stream outlines and reenactment models in shared advancement activities.

9.6.2. External Collaboration What Is It?

It is the capacity to impact and lead change past business limits and crosswise over orders and fields. A coordinated effort can be between organizations, and governments, and NGOs (non-administrative businesses), and multi-on-screen character organizations among each of the three. It empowers businesses to mutually create arrangements and cooperate for the soundness of the entire framework:

1. **For What Reason Does it Make a Difference?** The present hierarchical and societal difficulties are too huge and complex to be tended to by people or businesses working alone. Systems of interdependency make common dependence in which coordinated effort is vital for advancement. An association's critical sustainability impacts are regularly found up or downstream of their operations, requiring communitarian exertion with providers, clients, business accomplices, contenders, and others to acknowledge arrangements.
2. Working cooperatively can produce unwaveringness and construct social funding to empower solid connections and cultivate authoritative flexibility. To research new market opportunities and shape the financial setting in which they work, businesses need to connect with others. Working crosswise over divisions and here and there esteem chains is turning into a business need as sustainability results must be accomplished through aggregate exertion that handles fundamental blockages crosswise over markets. It empowers an organization to open innovativeness and advancement and access different information, abilities, and systems while sharing danger and pool speculation.
3. **What Capabilities Does it Expand Upon?:** Internal collaboration, relationship building, and conflict resolution.

9.6.2.1. Foundational

Stakeholder issue recognizable proof and discussion:

- Understands the business case for viable outside coordination effort-including opportunity costs (of teaming up versus not teaming up);
- Understands the key partners that affect and are affected by the association (emphatically and adversely, specifically or in a roundabout way) and comprehends their essential advantages, concerns, and desires; can portray accomplishment from the points of view of differing partners;
- Engages partners through meeting and discourse to recognize issues, resolve exchange offs, adjust contending requests and enhance products and administrations;
- Gains alternate points of view and experiences from systems administration and banding together with different people and

businesses; adopts a key strategy to systems administration; comprehends the estimation of systems for learning, information spread, and social change;

- Cross-prepares thoughts and cultivates choices and crossbreeds by working crosswise over business orders and segments (e.g., creators, and product engineers from one organization cross-treat with sustainability, deals, and advertising specialists from another);
- Understands the parts of various businesses, to figure out who has basic leadership specialist and to build up administration, responsibility, and correspondence measures;
- Understands issues at the convergence of business and society;
- Develops banding together and joint effort methodologies;
- Understands how to assemble communitarian exercises that advance the value and horizontal reasoning in the decision-production process where every on-screen character contributes similarly, with a comparable level of engagement (i.e., sidelong rather than various leveled); and
- Possesses abilities in advanced, web-based social networking and in-person correspondence and coordinated effort apparatuses and methods.

9.6.2.2. Advanced

Multi-partner co-made arrangements:

- Builds multi-party, activity arranged, commonly gainful coordinated efforts with differing divisions, enterprises, providers, clients, ages, disciplines, capacities, societies, groups, and businesses, including eccentric partners and contenders.
- Harnesses systems to achieve societally and frameworks change objectives.
- Fosters put stock in, commonality, and shared comprehension to construct an aggregate vision, produce a typical purpose, and encourage aggregate imagination to enhance business and social results.
- Understands and bridles various plans of action and societies from tri-segment involvement in business, government, and common society.

- Navigates crosswise over various institutional and social limits and all divisions of society (counting academia, of all shapes and sizes social businesses, nebulous systems, instructive establishments, and so on.), drawing in with on-screen characters all through frameworks, incorporating people with significant influence and those in more negligible or defenseless positions in the public eye, to address foundational challenges.
- Understands and is touchy to power and benefit (i.e., has pondered social disparity, their own history, and social position/rank-by and by, professionally, hierarchically, sectorally) and distinguishes and portrays key cases of how people and social gatherings encounter imbalance; outlines and executes procedures or medications that enhance the essentialness of energy and benefit.
- Understands how to address focused limits and rivalry-related lawful issues.
- Leads virtual, cross-hierarchical groups.

9.6.3. Social Innovation What Is It?

It is the capacity to produce and empower plan of action, association, and framework level development to progress both business and social esteem. It moves the aggregate concentration from receptive critical thinking to co-making the future with partners.

1. **For What Reason Does it Make a Difference?:** How businesses respond to sustainability superpowers will influence their capacity to succeed and flourish. All segments, esteem chains, plans of action, and capacities should be re-designed to empower synchronous business and societal advance.

   Aptitudes in development age and usage are expected to acknowledge authoritative and substantial scale change. The capacity to transform many-sided quality into circumstance will give businesses a future upper hand.
2. **What skills does it expand upon?**: Change Leadership, Creativity, and Innovation.

9.6.3.1. Foundational

Incremental bits of knowledge and arrangements:

- Identifies and actualizes chances to enhance and update products, administrations, and procedures to make incremental business and social esteem.
- Questions existing conditions, suspicions, aggregate standards and got knowledge; considers unheard of options and regards authoritative imperatives and discernments as discussable and transformable.
- Encourages a scrutinizing outlook and welcomes workers to challenge presumptions because of past encounters; backings remunerate and incorporates assorted and whimsical perspectives.
- Explores limitations in innovative ways and reclassifies difficulties to benefit from businesses crosswise over them; reframes issues as circumstances.
- Pushing ahead:
- Connects inconsequential inquiries, issues, or thoughts from various fields to develop new bits of knowledge;
- Experiments and gains from disappointment.
- Learns from innovative accomplishments outside the business and consistently examines cases from different ventures in group gatherings; remains side by side of sustainability drifts that are changing different divisions and thinks about how to apply them.
- Provides partners with open access.
- Makes choices when enough is known and fights the temptation to know everything; alters activities in light of what is found out.
- Confidently utilizes on the web and virtual instruments and assets to source and execute thoughts from outsiders.

9.6.3.2. Progressed

The association and framework change:

- Builds and acknowledges optimistic dreams that encourage long-haul authoritative and framework change.
- Leads the advancement of, and conveys, a convincing future that creates social and business esteem; drives association-wide activities to imagine and create answers for foundational issues and difficulties; outlines and oversees leap forward systems and plans amid unexpected difficulties and impacts.

- Shifts the aggregate concentration from responding to issues to co-making and building positive dreams for what is to come.
- Encourages experimentation and development all through the association and deliberately utilizes fast prototyping systems to cultivate learning and assemble hierarchical energy.
- Embraces vulnerability as an impetus for new thoughts and plans of action; utilizes versatile administration to progressively control complex change activities, changing the outline or system as the setting shifts.
- Embraces imaginative pulverization as an open door, seeing astuteness in consider the development of insecurity keeping in mind the end goal to cultivate transformative change; goes out on a limb to upset inheritance plans of action.
- Encourages social business enterprise in the association and empowers huge scale advancement; invigorates and augments the group of trailblazers; moves aggregate experimentation.
- Creates interdisciplinary groups and community procedures to develop sympathy through discussion, perception, or encounters; utilizes human esteems and individuals driven methodologies, (e.g., human-focused plan techniques) to enhance or make new products and administrations.
- Surfaces, supports, and deals with the dynamic strains of the association and partner framework and defies troublesome certainties about the present reality; deals with the imaginative pressure amongst vision and reality to move new methodologies and grow new systems; creates change procedures that distinguish unwanted states and elements and imagines attractive results.
- Harnesses pressures as a wellspring of development and imagination.
- Exploit's opportunities in different parts of the framework to make change around an issue by working crosswise over scales or authoritative/area limits.

9.6.4. Sustainability Literacy What Is It?

It is the learning of how ecological, monetary, and social sustainability impacts the association and how the association impacts sustainability. It includes attention to how to enhance the association's sustainability execution and how the association and plan of action can be adjusted to produce positive business and societal advantages.

1. **For What Reason Does it Make a Difference?:** Sustainability powers will influence business and societal accomplishment over the medium to the long haul. Foresighted organizations will use the sustainability patterns to plan new plans of action, construct their social permit to work, and develop and emphatically impact societal results. Connected sustainability learning can improve esteem security and creation- and cultivate an upper hand for the firm.
2. **What Capabilities Does it Expand Upon?:** Business Acumen and Financial Leadership.

9.6.4.1. Foundational

Sustainability procedure and practical information:

- Familiar with foundational ideas of sustainability; learning of reasonable advancement and central socio-environmental ideas and standards;
- Aware of rising ecological and social patterns (counting little patterns and frail signs) and the dangers and opportunities they make for the association and its clients, providers, part, and general business working setting over the medium to long haul;
- Knowledge of the association's immediate and circuitous social and natural effects;
- Aware of how partners and their associates are reacting to sustainability superpowers and can distinguish and organize important partner interests or concerns;
- Understands the changing part of business in the public eye;
- Aligns social and ecological destinations with money-related objectives and explains the business benefits for seeking after social and natural goals;
- Designs and executes procedures connected to the association's center business methodology that enhance the association's social and ecological execution, with long term dreams, medium-term objectives, and here and now designs and strategies;
- Applies sustainability to their part, capacity, and everyday choices and components sustainability learning into key, money related and operational basic leadership;

- Implements sustainability standards into authoritative capacities, approaches, and objectives; and
- Uses situation arranging, back-throwing, and problem area and materiality investigation devices.

9.6.4.2. Progressed

Social reason and installation learning:

- Aware of how the organization makes, upgrades, or decimates normal, social, relationship, and human capital and its significance to business and societal achievement.

9.6.5. Active Values What Is It?

This portrays self and entire framework learning and mindfulness. It envelops the capacity to create and seek after higher reason inside self, groups, and business; to rehearse care, and to cultivate and empower individual and hierarchical change.

1. **For What Reason Does it Make a Difference?:** High passionate knowledge cultivates strength, responsibility, trust, and correspondence between colleagues and outside partners, every one of whom is fundamental to empower business, societal, and transformational change. Similarly, dynamic esteems are expected to manufacture versatile abilities and strong businesses, enhance cooperation, and coordinate effort and surface, acknowledge, and receive advancement. Care and pondering practices help change existing mental models and upgrade center and responsibility amid testing, vague, and quickly evolving circumstances. An empathic and merciful outlook can create a product and administration development lined up with center human esteems that are pertinent to clients' authentic needs and interests. Arrangement of profound individual esteems with business, society, and the planet's needs can diminish pressure, enhance profitability, and make opportunity and success.
2. **What Abilities Does it Expand Upon?**: Decent variety, Integrity, and Self-Management.

9.6.5.1. Establishment

Individual mindfulness and qualities arrangement:

- Regularly self-reflects structurally; perceives and beats oblivious presumptions, blindsides, constraints, and individual protection from change;
- Actively encounters and watches an idea or an inclination (particularly those that are negative and constraining), supposition, judgment, propensity, feeling or sensation, for example, fear, perplexity, strife or want, and after that forgoes quickly responding or reacting to the circumstance;
- Complements balanced idea with instinct, goals, fears, qualities, recollections, and a feeling-based approach;
- Understands possess feelings and needs and those of others (enthusiastic knowledge) and can see their own particular place in, and effect on, a circumstance (reflexiveness);
- Exhibit humbleness-can state, "I don't have the foggiest idea" and request help; is guided by modesty and a feeling of appreciation and sympathy.
- Open to gaining from others and can let the unforeseen (and frequently exceptionally imaginative) develop amid direness and time weights; open to thoughts that appear to be remote and notwithstanding undermining;
- Is a positive esteem a good example inside and outside the association and show adherence to an arrangement of qualities in great and awful circumstances; advocates for dependable business administration inside and remotely;
- Aligns profound worry for social-biological trustworthiness to business parts and choices and is guided by a pledge to genuineness, truth, and straightforwardness in choices, systems, and plans;
- Transcends self-intrigue and concentrates on the group or more prominent great; and
- Involved in businesses and occasions progressing biological and social sustainability.

9.6.5.2. Progressed

Individual change and higher reason:

- Is completely mindful and show at the time and consequently watches their considerations and sentiments and how they are relating, detecting, and judging through purposeful perceptions of different measurements of their self (counting the physical, mental, shadow, enthusiastic, and otherworldly domains).
- Demonstrates genuine acknowledgment and graciousness toward every one of the measurements of themselves as well as other people, paying little heed to the situation; reflects upon others without judgment.
- Possesses an attitude that sees the world, other individuals, and all circumstances as a component of an entire in which everything is associated and settles on decisions and seeks after activities in light of the conviction that everything is between associated-moving past mindfulness to extraordinary mindfulness.
- Seeks individual change and seeks after formative encounters which challenge their reality sees.
- Engages in transformational change activities that expand upon a profound association with themselves, the general population they work with, the planet, and the more extensive world.
- Pursues work for a reason more noteworthy than themselves and sees work and business as a coordinated method to help change society; shows an inheritance outlook to tackle business to enhance prospects for present and who and what is to come.
- Creates a higher reason for themselves and adjusts their true nature to activities inside and outside the business and, if what they are doing does not line up with a reason, modify, and upgrade it until the point when it does.
- Supports groups to take advantage of their instinct and develop aggregate knowledge; makes and catalyzes higher reason for others, drawing upon this for motivation and understanding.
- Fosters intelligent and generative discussions through the formation of precisely organized procedures of examination and reflection; makes opportunities for individuals and groups to address, research, and make the importance of the qualities and presumptions that advise the basic leadership process.

- Cultivates their own particular mindfulness and extends their reasoning through pensive and physical practices, for example, reflection, yoga, journaling, nature strolls, instructing, playing a melodic instrument, workmanship, judo, withdraws, peer coaching, and groups of training.

Rehearsed together, these five skills will fabricate solid leaders, groups, businesses, and social orders and position the business for progress over the medium to the long haul. Businesses that enlist, select, create, boost, and convey ability with these attributes will not just receive business rewards; they additionally make sound working environments, resolve individual business strains and acknowledge more amicable groups and social orders inside the biological limit of the planet.

9.7. RELATED COMPETENCIES

The five abilities distinguished through this exploration are exceedingly interlaced. One arrangement of practices fortifies another set, making an upright circle whereby one competency empowers and upgrades the others in a commonly gainful manner. This blend shows the basic idea of these five limits and their reliance as outlined beneath: Systems thinking → reveals more instrumental relationship → opportunities for strategic collaboration → social innovation which is enhanced by → systems thinking and seeing a system from different viewpoints → sustainability knowledge helps prioritize strategic investments and embed sustainability → values-based self and system awareness → fosters open-mindedness and enhances the ability to collaborate → social innovation, etc.

9.8. SUSTAINABILITY COMPETENCIES

Creativity and development are acknowledged through a sense-production-the capacity to interface things to make new thoughts. To encourage social development, it is basic to team up with external accomplices and to see a framework unexpectedly. It is critical to know about and defeat, existing mental models because of prior time and experience. Too, sustainability learning advises the key concentration and catalyzes hierarchical change. This association recommends that pioneer competency models ought to mirror every one of the five credits to guarantee an adjusted and compelling outcome.

9.9. ADVANCE TOWARD EMBEDDING SUSTAINABILITY

As businesses advance with sustainability and CSR, they ceaselessly insert sustainability advance into their human asset frameworks, corporate reason, and plans of action. The figure beneath demonstrates a run-of-the-mill development way businesses seek after. It is a device that administrators, directors, and sheets can use to stock their advances (Figure 9.1).

Figure 9.1. Sustainability embedment path.

9.10. WHAT'S NEXT?

These capabilities do not characterize what makes individuals and firms fruitful today.

They expect the ability ventures organizations should make to encourage business and social accomplishment throughout the following 10 to 20 years. They perceive that what made leaders fruitful in the past may not prepare them to be viable later on.

These five abilities are regarded as the best ability speculations organizations should make to encourage both business and societal achievement in the decades to come.

While change begins at the best and requires vision, everybody has a part to play: sheets, officials, sustainability chiefs, and HR experts are urged to fuse them into their competency models and utilize them to choose, create, send, remunerate, perceive, and advance leaders.

By utilizing these five sustainability capabilities to characterize and drive superior, organizations will have the capacity to assemble an administration establishment to outline an effective course to what is to come.

Proficient affiliations, administration training, and business colleges ought to think about their part in outfitting future leaders with these capabilities. HR, ability, and learning, and improvement experts can recognize gaps in their present way to deal with administration advancement and fabricate these authority qualities to empower future practical and business achievement.

Businesses can utilize these skills to improve the ability pipeline and build up the up-and-coming age of leaders and the authoritative abilities to control enterprises toward a sustainable future for all.

9.11. EXAMPLE OF SUSTAINABILITY PROFILE

9.11.1. Sustainability and Sustainable Development Expert

9.11.1.1. Responsibilities

The following responsibilities apply to project-wide activities as well as to specific pillars of the project if it were necessary:

1. Project implementation and activities:

a. Coordination and management support on specific areas of the project, namely:

i. An Action Plan Framework for the Sustainability Strategy Initiative.

ii. A Monitoring and Evaluation Framework for the Sustainability Strategy Initiative, including if necessary individual frameworks for the core components and key performance and reporting indicators.

iii. A clear methodology for how the Sustainability Strategy Initiative will be monitored over time, with a reporting timeline to include the final evaluation.

iv. A mid-term review of the Sustainability Strategy Initiative including a brief report on the preliminary results of the mid-term review, to validate preliminary findings and test tentative conclusions and/or recommendations during the final evaluation.

v. A final evaluation of the Sustainability Strategy Initiative, including a comprehensive report on the results and recommendations for all stakeholders. The report will be clear and simply written.

b. Assist with relationship management:

i. Designing a Stakeholder Engagement framework and procedure to ensure long-term relationships are forged and the needs of all involved taken into consideration.

ii. Implement a Materiality Analysis framework to establish priority areas to be addressed throughout the project.

2. Communications:

a. Assist with the development and implementation of marketing and communications activities, incl. social media, newsletters, website, articles, and events for it to be aligned with the Sustainability component of the project.

b. Putting together materials containing resources, trends, and insights.

c. Support with opportunities to feature the project and team. This work can include research, submission of pitches for conferences, articles, etc.

d. Support and coordinate internal communication systems.

4. Partnerships and Awareness:

a. Assist with the setting up and development of partnerships.

b. Support the development of broader awareness about the Project.

c. Use an entrepreneurial approach, working with other members of the team, to identify funding opportunities in different areas of the project.

9.11.1.2. Availability

The Responsibilities described will be performed on an online basis, as I will be traveling and will be available to go onsite as of September 2018.

9.11.1.3. Language Capacity

i. The work will be delivered in English.

ii. apacity to discuss and have meetings in French, Spanish, and Portuguese if required.

9.12. CEO COMPETENCES

9.12.1. Introduction

The present corporate sheets have a major duty. With 16% CEO turnover and retirements the best driver of CEO renewal, their undertaking is to enlist the leaders of tomorrow. These new leaders will confront sensational change. They should explore the dangers and chances of fast population development and every one of those accompanies it on the grounds that by the year 2050, our planet will have 9 billion individuals.

As of now investors, customers, employees, governments, and host groups request that organizations successfully deal with their social and natural effects and help diagram a practical course for society. Deliberately shrewd organizations will upgrade their CSR and sustainability execution if they wish to succeed and flourish in the 21st century. To steward an organization through this changing landscape- and profit by the business advantages of doing as such-organizations will require CSR-skilled leaders in charge.

As this is a current business wonder, CEO progression arranging and enrollment programs regularly neglect to consider CSR qualities. To create and draw in leaders with CSR esteems and capacities, board HR and enrollment advisory groups should refresh CEO position profiles and progression designs with new CSR criteria. In any case, while an ever-increasing number of sheets understand the significance of viable CSR initiatives, they do not have the instruments and direction on the qualities required by this new organization official.

This guide tends to the holistic view. It assembles worldwide bits of knowledge into the best qualities CEOs and their successors should secure and make investor esteem through the quest for sustainability and CSR.

This guide furnishes sheets of executives with:

- The method of reasoning for including CSR and sustainability contemplations in CEO progression arranging and enrollment; and
- Recommended CSR criteria for incorporation in the determination models for the President and CEO. The rules depend on a writing review of pioneer CSR qualities (recorded in the reference section) and an output of driving organization practices here.

The proposed criteria are intended to supplement not dislodge conventional business enlistment necessities. Indeed, some of the criteria expand and improve customary qualities. A perfect CSR position profile would incorporate at least one of these CSR criteria. At times existing criteria can be revised to factor in the significant CSR segment, while in different cases the CSR criteria may bring about new competency necessities. Emphatically dedicated CSR organizations may wish to incorporate them all. The primary segment gives six reasons why CSR ought to be joined into CEO choice models. The second segment points of interest the accompanying six CSR choice criteria for CEO progression arranging and enrollment:

- "Values" good example;

- Externally mindful;
- CSR strategist and change administrator;
- Collaborates with partners;
- Catalyst and backer; and
- Develops dependable leaders.

Forward-looking sheets and those engaged with CEO determination are urged to consolidate the CSR criteria most important to their plans of action and esteem insurance and creation procedures. Future-sealed businesses will require CEOs with the vision, duty, and know-how to deal with the dangers and grab the opportunities introduced by the changing business setting.

Here are six reasons why your board and HR advisory group ought to be engaged with refreshing the CEO progression arranging and determination criteria.

9.12.2. Six Motivations to Add CSR Criteria to CEO Progression Arranging and Choice

1. **Successful CSR Execution:** Research uncovers that CEO administration is a basic achievement factor for successful CSR usage. Since CEOs set the "tone at the best" they have to show an individual sense of duty regarding, and faith in, the significance of CSR, so different leaders and all staff can turn out to be completely engaged with CSR execution.

   Keeping in mind the end goal to encourage CSR purchase in and take-up, CEOs need to reliably strengthen the organization's CSR duties and bearing through their own behavior and desires of others. Chiefs who just play lip administration to CSR will breed a culture of negativity and could cause a bargain of the organization's center esteems.
2. **Brand and Notoriety Administration:** Since society anticipates that business will show great CSR administration, the CEO must comprehend and models CSR states of mind, practices, and abilities that are lined up with partner esteems. Disregarding these authority limits may endanger the organization's image and notoriety. Research shows that numerous supervisors (43%) have been requested to accomplish something against their association's esteems. To keep this circumstance, it is vital that

the CEO models for different leaders and staff how to settle on choices that consider.

To be sure scholastic research into the 2008 worldwide budgetary emergency uncovered that administration and administration character disappointments added to the unreasonable development of use in money-related markets and the ensuing meltdown. These character imperfections included carelessness prompting unnecessary hazard-taking practices; absence of straightforwardness and now and again, an absence of uprightness; heedlessness to basic issues; absence of regard for people; and unreliability toward investors and the social orders inside which these businesses worked.

Chiefs with solid CSR esteems, arrangement, and limit are less inclined to have these character qualities and more averse to put their businesses and society in danger.

3. **Employee Fascination, Maintenance, and Engagement:** In a tight work showcase a solid CSR-adjusted pioneer can better draw in and hold top staff. Research uncovers that CSR is additionally one of the key factors in worker engagement. CSR can rouse worker devotion and profitability where it exists and can be the best danger to employee fulfillment where it is not bolstered. Workforce soundness can be upgraded if the business shows a solid CSR responsibility in both word and deed. Chiefs need to "walk the discussion" to set a good example for staff and conquer inner skepticism or uncertainty, particularly for those staff whose preparation and foundation make it troublesome for them to value the esteem and significance of CSR.
4. **Changing CSR Prerequisites:** Presidents need to comprehend that CSR is never again the consistent, magnanimous, and advertising exercise it used to be. It is currently an expert business teacher and board concern. More noteworthy desires, more open examination, and expanded weights elevate concentrate on how organizations profit, the effect they have on the groups they work in, and the significance of making long-term shared esteem.

   Various CSR dangers undermine business practicality, as recognized by the World Economic Forum. Later on, organizations should be stronger in an unpredictable, dubious, mind-boggling, and questionable world. Although not a CSR master, a keen CEO needs to comprehend CSR dangers and regard their importance to the organization, its market, its groups, and particularly its clients.

A CSR focal point on business can encourage advancement and opportunity creation, making CEO authority and support for CSR development a critical quality.

Today a CSR-proficient CEO needs to comprehend, oversee, and advance the material social, natural, and monetary dangers and chances of their business and those of its providers and clients. To guarantee their business has the limit and know-how to contend in this new working condition, the CEO needs a la mode thankfulness for the pertinence of CSR to business achievement.

5. **President as Open Face:** Progressively the general population anticipates that organizations will lead on issues identified with thriving and versatility in the groups and markets in which they work. As organizations turn out to be all the more unmistakably connected with, the CEO likely will turn out to be more engaged with the general population exchange on CSR matters that influence its working condition. Having a CEO pioneer who can go about as a viable employee of the organization's social image will both improve its business and social objectives.

6. **Better Choices:** Chiefs who have CSR capabilities can settle on and cultivate more compelling basic leadership inside the association. By applying a CSR point of view, their choices and those they bolster are more receptive, all-encompassing, and long haul, profiting the supported accomplishment of the organization. Truth is told; CSR capabilities improve and fortify conventional business keenness and other alluring initiative characteristics, for example, a long term sees all-encompassing basic leadership, a hazard administration point of view, and successful individuals' authority. Chiefs with solid CSR capacities are more viable leaders in general.

These are six reasons a directorate may wish to incorporate CSR criteria in their CEO progression arranging and enlistment endeavors. Practically speaking, there are three CSR administration styles: CEOs who straightforwardly expel CSR; the individuals who express a nonexclusive responsibility, yet there is a gap between their words and activities; and CEOs who possess and are exceptionally engaged with CSR. The CSR criteria recorded in the following segment are intended to enable sheets to enroll CSR-equipped leaders-the individuals who claim and are engaged with CSR. They are proposed for thought by sheets, their HR advisory groups, and the individuals who exhort them.

9.13. CSR LEADERSHIP CRITERIA FOR CEO SELECTION STANDARDS

The accompanying six CSR authority criteria can be utilized as a part of CEO progression arranging, initiative improvement, evaluation, and enrollment. The criteria can be utilized to educate CSR training for developing leaders, inner CEO successors, and as a focal point while picking another CEO.

The CSR authority criteria ought to be consolidated alongside exemplary and ordinary administration capabilities, a large number of which have a CSR or qualities-based measurement, for example, morals, and uprightness. The accompanying criteria are drawn from worldwide research and a best-rehearse check. They include:

- "Values" good example;
- Externally mindful;
- CSR strategist and change administrator;
- Collaborates with partners;
- Catalyst and backer; and
- Develops mindful leaders.

A great part of the accompanying substance is verbatim from worldwide research. CSR, values-based, dependable business, and sustainability terms are utilized reciprocally. The CSR administration qualities incorporate a blend of learning, ability, practices, and states of mind.

Two of the criteria interface with regular or built-up criteria, while the other four are new criteria for thought. Sheets and others engaged with CEO determination may wish to survey the accompanying criteria and select those (or parcels thereof), which are pertinent to their corporate setting for consideration in CEO enrollment and progression arranging forms. Businesses would thus be able to utilize the criteria to build up a tweaked CSR initiative approach.

9.13.1. Administration Development

The six CEO CSR Leadership Criteria can be utilized for senior administration ability enlistment, choice, improvement, maintenance, and examination and progression administration.

9.13.2. President CSR Leadership Defined

The CSR-able CEO makes an unmistakable vision in which individual esteems and business practices are firmly adjusted. The vision is conveyed reliably through their activities and choices and in the desires of others. They fabricate viable and incorporated administration that diagrams a course for business and societal achievement and those backings the top managerial staff to improve its sustainability limit and oversight. They support customary official discussions that distinguish and address the opportunities and dangers postured by worldwide sustainability patterns. They build up frameworks that reward sustainability advancement and execution. They guarantee credible engagement with partners, understanding that the result could impact the association's course. They champion sustainability to governments, industry leaders, and the speculation group. They understand this is a voyage that requires genuineness and fearlessness.

With bits of knowledge from business in the community:

1. **"Qualities" Good Example (New Criteria):** Is a qualities-based pioneer. Individual esteems are lined up with hierarchical esteems. An extension esteems/esteem proclamations to real business practices and practices. Shows others how it is done in exhibiting the association's esteems and culture and is energetic about consolidating business and societal achievement. Works as per the most astounding social, natural, and moral models.

i. Acts as a good example inside and outside the organization. Models the way for other workers by demonstrating how they show the organization's esteems in their decisions and practices. At the point when vital choices are made, they indicate how they mirror the association's esteems and impart this to staff. Examines with staff difficulties they look in maintaining the business and supports open, two-path correspondence on issues that emerge.

ii. Recognizes they give a noteworthy shadow a role as a pioneer and know about the effect of their shadow. In this manner, they both express a convincing and intelligent method of reasoning for the conduct they need to see and exhibit it in what they demonstrate enthusiasm for, and how they invest their energy inside and outside work.

iii. Is clear regarding why capable conduct matters to them, the business, and to society. Knows that while discussing capable business is simple, openly conferring and finishing as a CSR pioneer requires strength.

iv. Is reason-driven and ready to electrify the association around a typical reason.

2. Externally Mindful (Associates with Ordinary Criteria):

i. Demonstrates strong attention to the mind-boggling sustainability issues that influence the business condition and sees the association between external patterns and the suggestions for the center business. Comprehends and factors in worldwide social and condition inclines in business arranging.

ii. Scans the skyline a long way past the organization and industry to understand what is occurring in business and society everywhere and recognize new opportunities. Invests energy with individuals inside and outside the organization gathering data from both formal and casual channels (counting sites and other online networking), and from systems of "various reasoning "individuals.

iii. Explores "jostling notes" (flags that are awkward, genuinely unclear toward the beginning, however, could be vital) and is set up to think the unfathomable, regardless of whether the suggestions may be distressing. Evaluates low likelihood/high effect hazards and entwined dangers that could endanger the organization's future. Considers "feeble signs" notwithstanding when their effect will not be promptly self-evident.

iv. Takes an all-encompassing way to deal with arranging an investigation that considers the way a framework's constituent parts interrelate, how frameworks work after some time and inside the setting of bigger frameworks-where the framework could be the organization's esteem chain, who, and what is to come, partners, ecological conditions, geopolitical elements, and different contemplations. For instance, they know about the association's long-haul relationship with the nearby/have group. They comprehend the organization's neighborhood impression and heritage over the long term and the part the organization can play to add to nearby thriving.

i. Positions the business for short-and long-haul accomplishment by driving the organization to adjust to- and impact-basic social, monetary, and natural patterns.

3. **CSR Strategist and Change Administrator (Associates with Customary Criteria):**

i. Leads the advancement of, and imparts, a convincing future (vision) for the business-one that mirrors the association's social obligations, makes an incentive for society and perceives the shifting goals and desires of partners, and searches out the business opportunities that sustainability offers. Stewards the improvement of a plan of action and system that adjusts social and natural targets to monetary objectives.

ii. Understands how to implant CSR into business choices. Sees the master plan, takes the long view, and comprehends both business and societal ramifications of choices. Parities budgetary, operational, and here and now business weights with the long-haul sustainability of the business and society. Chief's CSR esteems are maintained in both great and awful circumstances and shape business choices at all levels (particularly troublesome choices like redundancies).

iii. Understands and can explain the business case for seeking after social and natural targets. Can clarify how CSR converts into esteem creation, particularly for the business. Distinguishes the cooperative energy between business movement and sustainability.

iv. Leads complex social change inside their businesses to implant sustainability. Encourages authoritative limit with respect to change and advancement to make feasible plans of action and answers for what is to come. Qualities assorted a variety of thought, foundation, point of view, and culture. Examinations with new thoughts and arrangements and invites radical discussions. Leads the advancement of practical products and administrations intending to have a beneficial outcome all through the esteem chain.

4. **Collaborates with Partners (New Criteria):**

i. Can recognize key partners that affect the association. Sees how the association impacts key partners emphatically and contrarily. Shows enthusiasm for and information of developing partner slant and desires and can react insightfully and consciously to contending partner interests.

ii. Can lead change past business limits? It includes partners to help characterize and make progress. Gets by and by included and draws in with communities, NGOs, scholastics, and other people who challenge with various perspectives and can be a wellspring of innovativeness and advancement. Has a reputation of delivering budgetary outcomes with due thought for the interests and worries of partners?

iii. Listens to individuals who question or do not concur with them or the organization's bearing and can extricate experiences from such dispute. Creates and keeps up assorted businesses with partners, currently inviting alternate points of view and esteeming distinction, producing innovativeness, and lessening bunch think.

iv. Understands and qualities the basics of teaming up with outside partners to address challenges that require aggregate fundamental arrangements. Guarantees the association has an interior limit with regards to successful partner joint effort on CSR issues.

v. Builds activity arranged, commonly gainful businesses and coordinated efforts incorporating with offbeat partners. Can work straightforwardly and successfully in organizations and joint efforts. Makes progress in building external impact and seeks after industry and partner administration and connections to make an incentive for the association and society.

5. Catalyst and Supporter (New Criteria): Is a supporter of capable business authority. Perceives that business must be a basic piece of the answer for the neighborhood, national, and worldwide social and ecological difficulties. Understands that gaining ground on issues like neediness, regular asset utilizes, unemployment, training, and building flexible and prosperous groups requires a joint effort among business leaders. Adds to open level-headed discussion on these issues with an educated perspective.

i. Promotes sustainability to governments, clients, providers, and business accomplices. Offers a dream on the social reason and obligations of the business and the business profits by this approach.

ii. Champions sustainability to workers and leads the association to be an impetus for a feasible society.

iii. Advocates with government and industry relationships on the requirement for an open arrangement that empowers a sustainable society. Plays an influential position in the industry and expert relationship in the advancement of sectoral and expert CSR gages.

iv. Challenges short-termism freely and secretly. Imparts long-haul sustainability and long-haul esteem creation to investors, financiers, and safety net providers and at AGMs.

6. **Develops Mindful Leaders (New Criteria):** Actively looks for individuals with a CSR and qualities-based authority viewpoint while enrolling into the association and makes this a need in administration advancement programs.

i. Mentors and creates future leaders who comprehend more extensive societal issues, their part, and the part of the business.

ii. Uses reward-and-acknowledgment frameworks and correspondences to reinforce positive practices and results. This implies coordinating CSR and value-based business practices into group targets, individual execution surveys, and KPIs. Conveys why these qualities are vital.

iii. Creates the conditions to energize administration, social enterprise endeavor, and better approaches for speculation to rise.

iv. Provides opportunities for supervisors and future leaders to increase social encounters and bits of knowledge by working with a societal association or activity. Perceives and gains by the esteem that social encounters and on-the-ground networks convey to the business.

9.14. CONCLUSION

Many executives are progressively embracing CSR commands and getting to be engaged with CSR oversight and stewardship. When they comprehend the hugeness of CSR to the company's future execution and CSR ends up installed in the corporate methodology, they will need to guarantee their CEO has the skills and qualities arrangement to empower powerful execution. This makes it essential for individuals who prompt them, to have the bits of knowledge they have to incorporate CSR contemplations in

CEO progression arranging and inquiry. Various reports have been created regarding this matter and driving organizations and administrators are demonstrating the way.

This is an emerging board governance topic that will continue to grow in importance as CSR becomes an increasingly significant driver of value creation for organizations. With CEO turnover due to retirements, this is the time for boards to enhance their knowledge of these critical competencies and embed them in their recruitment criteria. Well-governed boards now have a tool to help them with this essential task.

Chapter 10

Strategic Reporting and Communications

CONTENTS

10.1. REPORTING AND COMMUNICATIONS

Sustainability reporting is a fundamental initial phase in the process by which businesses make a move to make a feasible worldwide economy; this conviction has been supported by GRI's main goal. Be that as it may, reporting is not static-it advances, through improvements like rising worldwide difficulties, innovations, and changing partner interests- and organizations need to think about this.

The Corporate Leadership Group (CLG) on Reporting 2025 was met by GRI to advance the worldwide dialog on the fate of sustainability transparency and divulgence, and to analyze how the act of reporting is developing.

Around 13 forward-looking organizations met up to research the patterns they predict will be more important later on. From the 17 patterns GRI displayed at the Sustainability and Reporting Trends Forum held in November 2015, the four were researched and better comprehend the impact they would have all alone organizations and sustainability reports (Figure 10.1).

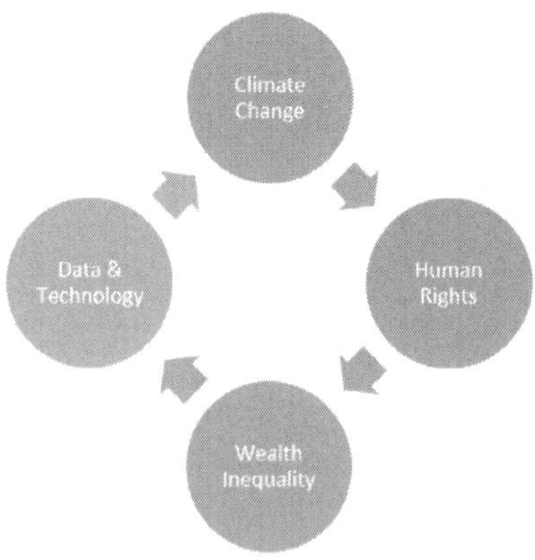

Figure 10.1. Reporting and communication areas.

Source: *GRI (2017).*

10.2. EXPLORING FUTURE TRENDS

To increase new bits of knowledge and a more profound comprehension of the potential impacts of these patterns all alone organizations and sustainability reports, the four patterns were dissected in four angles.

Diverse specialists were welcome to impart to the gathering their considerations on the fate of reporting, and sustainability gave content and encouraged the talks. In the Labs, the gathering adopted an organized strategy to investigating the patterns, covering the accompanying four viewpoints: (Figure 10.2).

Figure 10.2. Reporting process.

Source: GRI (2017).

10.3. EXAMPLE OF CLIMATE CHANGE

10.3.1. Current Landscape

Environmental change is currently the worldwide plan and is a standout amongst the most develop yet advancing patterns in sustainability and corporate reporting. In 2016, the World Economic Forum named the inability to alleviate and adjust to environmental change the top worldwide hazard regarding sway. The environment is highlighted noticeably in the 17 sustainable development goals (SDGs), which are now accumulating noteworthy intrigue and early take-up. Many transparency businesses as of now unveil data on environmental change; the Organization for Economic Co-operation and Development (OECD) and the Climate Disclosure Standards Board (CDSB) took supply of environmental change divulgence in the G20 nations to locate that corporate reporting practices are enhancing quickly, with a practice that was considered spearheading in 2010 getting to be noticeably standard in 2015.

The point of interest made at COP21 in Paris in December 2015 brought about:

- A more tightly atmosphere strategy condition;
- A long-haul objective being set for worldwide de-carbonization;
- Momentum in financial specialist enthusiasm for the issue, so far playing out by segment lines;
- The sureness that administrations cannot accomplish worldwide targets alone.

The following stride of taking a load of governments' Intended Nationally Determined Contributions (INDCs) to environmental change is in progress.

Various related activities have additionally risen in 2016:

- The OECD has been appointed to evaluate the past responsibility of a $100 billion store by 2020 to help developing nations adapt to environmental change;
- The Breakthrough Energy Coalition of innovation leaders is giving $1 billion to development to people in the general research pipeline;
- 120+ organizations have focused on creating science-based targets.

Corporate authority on environmental change should be driven in various regions. The top variables driving organizations to address environmental change are:

- Using elective and sustainable power source;
- New advancements/development;
- Setting targets and having an atmosphere methodology;
- Communicating and supporting on atmosphere;
- Supportive administration;
- Leadership from the top;
- Committing and conveying genuine outcomes;
- Reviewing products and administrations for atmosphere impacts.

"The Bank's commitment to the Paris Ascension is an essential piece of our need setting. Atmosphere related, green fund, green securities are issues where the Bank has been centering for a considerable length of time, and positively that concentration is not going to leave."—Parminder Plahe, European Investment Bank (EIB).

Besides, environmental change is being regarded money related: The Financial Stability Board presented the Task Force on Climate-related Financial Disclosures to create intentional predictable atmosphere-related monetary hazard exposures for organizations to give the correct data to speculators, moneylenders, backup plans, and different partners.

10.3.3. Implications for Business

There was clear agreement in the gathering that it is not a matter of if business ought to or can follow up on environmental change however how and how quickly they convey change. The accompanying focuses were exhibited in the Lab for the CLG to talk about:

- Companies are arrangement suppliers: they are relied upon to be a piece of the arrangements, from new energy models to efficiencies in the generation and dispersion of products.
- Climate change is interrelated with different issues: how does environmental change communicate with and affect different issues, for example, human rights?
- Clear, hunger, science-based targets are required: new indicators on environmental change impacts and related externalities are developing yet deficient even with concurred worldwide cutoff points.
- Linking to INDCs is vital: more prominent organization and nation engagement is relied upon to be required with the Paris understanding.

"Environmental change impacts horticulture. For our sourcing, the test is how to draw in ranchers and those included in rural creation on environmental change. Our report ought to be more unequivocal, more realistic, and clearer in its objectives to make it more conceivable for our own particular partners, particularly for our accomplices in horticulture."—Sol Beatriz Arango, Grupo Nutresa.

10.3.4. Examples: Business Addressing Climate Change

Cases of how organizations incorporate atmosphere related data in their sustainability reports:

- CEMEX has detailed widely on environmental change, ordering advancement, and future course into an independent position, which incorporates advance against targets and flags a move to inner carbon valuing.

- Power organization CLP set an objective in 2007-which still stands-to lessen the force of carbon outflows by around 75% by 2050.
- Food and refreshment organization PepsiCo is working towards a flat-out lessening in ozone harming substance emissions over the business and utilizes the focal point of the PepsiCo esteem bind to demonstrate the limits of this material issue.
- EIB, the world's biggest multilateral lender, has focused on straightforward and nitty-gritty giving an account of the atmosphere advantages of its speculations, by catching the GHG emissions of 95% of its venture ventures while screening out activities whose GHG outflows surpass a stringent edge level.
- Renewable energy bunch Gamesa plans to accomplish carbon lack of bias by 2025. This test includes singular duties on the estimation, lessening, and additionally counterbalancing of the CO_2 starting from the Group's immediate and roundabout discharges from 2015 to 2025.

To see other driving cases, see the GlobeScan/Sustainability 2015 Climate Survey, which recognizes driving corporate environmental change objectives. One territory where there is wide accord is setting aggressive targets: RE100 is turned out to be an intense activity, through which a developing rundown of organizations has focused on 100% sustainable power.

10.3.5. Priorities and Next Steps

Priorities for exploring and improving their reporting on climate change:

- Contextualize and disguise the test of environmental change more: Learn what you can from best practice yet guarantee you think about your materiality examination and the parts of environmental change most important to your division and association and enhance information, measurements, and reporting as needs be, for example:
- if the accentuation is on your inventory network, your need may comprehend the dangers in your store network and computing your extension 3 emissions.
- if your products and administrations impact the energy utilization

and discharges of others, their plan and conveyance might be generally intense.

- Aim to comprehend the interconnections, or nexus, of environmental change and different issues.
- Set and accomplish long-term (past 2020), science-based targets (endeavor to get at 'what's coming to you'), which likewise separates organizations.
- Determine how to adjust the interests and exercises of transparency businesses on governments, given national anticipates environmental change and the multinational way of many reporting businesses.
- Develop a reasonable and compact story of the helplessness of your association in light of environmental change and the common test it presents.
- Focus on conduct change: what will people and businesses need to do any other way to address the difficulties around energy utilization and emissions? "In a resource-constrained world, CEMEX understands the importance of reducing emissions and the need to quickly incorporate clean energies in the elaboration of our product. We understood we had to come to solutions quickly to contribute to a cleaner product and decrease our footprint."—Martha Herrera, CSR Director, CEMEX.

10.4. EXAMPLES OF HUMAN RIGHTS

10.4.1. Current Landscape

Human rights insurance is a key, and developing, societal concern, especially in light of ongoing clashes (e.g., in Syria) and relocation and displaced person streams. For the greater part of the advanced business has made human rights manhandle still happen. Many organizations are as yet pondering worries in their supply chains, specifically-be the unprotected transient workers in the palm oil or fish supply chains in Asia, the worry for Syrian outcast youngsters working in clothing production lines in Turkey, or present-day bondage in the UK. We see significant improvements with respect to human rights moving towards national execution and responsibility:

- Human rights are implanted over the SDGs: the Danish Institute for Human Rights proposes we can "… utilize human rights as a driver for understanding the SDGs… and utilize the SDGs to acknowledge human rights…"

- Various countries-presently including the UK, Italy, Spain, and Colombia-have created National Action Plans particularly for human rights.
- The UK's Modern Slavery Act was viewed as historic point enactment, influencing an expected 17,000 organizations: huge UK-based firms are required to distribute confirm on their sites showing that their operations are not dependent on universal subjugation.

10.4.2. Drivers of Corporate Performance on Human Rights

Phil Bloomer, Director of the Business and Human Rights Resource Center, specified two patterns that will be basic to business operations and show the interconnectivity of the patterns:

1. **The Ascent of Hyper-Disparity and Chance of Shared Thriving:** Business assumes a crucial part in the route in which riches are made, additionally in how riches are conveyed. Regarding and securing human rights is major to the equivalent conveyance of assets.
2. **The Compounding Biological Emergency:** The need to move to a low carbon economy makes a chance to discover arrangements that added advantage the most powerless-those frequently left unprotected earth or naturally likewise regularly encounter an absence of human rights and social insurance, particularly in long and complex supply chains.

10.4.3. Implications for Business

Desires of corporate providing details regarding the numerous features of human rights are developing and the issue may quickly develop:

- Human rights due persistence are presently the normal least.
- Benchmarking and positioning will empower simple and fast examinations between businesses.
- Investors, rating offices, and controllers are progressively looking for this data.
- Greater required straightforwardness and due steadiness: This

is obvious all around with requests from common society and expanding arrangement and control.

- An emphasis on work rights as basic: Modern subjection is another type of extreme work manhandle, and is prompting a more extensive development from attention on review and consistency to due tirelessness and cooperation.
- Stakeholders are stressing the requirement for least living wages, hence influencing brands and unions, modern aggregate understandings and possibly making compensation pre-aggressive. Well-being and security, the flexibility of affiliation, and the privilege to aggregate haggling likewise remain concerns.
- Conflict over common asset riches: Land rights are progressively debated and, as water shortage declines, questions are required to develop. Extraordinary air contamination is likewise picking up consideration. As the world moves to low carbon economies, there is support to guarantee that the move is quick and reasonable. At long last, corporate duty and assessment asylums have a part to play to guarantee expense is paid where asset riches are separated.
- Emerging zones of solid corporate promotion: various companies have talked and acted to end segregation by sex or sexual introduction, for example, while in a few divisions, for example, assembling, extractives, and innovation-support for the regard of fundamental rights all through the inventory network remains a need.

"Ensuring that compensation and remuneration programs do respect and improve minimum wages established in different markets and countries, or reducing the gender wage gap becomes a key challenge for multi-located companies like ours."—Isaac Ruiz, CSR Director, Gamesa.

10.4.4. Examples: Business Addressing Human Rights

Cases of how organizations incorporate human rights-related data in their sustainability reports:

- ICT organization Telefonica concentrates on the human rights issues around computerized trust, which incorporate security and security, the flexibility of expression, and youngster insurance. Telefonica is chipping away at the execution of its 10 Guiding Principles on Privacy and Freedom of Expression.

- Grupo Nutresa has a structure of activity-a reasonable independent correspondence on where the organization remains on human rights and how they conform to their human rights arrangement.
- Renewable energy organization Gamesa and IndustriALL Global Union consented to a worldwide structure arrangement (GFA) including a pledge to regard fundamental social rights, human rights, and common freedoms, level with circumstances, justify, and non-separation.
- Indian iron and steel maker JSW trusts a various workforce is a key element for a creative biological community. They exhibit the breakdown of the workforce by age, sex, classification, level, and turnover.

10.4.5. Priorities and Next Steps

- Better comprehend human rights, not just as a material issue for some organizations, however a greater comprehension of striking nature and which rights are in danger of the most serious effects through the organization's exercises and business connections.
- Consider doing this through human rights impact evaluations.
- Consider receiving the UN Guiding Principles on Business and Human Rights Reporting Framework.
- Building mindfulness and spreading learning all through an organization and its inventory network is crucial.
- Companies are engaged with investigating how their HR offices can help serve human rights.
- Integrating regard for human rights all through the production network is viewed as the greatest test.
- Companies are additionally intrigued by stages to share store network data, as a huge number of providers in any one inventory network cannot be checked or inspected by a solitary association viably.
- Multi-partner coordinated effort for aggregate activity around a range of human rights, regardless of whether ware particular or a neighborhood area, is testing yet worth handling.

- Supply chain chance investigation work and inspecting is an initial step to distinguishing dangers in human rights.

10.5. EXAMPLES OF WEALTH INEQUALITY

10.5.1. Current Landscape

As per Oxfam, the wealthiest 1% on the planet now have more riches than whatever is left of the world consolidated. In the sustenance and drink industry, for instance, 60% of ranch workers live in neediness. Little scale ranchers create 80% of the world's nourishment, yet together with horticultural laborers, they make up the lion's share of the ravenous individuals.

The OECD characterizes riches imbalance as "monetary disparity… the distinction in how resources, riches, or pay are circulated among people as well as populations." It is likewise portrayed as the gap between rich and poor, pay imbalance, riches divergence, riches, and pay contrasts, and the riches gap.

Tending to riches disparity is progressively observed as a crucial essential of a feasible economy, with various key partners and specialists concentrating on the issue and how it interfaces with get-to-monetary assets, instruction, wellbeing, and so forth. With the ascent of hyper imbalance and every one of the dangers it presents, there is a significant chance to concur and re-adjust on what is more equivalent and shared success.

Examining the sustainability reporting of a few organizations, it is clear that riches imbalance is infrequently tended to straightforwardly as a pattern or some portion of the more extensive working setting impacting business. There are signs that more organizations are perceiving the potential and desire for them to impact financial difficulties through particular business exercises, for example, work, wage levels, and proportions, and neighborhood sourcing.

10.5.2. Drivers of Corporate Performance on Wealth Inequality

As indicated by Ioan Nemes, Policy Lead CSR, and Sustainable Agriculture at Oxfam Novib, there are two key measurements of driving worry for riches imbalance and picking up organizations' consideration:

- An expanding offer of the estimation of our worldwide economy is going to capital, as opposed to work, which addresses the difference between lower-wage specialists and high riches people. Many expense frameworks do not guarantee the reasonable dispersion of riches from capital or benefit-producing exercises to whatever remains of society-in creating markets, as well as in developing ones.
- Inequality is reflected in the way that power, benefit, and impact are utilized as a part of the linkages in supply chains (delineated by the Oxfam Behind the Brands battle).
- What is more, there are empowering signals from worldwide organizations driving interest and consideration on riches balance:
- UN Sustainable Development Goal 10 decisively concentrates on decreasing disparity with particular targets including continuously accomplishing and supporting salary development of the last 40% of the population at a rate higher than the national normal by 2030.
- The World Economic Forum additionally recognized riches disparity as a top pattern in 2015 and attempted a local investigation of the issue to better comprehend which imbalance-related angles are needs in which districts (e.g., defilement, instruction, urbanization), which can better educate corporate comprehension of key markets. Implications for business.

Oxfam sees different difficulties ahead for the business identified with riches disparity, including:

- Radically expanding the share of significant worth caught by laborers and little scale makers.
- For example, accomplishing living wages for workers (and living earnings for little scale makers).
- Eliminating financial gender equality imbalance and sex segregation.
- Tackling the race-to-the-base on open administration to pull in speculation.
- Calling for a conclusion to the period of duty shelters.
- Breaking market fixation and tending to the unequal conveyance of energy.

- For instance, new plans of action ought to be quickly settled to share esteem more impartially in supply chains.
- Examples: business addressing issues related to wealth inequality.
- Cases of how organizations incorporate human rights-related data in their sustainability reports:
- Ferrero shows expanding straightforwardness and broad reporting at the national level (for key nations), exhibiting through transparency how business operations affect nearby economies. The report by the nation on wage proportions (and kind of laborer), nearby administrative contracts, and neighborhood provider spend.
- Mosaic presents giving an account of its worldwide group speculations-which are organized and arranged as identified with nourishment, water, and nearby-making utilization of a microsite, Mosaic's Giving Map.

10.5.3. Priorities and Next Steps

Needs to explore and enhancing their providing details regarding riches imbalance:

- Start some place-take a gander at your own operations and employees with a social rights point of view and after that consider extending the limits of this evaluation to incorporate the store network. Ask yourself: are there aberrations in the path in which the organization values individuals and exercises in the inventory network?
- Seek more data and detail on where the organization has made group-level ventures and following going ahead.
- Consider how your organization as of now does, or can, impact access to fundamental products and administrations (e.g., sustenance, water, energy) on a worldwide premise or in the neighborhood groups in which you work.
- Explore effect and results-based estimation, regardless of the difficulties of middle people in supply chains, diverse purviews, distinctive exercises, and so on.

- Consider what your organization's most material effect identified with riches imbalance might be and create effect-related KPIs.

10.6. EXAMPLES OF DATA AND TECHNOLOGY

10.6.1. Current Landscape

Information and innovation are a piece of a steadily developing field of improvements. The CLG watches a speeding up of the measure of information being made accessible, incorporating into constant: more information has been made in the previous 2 years than in the WGAP history of humankind. There are more methods of utilization of information crosswise over esteem chains, including systems of systems and a web of things.

However numerous corporate columnists indicate a requirement for more connection amongst information (and innovation) to comprehend impacts. For sure, for the world to meet SDG target 12.6 is to "empower organizations, particularly expansive and transnational organizations, to embrace sustainable practices and to coordinate sustainability data into their reporting cycle"—we should better comprehend and utilize information. The UN knows this and requires an information insurgency to make information bolster improvement and exhibiting why it truly matters. We know certainly that better accumulation of and access to information (frequently through innovation) empowers transparency that depends on increasingly and better information. Better information empowers partners to comprehend an organization's execution and thus settle on better choices. Innovation can likewise empower partners to get to information more successfully. We watch corporate reporting utilizing information and innovation from multiple points of view: how organizations are straightforwardly exhibiting and imparting information remotely, how innovation can empower information openness and introduction, and how information can educate partner basic leadership.

10.6.2. Drivers of Corporate Execution on Information and Innovation

Pavan Sukhdev, Founder, and CEO of GIST Advisory joined the Lab on information and innovation as a specialist to extend individuals' reasoning on information and particularly what information organizations may as of now have on the off chance that they choose to esteem it, displaying a multi-capital esteem system. As far as he can tell with organizations, sparking alight by gathering information on human, physical, regular, and social capital can accomplish a multi-dimensional feeling of significant worth that is reflected in sustainability contemplations being better coordinated into organizations and reporting.

Understanding these perspectives better- and for a few, connecting a money-related incentive to them-will empowers organizations to recognize potential territories to enhance, to expand positive effects, diminish negative effects, and at last increment business esteem.

10.6.3. Suggestions for Business

With regards to corporate detailing, information, and innovation are regularly observed as an open door and a test in equivalent measure.

10.6.4. Challenges

- Securing adequate internal purchase in.
- Promoting the way of life: making mindfulness for good utilization of the internal frameworks that convey high caliber, practically identical information.
- Availability of delicate and classified information.
- Need for more scientific instruments to better comprehend information.
- Manually ordering information crosswise over spreadsheets or decentralized frameworks, or transitioning to new, more imaginative frameworks to oversee information and data.

10.6.5. Opportunities

- Online transparency is an innovative device to impart information adequately.
- Embedding sustainability information (counting gathering and auspicious accommodation) into targets and execution administration frameworks.
- Being proactive and keeping associates educated around the procedure and results.
- Monitor- and give criticism circles to information suppliers-both the positive and the negative effects of sustainability issues followed.
- Understand the flow and different requests on similar information to enhance the data channels and lower the weight for associates, where conceivable.

10.6.6. Cases: Business Tending to Information and Innovation

Cases of how organizations exhibit information in their detailing, concentrating on internet reporting, intelligent transparency that utilizations information to give the client a chance to pick how and what they read, infographics that present mind-boggling or a lot of information in a simple to peruse design, and regular execution refreshes:

- TIM presents its 2015 online report also outlined and takes into account a simple route to its key concentrate on social advancement, natural assurance, and computerized culture and presents the report with a video.
- CLP opens up a few datasets to enable searchers to interface with and redo their perspective of CLP's information, and it covers money-related, operational, natural, and social and administration execution information.
- Grupo Nutresa presents complex information in a simple to peruse design by outwardly mapping the organization's exercises and commitments crosswise over many issues to particular SDGs.

10.6.7. Needs and Next Strides

Needs to explore and enhancing their transparency using information and innovation:

- Use information and innovation to approach partners in various ways.
- Use innovation to facilitate the gathering of information by moving towards more advanced and brought together information frameworks.
- Explore and better comprehend the requirements of various partner gatherings and tailor the introduction of information in a like manner.
- Present data to partners (e.g., infographics, report microsites) more successfully.

10.6.8. Future Focus

- Greater desires: Overall, organizations are encountering more prominent weight from partners on sustainability issues, as confirm by improvements, for example, expanding direction.
- Explore and test partner enthusiasm for transparency in various arrangements and frequencies and consider how reporting businesses may deal with this.

- Closely screen and research the four patterns (environmental change, human rights, riches disparity, and information and innovation), particularly the less developed regions of human rights and riches imbalance.
- Convey the estimation of the development towards GRI Standards in connection to new or rising ranges: GRI can give more prominent clearness and direction on divulgences and guidelines however ought not to be prescriptive on the transparency procedure.
- Reset targets: Companies are resolved to return to their objectives; how might they be made longer-term and drive sustainable results? Will more effect and results-based estimation be actualized?
- Provide direction to organizations on targets. Would it be advisable for them to be science-based? Setting based? Speak to a what is coming to the organization of a test or effect?
- Country-level and nearby focal points: There is a craving to search out more national level and neighborhood information over these patterns-on wages, on striking human rights, to line up with government anticipates atmosphere, and so on.
- Explore promote direction on the most proficient method to report adequately on expense rehearse crosswise over various wards, which governments can bolster this.
- Support inquiring about, benchmarking, and direction on ranges, for example, least wages and living wages in various locales or human rights benchmarking to help organizations look at and report.
- Deepen the comprehension of consequences and effects: The need to better comprehend dangers and effects is foremost, regardless of whether that is scope three emissions, leading human rights effect appraisals, or investigating how riches imbalance plays out.
- Support business transparency enthusiasm when estimating effects and consequences.
- Improve information: There are enhancements to be made to internal information accumulation procedures to enhance transparency against these patterns and bolster better understanding.
- Pursue further or more profound arrangement (e.g., GRI with different systems) so information is gathered once for various purposes.
- Encourage peer learning and sharing of best practices.

- SDGs matter: There is a solid accord that the understanding of the SDGs is critical and will affect corporate sustainability motivation.

10.7. TRENDS OF GLOBAL REPORTING

10.7.1. History of Reporting

- 1994–2000 Birth of reporting:
- First movers;
- Origins of GRI.
- 2000–2006 Era of innovation and rapid growth:
- GRI G2 and G3;
- AA1000AS.
- 2006–2012 Era of calm and steady growth:
- GRI only game in town;
- Shared sense of best practice.
- 2012–2015 Era of disruption and questioning:
- G4, SASB, IIRC;
- Regulation and customer scrutiny.
- 2015-plus Era of digital technologies.

10.7.2. Three Key Global Reporting Trends

1. **Materiality:** Companies are focusing on sustainability management and disclosure through reporting on topics of highest priority (and most relevance) to the company and stakeholders.
2. **Integration:** Several companies are integrating sustainability management into the core of the business, and producing integrated reports as an output.
3. **Interactive:** Companies are thinking about the difference between report and reporting; a report is static; reporting is more dynamic: multi-channel, ongoing, and/or social.

10.7.3. The Different Dimensions of Materiality

Multiple criteria can be used when applying the materiality principle and prioritizing sustainability issues. Here are some of the most common examples:

- Importance to business success;
- Importance to sustainability and/or stakeholders;
- Changing importance over time;
- The ability of the company to influence;
- The extent of current management.
- **Materiality Analysis:** Aims to identify the societal and environmental issues that present risks or opportunities to a company while taking into consideration the issues of most concern to external stakeholders. The process of labeling material topics in a company requires a comprehensive framework that methodologically identifies and prioritizes issues, risks, and opportunities (Figure 10.3).
- **How it Works:** Define important areas/issues and internally organize these issues in order of importance. Ask stakeholders (contractors, suppliers, clients, and community) to organize the same issues in order of importance.

  Use the results to create a Materiality Matrix that will order the issues according to the importance of all stakeholders confronted with the importance that the company has established.

  Those issues that are found to be important for the company and the total of other stakeholders (top right of the image) will be further developed into actions to maximize our positive impact and increase the added value provided.

  Here you have an example of a materiality matrix in Figure 10.3.

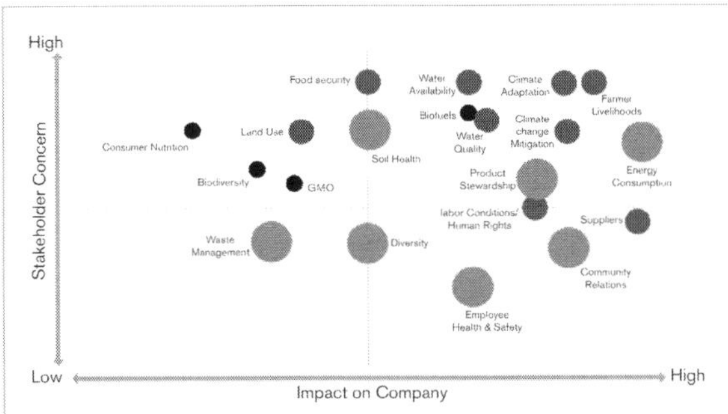

Figure 10.3. Materiality analysis example.

Source: *ISO (2017).*

10.7.4. Features of Integration

- Integrated thinking, not combined reporting. An integrated report is not about just combining two previously separate publications into one; it is about weaving together a single, integrated narrative.
- A single approach to materiality. An integrated report requires one single threshold for information considered important enough to include.
- An entry point to more detailed information. Rather than pack in every detail, an integrated report should be logically structured with effective navigation and cross-referencing to more information available elsewhere.
- Based on concepts of value creation and capitals. An integrated report explains how the organization interacts with the external environment and six capitals (financial, manufactured, intellectual, human, social, and natural) to create value over the short, medium, and long term.

10.7.5. Pathways to Integrated Reporting

An integrated set of reports-not one report alone meets the needs of diverse report users.

Same look and feel: Have common branding, design, and format.

- **Same Theme:** Highlight the same basic narrative, conveyed in a CEO letter.
- **Same Performance Overview:** Contain one performance dashboard, covering financial and sustainability.
- **Same Approval Process:** Follow identical review and sign-off protocols.

10.7.6. Interactivity

Thinking through the difference between a report and reporting:

- Some stakeholders want a "single moment in time" annual sustainability report, while others expect a depth of analysis that cannot be contained in a printed report. Companies are responding through the creation of a reporting system to satisfy multiple stakeholders and allow for customization.

10.7.7. Leveraging Web 2.0

Companies recognize the dynamic debates and insights are to be found on social media. Some are sharing their sustainability agenda and inviting contributions from stakeholders. Many are translating data into pictures, videos, snippets, blogs, contacts, and posts.

10.7.8. Key Takeaway

We are in the era of disruption (and innovation), where one size does not fit all companies are rethinking reporting approaches and forging new reporting trends which deliver value across multiple dimensions.

Chapter 11

Certifications Bodies and Standards

CONTENTS

11.1. UNITED NATIONS

The UN Global Compact intends to prepare a worldwide development of feasible organizations and partners to make the world they need. That is their vision.

To get this going, the UN Global Compact backings organizations to:

- Do business dependably by adjusting their techniques and operations to 10 Principles on human rights, work, condition, and against defilement; and
- Take key activities to progress more extensive societal objectives, for example, the UN sustainable development goals (SDGs), with an accentuation on cooperation and advancement.

11.2. UNITED NATIONS GLOBAL COMPACT: 10 PRINCIPLES

11.2.1. Human Rights

- **Principle 1:** Businesses should support and respect the protection of internationally proclaimed human rights.
- **Principle 2:** Make sure that they are not complicit in human rights abuses.

11.2.2. Labor

- **Principle 3:** Businesses should uphold the freedom of association and the effective recognition of the right to collective bargaining;
- **Principle 4:** The elimination of all forms of forced and compulsory labor;
- **Principle 5:** The effective abolition of child labor;
- **Principle 6:** The elimination of discrimination in respect of employment and occupation.

11.2.3. Environment

- **Principle 7:** Businesses should support a precautionary approach to environmental challenges;
- **Principle 8:** Undertake initiatives to promote greater environmental responsibility;

- **Principle 9:** Encourage the development and diffusion of environmentally friendly technologies.

11.2.4. Anti-Corruption

- **Principle 10:** Businesses should work against corruption in all its forms, including extortion and bribery.

11.3. RESULTS (FIGURE 11.1)

9,269	166	43,142
COMPANIES	COUNTRIES	PUBLIC REPORTS

Figure 11.1. UNGC certifications figures.

Source: *UNGC (2017).*

11.3.1. Sustainable Development Goals (SDGs): 17 Goals to Transform Our World

Governments, businesses, and civil society together with the United Nations have started to mobilize efforts to achieve the Sustainable Development Agenda by 2030. Universal, inclusive, and indivisible, the Agenda calls for action by all countries to improve the lives of people everywhere. In 2015, countries adopted the 2030 Agenda for Sustainable Development and its 17 SDGs. In 2016, the Paris Agreement on climate change entered into force, addressing the need to limit the rise of global temperatures (Figure 11.2).

Figure 11.2. UNGC sustainable development goals.

Source: *UNGC (2017).*

11.4. ISO 26000

11.4.1. What Advantages Can Be Accomplished by Updating ISO 26000?

An association's execution on social obligation can impact, in addition to other things:

- Competitive preferred standpoint;
- Reputation;
- The capacity to draw in and hold laborers or individuals, clients, customers, and clients;
- The upkeep of worker resolve, duty, and profitability;
- The impression of speculators, proprietors, givers, supports, and the money related group;
- Relationships with organizations, governments, the media, providers, companions, clients, and the group in which it works.

11.4.2. Who Can Profit by ISO 26000 and How?

ISO 26000 gives direction to a wide range of association, paying little respect to their size or area, on:

- Ideas, terms, and definitions identified with a social duty;
- Foundation, patterns, and qualities of social duty;
- Standards and works on identifying with a social duty;
- Center subjects and issues of social duty;
- Coordinating, executing, and advancing socially capable conduct all through the association and, through its approaches and practices, inside its range of prominence;
- Recognizing and drawing in with partners;
- Conveying duties, execution, and other data identified with social obligation.

ISO 26000 is proposed to help businesses in adding to sustainable improvement. It urges them to go past legitimate consistency, perceiving that consistency with the law is a key obligation of any association and a fundamental piece of their social duty program.

The standard tries to advance a typical comprehension of social obligation while supplementing-however, not supplanting other existing instruments and activities. While applying ISO 26000, businesses ought to consider societal, natural, lawful, social, political, and hierarchical assorted qualities and contrast in monetary conditions, while being predictable with global standards of conduct.

Not for confirmation ISO 26000 is not an administration framework standard. It does not contain necessities and, all things considered, cannot be utilized for confirmation. Any offer to affirm, or claims to be ensured, against ISO 26000 would be a deception of its goal and reason.

What specifically does ISO 26000 contain? ISO 26000 addresses seven core subjects of social responsibility defined in the standard and portrayed in the following graphic (Figure 11.3).

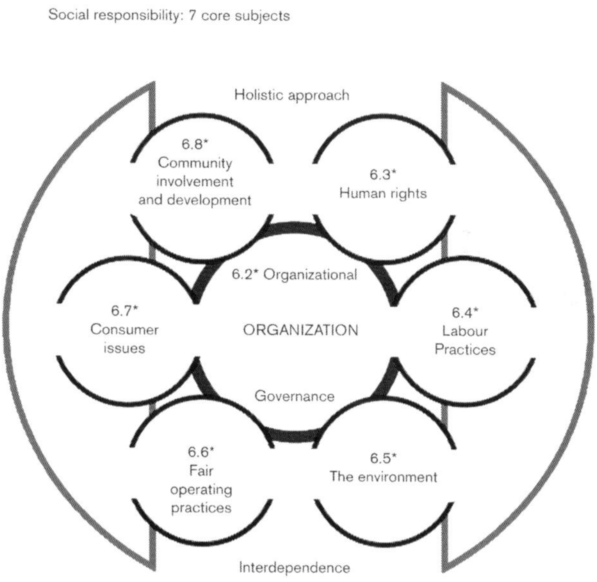

Figure 11.3. ISO 26000 framework.

Source: *ISO (2017).*

11.5. GRI

Global reporting initiative (GRI) that helps organizations, governments, and different businesses comprehend and share the impacts of business on basic sustainability issues, for example, environmental change, human rights, defilement, and numerous others. Their vision is to make a future where sustainability is essential to each association's basic leadership preparation.

Their central goal is to engage leaders all over the place, through our sustainability models and multi-partner system, to make a move towards a more economical economy and world.

They accept:

- In the energy of a multi-partner handle and comprehensive system;
- Transparency is an impetus for change;
- Our measures engage educated basic leadership;
- A worldwide point of view is expected to change the world;
- Public intrigue ought to drive each choice an association makes.

11.5.1. Vital Needs

GRI is based upon a novel multi-partner rule which guarantees the interest and aptitude of assorted partners in the improvement of its gauges. The advantage of this expansive and comprehensive approach is that businesses can have trust in the vigor of partner cooperation while considering an extensive variety of sustainability issues. GRI is seeing a more prominent interest in sustainability data for particular uses exhibited by the development of new reporting activities. Although the utilization of the data varies, the inspiration for giving it is regularly the same: to assemble trust. (Figure 11.4).

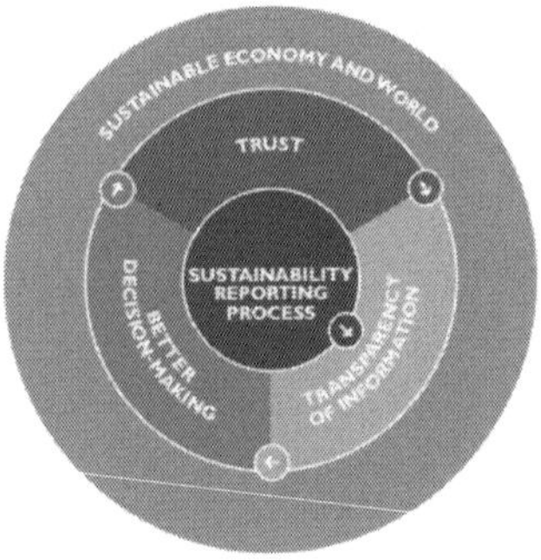

Figure 11.4. GRI framework.

Source: *GRI (2017).*

11.5.2. Empowering Smart Policy

GRI's worldwide group traverses a large number of columnists yet our degree stretches out past topography and into different fields of work. They work with governments, worldwide businesses, and capital markets. Thus, in this work, 27 nations utilize GRI in their sustainability approaches and seek us for direction as the universes most broadly utilized sustainability detailing benchmarks. Furthermore, they have long-standing joint efforts with more than 20 universal businesses, for example, the UNGC, OECD, and the UN Working Group on Business and Human Rights.

GRI teams up with different businesses on various worldwide driving edge activities which concentrate on handling a portion of the world's most squeezing difficulties, for example, environmental change, human rights, and defilement. Through this sort of joint effort, they are finding imaginative methods for utilizing sustainability detailing data to help bolster organizations specifically.

Consistently they help developed nations put millions in sustainable improvement exercises in developing markets to address neediness-related issues, for example, water utilizes, arrive utilize and gender equality correspondence. GRI's Standards keep on playing an imperative part in these sorts of speculation streams guaranteeing that sustainability issues are mulled over by these businesses as they improve their aggressive edge in the neighborhood and global markets.

11.5.3. More Reporters, Better Reporting

GRI is best known for driving the improvement of the sustainability transparency procedure and keeps on building their worldwide group which incorporates a great many prepared professionals and columnists. Among this differing group, they additionally have many center individuals who work straightforwardly with them to champion their central goal.

As a worldwide autonomous association, the provincial centers empower them to address novel issues crosswise over topographies and set up a genuinely worldwide nearness. GRI works with a developing group to create industry-driving exercises to promote the estimation of sustainability detailing. They support and empower those businesses that do not right now answer to do as such, particularly advancing the take-up of transparency among small and medium-sized ventures.

GRI persuades and underpins those that as of now do answer to make progress toward a superior nature of transparency through our preparation and information sharing exercises. What is more, for those that are driving the way, they work in a coordinated effort to research and imagine enormous picture difficulties, for example, the eventual fate of transparency through their corporate initiative engagement exercises.

GRI is focused on giving worldwide models to sustainability detailing and keeps on strengthening their believability and part as a standard-setter through late changes to administration structure. This incorporates the production of a different administration body to create and support GRI's Sustainability Reporting Standards to expand the autonomy of these exercises.

Guaranteeing that more organizations and governments' esteem sustainability data will remain an essential piece of GRIs DNA, however, the time has desired them to expand on this inheritance and catalyze another time where organizations and governments settle on vital choices in light of these vital sustainability issues.

11.5.4. Moving Beyond Reports

GRI's concentrate has dependably been on the detailing procedure and the estimation of the data that originates from it. While the sustainability report remains a vital yield of the detailing procedure, they should now move past the report itself to guarantee that chiefs have entry to the high caliber and solid data they are progressively requesting.

From the utilization of sustainability data in business insight to the real formation of new lines of business, unmistakably, this data is not only for sustainability experts. It is for financial specialists to empower more prominent trust in their ventures, clients in their products and administrations, subjects in their legislatures et cetera.

These gatherings and people all need distinctive data and need to get to it in various ways. Today we are seeing a rush of new routes in which data from the sustainability detailing procedure is being utilized by differing gatherings of partners to address their particular needs.

Yet, for this data to genuinely enable economical choices in each association, it must be more open, equivalent, and accessible progressively. GRIs part in deduction past the sustainability report is to help the inexorably various scope of clients take advantage of the sustainability data they require, empowering them to utilize this data in more imaginative ways.

11.5.5. Advancement and Collaboration

The sustainability scene is continually changing and GRI has dependably trusted in the requirement for development. GRI's Standards are a free, open great which have effectively motivated the making of new systems, businesses, arrangements, and professions all centered around enhancing the estimation of sustainability data.

GRI keeps on driving the exchange on incorporating sustainability and monetary data, working with various businesses and partners to further this plan. Effective development requires another soul of joint effort and comprehensiveness in the reporting field, guaranteeing businesses cooperate towards a shared objective of building trust in organizations and governments. A portion of the best developments, be that as it may, will originate from coordinated efforts past the detailing field.

This is the place innovation and enormous information have a gigantic part to play and we are working with the world's driving innovation organizations to move to future 'past reports.' This will help all partners get to the data they have to settle on better business and approach choices, in light of the world's most generally utilized and trusted sustainability detailing benchmarks.

11.5.6. Global Reporting Initiative (GRI)-G4

Drivers:

- Increasing understanding of the connection between ESG issues and sustainable business value;
- Increasing interest in organizational focus-what and where.

Chapter 12

Policies and Templates

CONTENTS

12.1. SUSTAINABILITY MODEL TEMPLATE

The Sustainability Model guides and ensures that procedures meet the intentions and that there is an effort to continue to address the principles in the day-to-day operation. This model is in itself one of the references used for working procedures, impact assessment methodology and continuous improvement actions. The Sustainability Model integrates the Sustainability Principles, the Vision and International Corporate Responsibility best practices. For example: Fellgroup.

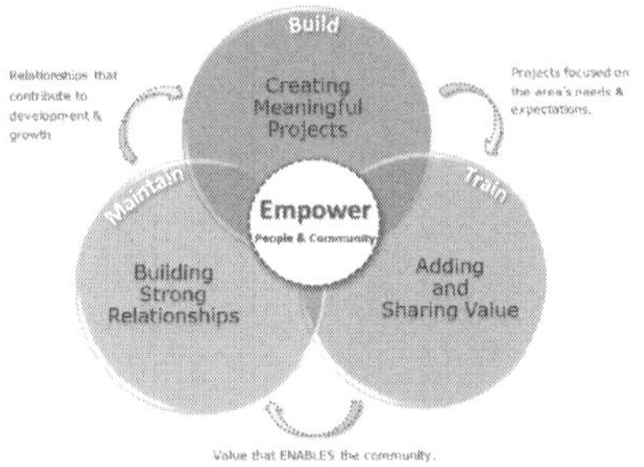

Figure 12.1. FELLGROUP Sustainability Model.

Source: *FELLGROUP.com (2017).*

CEMEX:

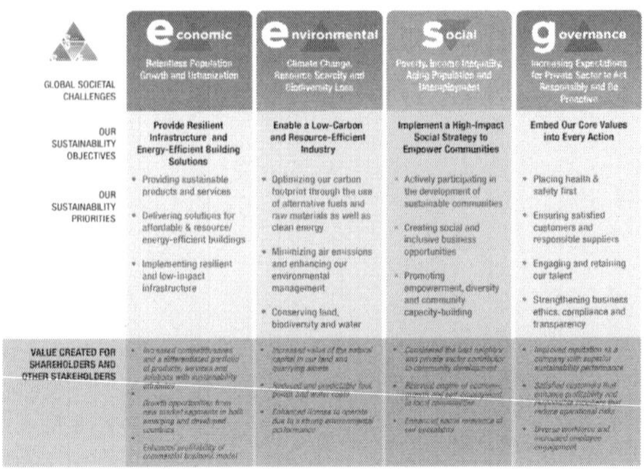

Figure 12.2. CEMEX Sustainability Model.

Source: *CEMEX.com (2017).*

TELEFONICA:

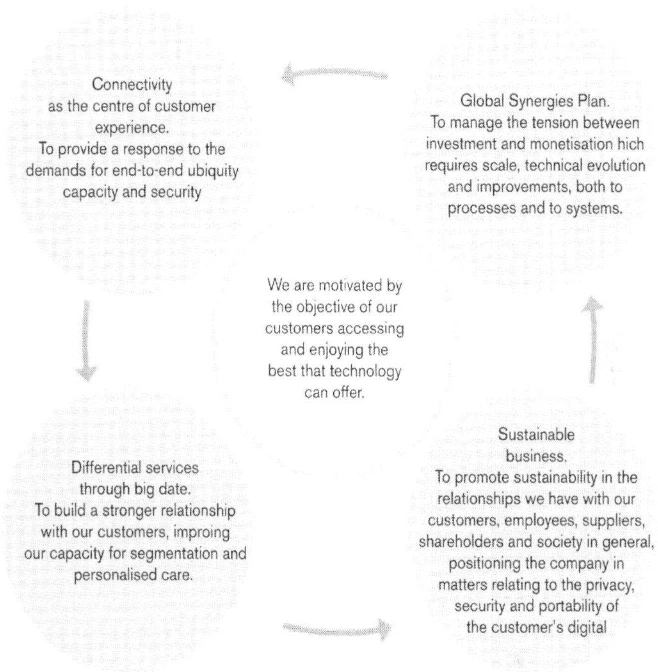

Figure 12.3. Telefonica Sustainability Model.

Source: *Telefonica.com (2017).*

Actions:

In this section, we will present to you with a given set of possible actions to include into the CSR action plan.

12.1.1. Environment

12.1.1.1. Energy Consumption and CO_2 Emissions

1. Reduction of energy consumption through employees' awareness programs.
2. Significant use (>20% of energy mix) of renewable energies.
3. Reduction of energy consumption through innovative technologies (please specify).
4. Monitoring direct CO_2 emissions.

5. Monitoring indirect CO_2 emissions.
6. Measures to reduce CO_2 emissions from business travel (i.e., teleconferencing, video-conferencing) Official program of Offsetting of CO_2 emissions (e.g., carbon-neutral program).
7. 75% of hardware is Energy Star rated or have enabled active power saving management capabilities.
8. Measures for Data Life Cycle Management (DLCM) to reduce inefficiencies in data storage
9. Server virtualization.
10. Adoption of alternative data center cooling practices (if applicable).

12.1.1.2. Waste Consumption

1. Work processes implemented to recycle paper/cardboard waste.
2. Work processes implemented to recycle toners and ink cartridges.
3. Work practices implemented to recycle IT equipment (laptops, desktop, printers, and monitors).
4. Work processes implemented to recycle Others (Please specify).

12.1.2. Sustainable Procurement

12.1.2.1. Sustainable Responsible Procurement

1. Choice of intellectual services suppliers based on environmental or social criteria.
2. Choice of data centers on environmental or social criteria.
3. Choice of office equipment (office supplies, furniture,) on environmental or social criteria.
4. Choice of IT equipment on environmental or social criteria.
5. Supplier CSR code of conduct in place.
6. Detailed risk analysis per purchasing category completed.
7. Company specific training of buyers on social and environmental issues within the supply chain.
8. Systematic integration of specific social or environmental contract clauses.

9. Regular supplier assessment on environmental or social issues.
10. On-site audits of suppliers on environmental or social issues.
11. Corrective actions to facilitate supplier capacity building on environmental or social issues.
12 .Integration of social and environmental principles into buyer's performance appraisal.

12.1.3. Health and Safety & Human Rights & Labor Practices

12.1.3.1. Health and Safety

1. Health and safety detailed risk assessment.
2. Procedure in place to anticipate health & safety risks related to change of operations (e.g., start-up of new operations, change of operations).
3. Provision of protective equipment to all impacted employees.
4. Specific procedures for handling of chemicals or hazardous substances.
5. Health and Safety procedures translated in major languages spoken by employees.
6. Formal targets to reduce occupational injury and illness.
7. Formal targets to reduce physically demanding work and repetitive strain injuries (RSI).
8. Joint labor-management health and safety committee in operation.
9. Active preventive measures for stress and noise.
10. Training of all relevant employees on health and safety risks and good working practices.
11. Mandatory health check-up for all employees.
12. Training on health and safety issues for subcontractors working on-premises (if applicable).
13. Regular inspection or audit to ensure safety of equipment.

Discrimination and Harassment

1. Proactive measures to prevent discrimination during the recruitment phase (please specify).

2. Awareness training to prevent discrimination and/or harassment.
3. Auditing of internal controls to prevent discrimination and/or harassment.
4. Provision of working conditions and infrastructure to accommodate employees with disabilities (e.g., work stations).
5. Whistleblower procedure on discrimination and harassment issues.
6. Measures to promote wage equality in the workplace (e.g., equal pay monitoring).
7. Measures to promote gender and racial equality in the workplace.

Working Conditions

1. Interactive communication session with employees with regards to working conditions (e.g., seminar, working groups).
2. Company-wide promotion of employees' initiatives regarding working conditions.
3. Official measures to compensate atypical working hours.
4. Official measures to promote work and life balance.
5. Additional rest periods or vacations, above legal requirements.
6. Company specific health care program for employees.
7. Bonus scheme for more than 70% of employees.
8. Transparency (process and criteria communicated to all employees) on remuneration system.
9. Policy to have fixed salary systematically above minimum legal (when applicable).
10. Company Chart or code of conduct on personal usage of IT by employees.
11. Transparency to employees on security and monitoring devices.

Social Dialogue

1. Company public commitment to promote and facilitate structured labor relations.
2. Local employee representatives' bodies for more than 75% of employees.

3. European Works Council (employee representative body covering the whole company).
4. Companywide collective agreement signed on working conditions, including agreement on remuneration.

Training and Career Management

1. Transparent recruitment process (communicated clearly and formally to all candidates).
2. Regular assessment (at least once a year) of individual performance.
3. Setting of Individual development and career plan for all employees.
4. Official measures promoting career mobility.
5. Policy to give priority to internal recruitment.
6. Provision of skills development training.
7. Official measures to anticipate or reduce layoffs and associated negative impacts (e.g., financial compensation, outplacement service).

Corruption & Bribery

1. Signature acknowledgment of anti-corruption policy required for all concerned employees.
2. Specific approval procedure for sensitive transactions (e.g., gifts travel).
3. Specific procedures for retaining and using third-party intermediaries (i.e., due diligence, certifications).
4. Structured mechanisms to deal with policy violations (e.g., potential sanctions).
5. Secure communication channel for employees to seek advice or voice concerns (e.g., hotline, whistle-blowing procedure).
6. Web-based or in-person training program on anti-corruption.
7. Internal audit on compliance with anti-corruption and bribery policy Internal controls (e.g., four-eyes principle, separation of functions, job rotation).

Anti-competitive Practices

1. Signature acknowledgment of anti-competitive practices policy required for all concerned employees.
2. Structured mechanisms to deal with policy violations, i.e., potential sanctions.
3. Secure communication channel for employees to seek advice or voice concerns (e.g., hotline, whistle blowing procedure).
4. Web-based or in-person awareness or training program on anti-competitive practices (e.g., cartels, price-fixing, bid rigging).
5. Internal audit on compliance with anti-competitive practices policy.

Respect Intellectual Property Rights

1. Conducting investigations on third parties patents/trademarks at initial stages of R and D.
2. Conducting investigations on third parties patents/trademarks at all stages of product development.
3. Systematic intellectual property audit to prevent/identify potential infringements.
4. Measures to prevent counterfeiting of other products.

Consumer/Client Data Protection and Confidentiality

1. Measures to limit types of data collected and stored.
2. Measures to protect customer/client data from unauthorized access or disclosure.
3. Measures to consult customers/clients on personal/confidential data.
4. Internal data protection audits.
5. Web-based or in-person training program on data protection and confidentiality.
6. Process to safely destroy confidential data of client/customers.

Community Relations

1. Implement a Volunteering Program for employees.
2. Engage in community related activities.

3. Donate Materials to institutions.
4. Proactively design programs that would provide and empower the community with skills and knowledge.
5. Sponsor local initiatives.

12.2. CODE OF CONDUCT POLICY TEMPLATE

12.2.1 Our Values

Examples:

- **Transparency**: We believe that transparency is essential to create long lasting relationships, built on trust and information; this is why we share information internally and with stakeholders. Transparency means openness, communication, knowledge and responsibility.
- **Innovation:** We believe innovation is the driver for change in today's competitive world. Opening up for change, continuous improvement and reinventing yourself on a regular basis is a must in becoming market leader.
- **Integrity:** We shall always work with honesty, fairness, ethically and in compliance with legal regulations. We will consistently treat all of our stakeholders with the respect and discreteness they deserve.
- **Quality:** We will always aim for excellence in all of our work, and through continuous improvement, we will keep optimizing our products and services whilst helping our clients and business partners develop.
- **Diversity:** We believe that the differences in gender, age, background and knowledge are valuable assets therefore we will work towards inclusion and diversity.

- **Accountability:** We will always account for our activities, accept our responsibility for our actions and disclose results in a transparent manner.

12.2.2 Our Principles

Our code of conduct establishes the principles we adhere to in our day-to-day work at XXX. This document aims to serve as a guideline and reference for everyone involved in our activities. Our Code is applicable throughout our organization; all employees must follow and enforce the guidelines established here.

12.2.3 Relations with our stakeholders

We are very committed to engaging effectively with our stakeholders: respecting, considering and responding to their interests the best we can.

Employees:

- **Recruitment;** Our selection and hiring processes are designed and implemented respectfully, without creating false expectations, and in adherence to local laws and practices. We select and recruit employees based on their ability, knowledge, career experience and personal alignment with our corporate values.
- **Work environment:** We aim at providing a safe and productive work environment for all of our employees, maximizing individual potential and creativity and fostering collaboration and teamwork.
- **Development:** We are committed to offering continuous training, development, and individual recognition, promotion based on merit, clear communication and effective feedback. Managers have a special responsibility in ensuring that all employees have clear roles & responsibilities, balanced expectations and the opportunity to express opinions and suggestions in a constructive and open environment.
- **Interpersonal Relationships:** We seek to ensure that interpersonal relationships in our workplace encourage collaboration and teamwork, which are essential factors to overcoming the challenges that we continuously face.

- **Human Rights:** We are each entitled to a workplace that observes and respects basic human rights. We must observe all applicable laws that govern our work, and never use or tolerate the use of child or forced labor. As a company that believes in the power of acting with integrity, XXX seeks to advance respect for human rights.

High priority is given to:

- Complying with labor laws and regulations
- Respecting individual differences and opinions: preventing all forms of discrimination and harassment.
- Safety equipment, systems and procedures that protect our people and facilities
- Preserving the environment and our occupational health.
- Defining, communicating and ensuring compliance with our policies and internal procedures.
- Fostering an environment of mutual respect, and complying with the laws, rules and regulations of the countries where we operate.

Customers

- **Market selection:** We do not discriminate against customers or markets for any reason other than to comply with legal provisions. Unlawful discrimination is a violation of our Code and global competition laws, and will not be tolerated. If you witness or suspect unlawful customer or market discrimination report the behavior immediately to Anonymous line or the **Legal & Compliance**
- **Customer Engagement:** We are committed to treat customers with integrity and professionalism and avoid arrogance at all times. To build and maintain customer relationships based on trust and credibility, we only make commitments that are commensurate with our abilities. If unforeseen circumstances make it impossible to meet a commitment, the person involved must inform his/her immediate supervisor, as well as the customer.
- **Sales:** Our sales activities will be free of false representations regarding product quality and/or availability, delivery dates and payment terms. We must market our products and services

honestly and accurately. Using deceitful or dishonest practices is a violation of our Code and our corporate values, and will not be tolerated.

Suppliers

- **Supplier selection:** We will provide suppliers with equal opportunities to bid on and win contracts. In addition, we will always conduct our procurement processes consistently, respectfully and confidentially. In all cases, we will base the selection of suppliers on established criteria. We encourage our suppliers to adhere to the standards of our Code and, therefore, strongly advise our suppliers not to perform or engage in any act prohibited by law or by our Code of Conduct.
- **Supplier Engagement:** We honor all of our agreements and commitments, including copyrights, licenses and other proprietary claims. Consequently, we will do business only with contractors or suppliers who prove the authenticity and legitimacy of their products and services.

Community

As a responsible member of the global community, we are engaged in participating directly or indirectly with organizations or programs designed to promote integration, development and improved quality of life worldwide.

Our participation may include counsel, management, sponsorships or any other support involving our products, assets and/or services.

Government

We advocate a policy of awareness and compliance with laws, regulations, standards and other legal provisions in every country in which we operate. No one at XXX may commit an illegal or unethical act, or instruct others to do so, for any reason.

If you believe any practice raises questions as to compliance with any applicable law, rule or regulation, or if you have questions regarding any law, rule or regulation, contact **Legal & Compliance.**

12.2.4 Operation of Our Activity

We are committed to operating in the most effective and compliant form: addressing all our stakeholders' needs and expectations while assuring the sustainability of the company.

It is the responsibility of each of us to make a report if we suspect that a violation of human rights has occurred. This includes any act of retaliation we may witness as the result of our colleagues standing up for their rights or the rights of others. Do not hesitate to reach out to your Human Resources Department, Legal & Compliance or Anonymous line to report such a concern.

Anti-bribery

We reject all forms of corruption. Paying or receiving bribes is illegal and highly unethical, and can lead to severe consequences for all parties involved, including jail for individuals and harsh penalties for the Company. We are committed to conducting our business with transparency and integrity, and will therefore ensure that all transactions comply with anti-bribery laws, including requirements to maintain complete and accurate books and records.

All gifts travel and entertainment expenses must be specifically recorded in exact accordance with applicable laws and established company procedures.

Preventing Money Laundering

We are committed to never facilitate or support money laundering: Always comply with applicable money laundering laws and regulations. We will aim at minimizing the risk of and avoid being involved in arrangements or operations that may be or are related to proceeds of crime. We will take appropriate actions to evaluate our business relationships to ensure their integrity.

Conflicts of Interest and Corporate Opportunities

XXX employees have an obligation to conduct themselves in an honest and ethical manner and to act in the best interests of XXX. All employees should endeavor to avoid situations that present a potential or actual conflict between their interests and the interests of XXX.

Safety and Security

Health and Safety

We give the highest priority to guaranteeing the health and safety of our workforce: preventing incidents. We are fully committed to carrying out our business activities in a safe and efficient manner.

Confidential Information

We respect the property rights and proprietary information of other companies. All XXX employees must respect such property and information. This means that we do not infringe upon any patented or copyrighted documents or materials. Never use, copy or disclose any confidential information without first seeking guidance from Anonymous line or **Legal & Compliance**. We all have an obligation to protect XXX's proprietary and confidential information even after we leave XXX.

> Only XXX's official spokespersons are authorized to provide corporate information to the media, analysts or other outside parties.

Information Security

To maintain the trust of our customers and business partners as well as our market position as a high-quality service provider and to protect our own business processes relying on the information system, XXX is committed to providing all employees and partners with a clear picture of their responsibilities within the scope of Information Security.

In order to ensure proper performance of our functions for the organization, it is vital to ensure that all employees and external parties, regardless of their hierarchical level, function and/or contractual relationship, have access to information necessary for the performance of their activities. In return, they need to respect the implemented Information Security policies and the commitment to the following values:

- **Confidentiality** – Ensuring that information is not made available or disclosed to unauthorized individuals, entities, or processes;
- **Integrity** – Ensuring the protection of the accuracy and completeness of assets;
- **Availability** – Ensuring the accessibility and usage of information wherever and whenever it is needed by the authorized entity;

- **Nonrepudiation** – Ensuring that evidence of the occurrence of a claimed event or action and its originating entities is available in order to resolve disputes about the occurrence or non-occurrence of the event or action and involvement of entities;
- **Legal compliance** – Ensuring respect for civil and criminal laws, regulations or contractual obligations and Information Security requirements.

It is XXX's legal and ethical obligation to guarantee to any entity which whom it holds any type of relationship that the previous values are upheld, namely to customers, partners, suppliers, and competent official bodies. If you have any questions or need to report an issue contact: info.sec@amplexor.com

Financial controls and records

We must ensure, within the scope of our responsibilities and duties, that our financial records are accurate and our financial controls effective. We must also ensure that our reports and documents filed with or submitted to securities regulators, as well as all other public communications, include full, fair, accurate, timely and understandable disclosure.

Preservation of Assets

The proper use and preservation of XXX's assets are essential for the fulfillment of our Company's mission. Assets may be tangible and intangible property owned by XXX, including, but not limited to: buildings, equipment, inventories, receivables, shares and securities. Assets also include our proprietary information, inventions, business plans, patents, brands, trademarks and names, corporate identity and information technology. Each of us is responsible for the custody and safekeeping of any assets under our direct control. We should never participate in, influence or allow situations and/or actions that involve the unauthorized taking, mistreatment, abuse, lending, disposal or sale of company assets.

We encourage all of you to report any suspected violation of the principles stated in this Code of Conduct. Keep in mind that our Company will thoroughly investigate all good-faith reports of violations. Open communication of issues and concerns by all employees without fear of retaliation is vital to the successful implementation of our Code. Each of us is required to cooperate in internal investigations of misconduct and unethical behavior. Any information supplied in regard to a particular case will receive professional and confidential treatment.

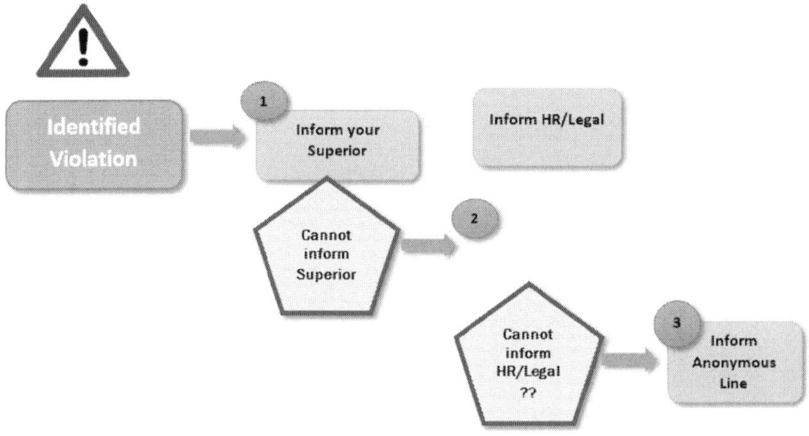

12.3. TRAINING POLICY

12.3.1 Statement

"INSERT COMPANY NAME" recognizes the importance of having a skilled workforce to achieve strategic and operational plans and is committed to providing an environment that is conducive to effective performance and promotes training and development opportunities for all staff.

12.3.2 Aim of This Policy

To provide a framework for training and development that ensures staff has the necessary competencies to deliver on "INSERT COMPANY NAME" 's strategic and operational plans.

12.3.3 Scope of This Policy

This policy relates to the Training and Development of all "INSERT COMPANY NAME" staff.

12.3.4 Policy Statements

- There will be equality of opportunity for all "INSERT COMPANY NAME" staff to develop their knowledge, skills, and abilities through a blend of learning methods including mentoring, coaching, on-the-job learning, courses, conferences, and seminars.

- The training needs of staff will be identified in line with best practice and legislative guidelines.
- "INSERT COMPANY NAME" will facilitate externally accredited training and development opportunities for staff subject to the availability of funding.
- All training, i.e., courses, workshops, seminars, and conferences will be coordinated through the Culture and Talent Team.
- All training will be evaluated to inform changes and improvements in training provision.
- The line manager will agree with each staff member on how knowledge/skills learned will be shared to inform team/ organizational learning.
- The line manager will support the staff member to transfer the knowledge/skills learned in training to the workplace.
- Staff participating in the training will satisfy all attendance, assessment, and evaluation requirements within the required timeframes.
- "INSERT COMPANY NAME" will develop internal trainer capacity to facilitate delivery of training programs in line with organizational needs and to provide development opportunities for staff.

Document Sections

- **Section 1:** Process.
- **Section 2:** Procedures:
  - Developing the training plan;
  - Developing new training;
  - Delivering training;
  - Evaluating training.
- **Section 3:** Training request form.
- **Section 4:** Application for external course/conference/education assistance.
- **Section 5:** Training evaluation form.

Section 1: Process (Figure 12.4)

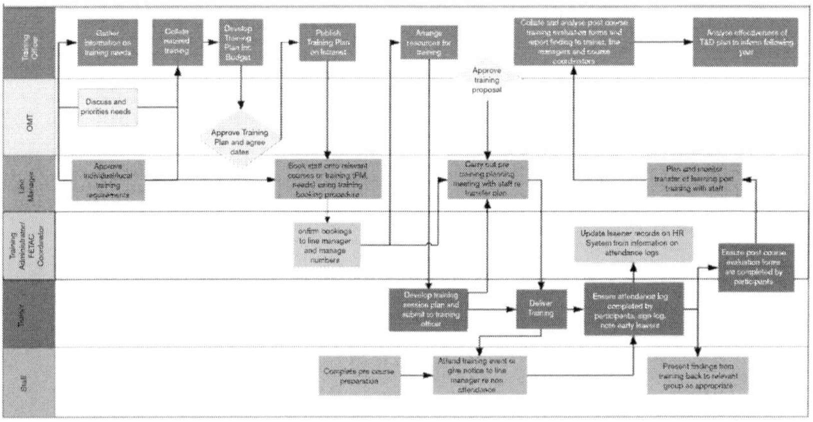

Process measures:
% variance expenditure versus budget re training
% training spend versus payroll
% training completed versus training planned

Figure 12.4. Process overview.

Section 2: Procedures (Figure 12.5)

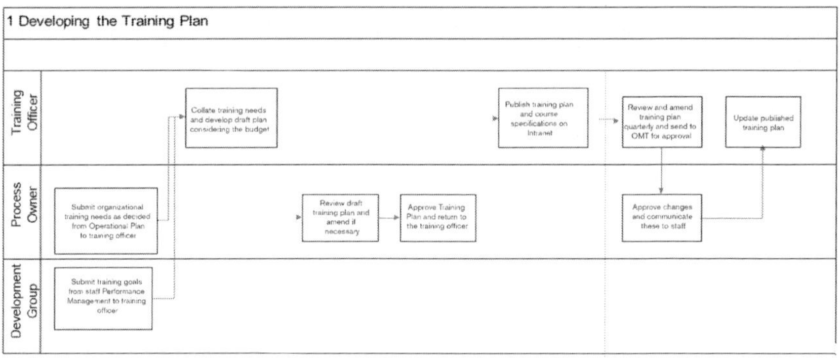

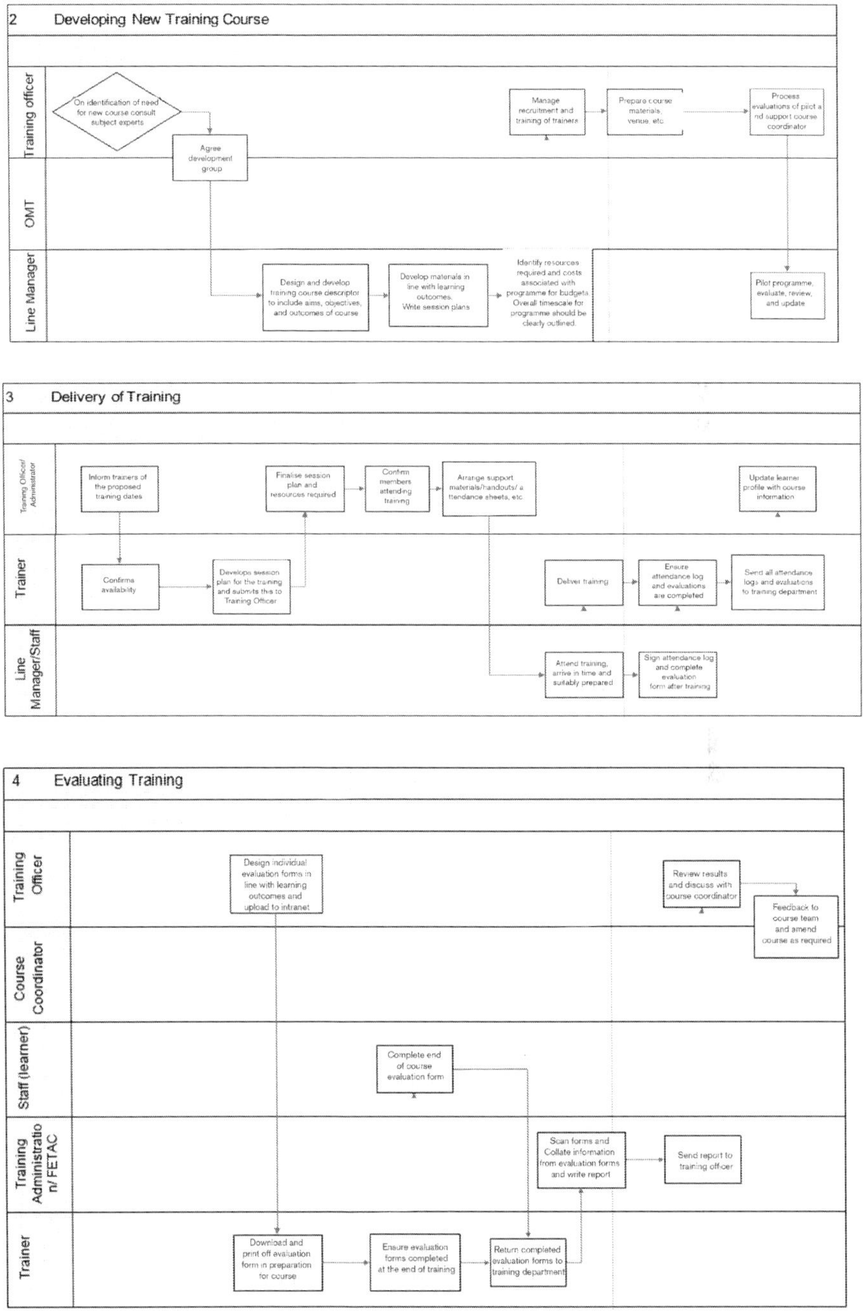

Figure 12.5. *Procedures.*

Section 3: Training Request Form-Training Plan

Applicant General Details	
Applicant Name:	**Job Title:**
Location:	**Email:**
Requested Course Details	
Name of Course and Description:	**Date of Course:**
Rationale:	
Have you conducted a Performance Management Meeting?	
Explain in detail why you want to conduct such training:	
Line Manager:	
I have read and understood all information provided and agree for the applicant to perform the course.	
Name and Date:	**Signature:**

Section 4: Application for External Course/Conference/Education Assistance

Section A-To be Completed by Applicant		
Personal Details		
Last name	First name	
Associate ID	Work location	
Region	Contact Number	
Home Address		
Job Title	Manager	
Course Details		
Course Title		
Desired Qualification	Accredited by/Awarding body	
Venue	Organizing Body	
Course Duration	Start date	End date
Course Cost	Per Year	In total
Closing date for application		

Study method	Part-time	Distance learning	Evening class
Have you researched this course?	No	Yes-information attached	
Please rate your level of knowledge on this subject matter	0% 25% 50% 100%		
Course relevance-please complete the following section in detail			
1. How does this course meet your professional needs?			
2. How will "INSERT COMPANY NAME" benefit from you gaining this qualification?			
3. Why did you choose this method of study?			
4. What are your expectations following the completion of this course?			
Section B-To be Completed by Line Manager			
Name	Contact number		
5. How will this course/conference benefit the service user? 6. Are you satisfied that this course will bring added value to the area and team and the applicant will share new information from this course to improve over-all service provision?			
7. Have replacement staff been organized for the applicant to attend this course?	No	Yes	
Agreement: I have read and understood the terms and conditions covered in the "INSERT COMPANY NAME" Training Policy and agree with the contractual arrangements outlined in the policy document. I have discussed this with my line manager. I have agreed to submit attendance and evaluation forms to the training officer on completion of the course.			
Applicant Signature	Date		
Line Manager	Ap-proved?	Yes	No	Date
Area Manager	Ap-proved	Yes	No	Date

Section 5: Evaluation Form (Generic)

Course Module	**Tutors**
Date	Where did the training take place?

☑ Please tick the appropriate response below based on your learning experience throughout the course and provide comments to support your choices.

Facility	**Not Good**	**Fair**	**Good**	**Excellent**
Heat				
Light				
Sound				
Parking				
Space/room to facilitate learning				
Location				
Comments:				
How do you feel that the tutors managed the delivery of the course?				
Comment-please circle the appropriate response: 1. Timing/pace of sessions (too quick/slow?). 2. Presentation skills, voice projection. 3. Interaction with your group and keeping you interested. 4. Giving breaks. 5. Answering questions, you had before leaving the session. 6. Putting students at ease. 7. Giving good examples to support the course information. 8. Using group work and discussions	Not good Not good Not good Not good Not good Not good Not good Not good	Fair Fair Fair Fair Fair Fair Fair Fair	Good Good Good Good Good Good Good Good	Excellent Excellent Excellent Excellent Excellent Excellent Excellent Excellent
Was there anything about the delivery of your course you felt could have been better?			Yes	No
Suggestions				

Course material and supports Please circle the appropriate response and provide comments to support your choices

Handouts				
1. Layout and presentation of information on the handouts.	Not good	Fair	Good	Excellent
2. Clarity and ease of reading.	Not good	Fair	Good	Excellent
Slides and overheads				
Tutors use of slides/overheads to support their presentation	Not good	Fair	Good	Excellent

Specific Learning Outcomes

Based on your training please tick the box to indicate if the training has developed your	**Yes**	**No**
Here the individual learning objectives of each course are listed to ensure they were met during training.		
Please support your statements with comments:		
Please outline the main learning outcomes you achieved in this training:		

Based on what you have learned, do you think that this training has been worthwhile? Yes/No Please give details:

Management System

We encourage our employees to strive towards continual improvement, and to establish, implement, and maintain recognized management systems and standards related to the areas described in Training Policy.

Monitoring

Training programs, results, and performance will be evaluated and monitored annually through the internal assessment policy principles. Those cases where training resulted in not being effective will be assessed to determine the root cause of the issue to prevent it from happening again.

Training Manager Job Description Template

Training manager duties and responsibilities:

- Evaluate employees and identify weaknesses;
- Identify training needs according to needs;
- Based on research, plan, and implement training programs that will prepare employees for the next step of their career paths;

- Recruit trainers;
- Lead, teach, onboard, and evaluate new trainers;
- Make other trainers' schedules;
- Build quarterly and annual training program;
- Present all the technical and supply training requirements;
- Prepare a budget for training programs and workshops;
- Encourage employees for training;
- Oversee employee attendance and performance;
- Track employee success and progress;
- Manage the production of program marketing material in collaboration with the marketing team;
- Communicate all the training programs on a timely basis;
- Have a program announcement marketing strategy;
- Prepare and deliver training courses;
- Bring guest presenters if necessary;
- Implement training KPIs;
- Prepare and present a report on training program KIPs.

Training manager requirements and qualifications:

- X years of experience as a Training Specialist or similar role;
- X years of experience with designing training programs and workshops;
- Ability to lead a full training cycle;
- X years of experience with learning management software;
- Knowledge of various training and teaching methods;
- Good knowledge of talent management and succession planning methods;
- Excellent decision making and organizational skills;
- Sense of ownership and pride in your performance and its impact on the company's success;
- Outstanding managerial skills;
- Great team leader;
- Good time-management skills;
- Great interpersonal and communication skills;

- Proficiency in MS Office and database software;
- BS degree in Education, Training, HR, or related field.

12.4. INDICATORS TEMPLATE

An indicator is something that helps you comprehend where you are, which way you are going and how far you are from where you need to be. A decent indicator alarms you to an issue before it gets too awful and helps you perceive what should be done to settle the issue. Indicators of a supportable group indicate territories where the connections between the economy, condition and society are frail. They enable you to see where the issue territories are and help demonstrate the best approach to settle those issues.

Sustainability indicators are unique in relation to conventional indicators of financial, social, and ecological advance. Customary indicators -, for example, stockholder benefits, asthma rates, and water quality – measure changes in one a player in a group as though they were totally free of alternate parts. Sustainability indicators mirror the truth that the three distinct portions are firmly interconnected.

Table 12.1. Indicators Examples

Economic Indicators		
Traditional Indicators	Sustainability Indicators	Emphasis of Sustainability Indicators
Median income Per capita income relative to the U.S. average	Number of hours of paid employment at the average wage required to support basic needs	What wage can buy Defines basic needs in terms of sustainable consumption
Unemployment rate Number of companies Number of jobs	Diversity and vitality of local job base Number and variability in size of companies Number and variability of industry types Variability of skill levels required for jobs	Resilience of the job market Ability of the job market to be flexible in times of economic change
size of the economy as measured by GNP and GDP	Wages paid in the local economy that are spent in the local economy Dollars spent in the local economy which pay for local labor and local natural resources Percent of local economy based on renewable local resources	Local financial resilience

Environmental Indicators		
Traditional Indicators	Sustainability Indicators	Emphasis of Sustainability Indicators
Ambient levels of pollution in air and water	Use and generation of toxic materials (both in production and by end user) Vehicle miles traveled	Measuring activities causing pollution
Tons of solid waste generated	Percent of products produced which are durable, repairable, or readily recyclable or compostable	Conservative and cyclical use of materials
Cost of fuel	Total energy used from all sources Ratio of renewable energy used at renewable rate compared to nonrenewable energy	Use of resources at sustainable rate

Social Indicators		
Traditional Indicators	Sustainability Indicators	Emphasis of Sustainability Indicators
SAT and other standardized test scores	Number of students trained for jobs that are available in the local economy Number of students who go to college and come back to the community	Matching job skills and training to needs of the local economy
Number of registered voters	Number of voters who vote in elections Number of voters who attend town meetings	Participation in democratic process Ability to participate in the democratic process

An indicator is a measurement that focuses on an issue or condition. Its motivation is to demonstrate how well a framework is functioning. On the off chance that there is an issue, an indicator can help figure out what measures need to be implemented to address the issue. Indicators are as different as the sorts of frameworks they screen. Nonetheless, there are sure attributes that powerful indicators have in like manner:

- Effective indicators are important; they indicate you something about the framework that you have to know.
- Effective indicators are straightforward, even by individuals who are not specialists.
- Effective indicators are solid; you can believe the data that the indicator is giving.
- Lastly, compelling indicators depend on open information; the data is accessible or can be assembled while there is still time to act.

Significant

An indicator must be important, that is, it must fit the reason for measuring. As indicators, the gas gage and the report card both measure truths that are important. In the event that, rather than measuring the measure of gas in the tank, the gas gage demonstrated the octane rating of the fuel, it would not help you choose when to refill the tank. Moreover, a report card that deliberate the quantity of pencils utilized by the understudy would be a poor indicator of scholastic execution.

Reasonable

An indicator must be justifiable. You have to comprehend what it is letting you know. There are a wide range of sorts of gas gages. A few gages have a lever that moves amongst "full" and "purge" marks. Different gages utilize lights to accomplish a similar impact. A few gages demonstrate the quantity of gallons of gas left in the tank. Albeit diverse, each gage is justifiable to the driver. Thus, with the report card, distinctive schools have diverse methods for detailing scholastic advance. A few schools have letter reviews A through F. Different schools utilize numbers from 100 to 0. Still different schools utilize composed remarks. Like the gas gage, these diverse measures all express the understudy's advance or absence of advance in a way that is reasonable to the individual perusing the report card.

Then again, a gas gage that demonstrated the quantity of BTU's left in the tank would most likely not be extremely helpful to you in choosing when to top off the tank. Moreover, a report card that gave reviews in old Greek script would be a puzzle to a great many people. With the goal for you to know when activity is required, you should have the capacity to comprehend what an indicator is letting you know.

Solid

An indicator must be solid. You should trust what the indicator appears. A decent gas gage and an exact report card give data that can be depended on. A gas gage that demonstrates the tank is vacant when in truth it is half full would make you stop for fuel before it is required. A gas gage that demonstrates the tank is half full when in certainty it is void would make you come up short on gas in a badly designed place. Additionally, if an understudy's review were accounted for wrong, a distinctions understudy could be sent for therapeutic work and an understudy who needs assistance would not get it. An indicator is just helpful on the off chance that you know you can accept what it is demonstrating to you.

Unwavering quality is not the same as accuracy. At the point when your gas gage registers discharge, you know there is as yet a gallon or so of gas left as a hold. The gas gage dependably under-reports the measure of fuel. An indicator does not really should be exact; it simply needs to give a solid photo of the framework it is measuring.

Available Data

Indicators must give convenient data. They should give you data while there is an ideal opportunity to act. For instance, envision a gas gage that lone gave you the measure of gas in the tank when the motor was begun. After you have been driving for a few hours, that perusing is no longer valuable. You have to know how much fuel is in the tank at every minute. Essentially, a report card conveyed seven days before graduation arrives past the point where it is possible to give an understudy healing help. All together for an indicator to be helpful in counteracting or taking care of an issue, it must give you the data while there is still time to rectify the issue.

One of the most serious issues with creating indicators of manageability is that often the best indicators are those for which there is no information, while the indicators for which there is information are the minimum ready to quantify sustainability. This has driven numerous groups to pick conventional information sources and measures for indicators. There are a few focal points to conventional indicators. To begin with, the information is promptly accessible and can be utilized to think about groups. Second, conventional indicators can characterize issue ranges. Third, customary indicators can be consolidated to make sustainability indicators. In any case, there is a genuine threat that conventional information sources and customary indicators will concentrate consideration on the conventional arrangements that made an unsustainable group in any case. It might entice to continue measuring 'number of occupations,' however measuring 'number of employments that compensation a reasonable wage and incorporate advantages' will prompt better arrangements. Exchanges that incorporate the expression 'however you can't understand that information' are not going to prompt indicators of sustainability. Truth be told, on the off chance that you characterize a rundown of indicators and find that the information is promptly accessible for each one of them, you presumably have not considered sustainability.

Attempt to characterize the best indicators and agree to less as a between time step while creating information hotspots for better indicators

Overall KPI Identification:

To meet the dual challenges of comparability and practicability for establishing KPIs by industry and sector, we have developed a six-step method as follows (see Diagram 12.6):

1. Assemble a broad universe of sustainability risks or opportunities that could apply to all industries.
2. Select an industry classification system.
3. Establish a definition of materiality to address non-financial issues.
4. Apply the materiality test to the sustainability issues potentially applicable to each industry sector.
5. Prioritize the issues
6. Develop industry-focused KPIs

Figure 12.6: Six step method to define industry specific KPIs.

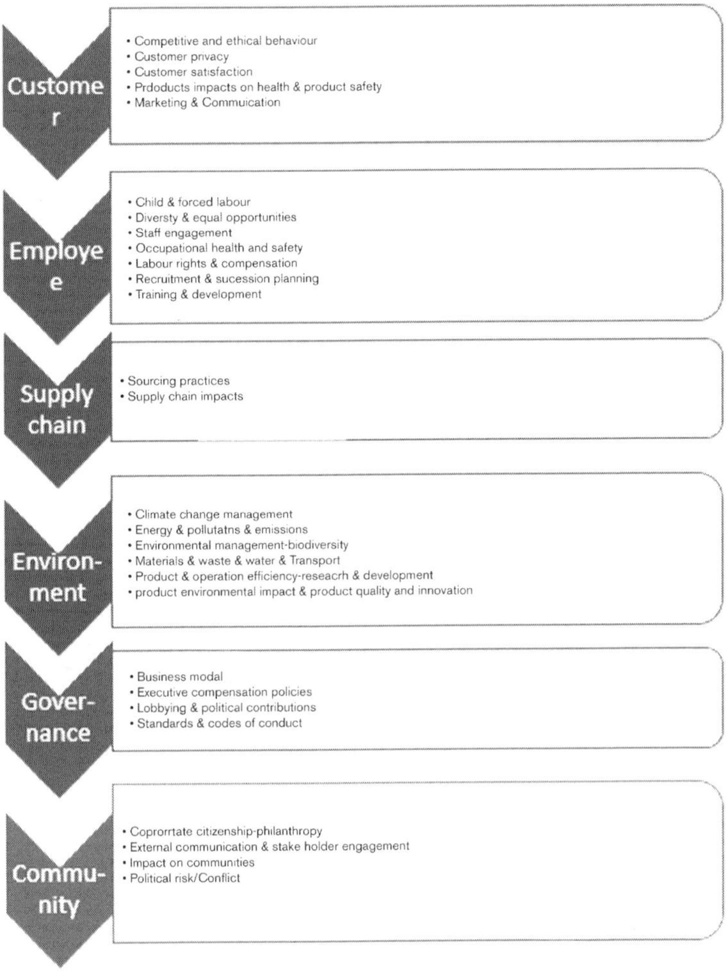

Figure 12.7. Universe of SG issues and opportunities.

Step 1: Assemble a broad universe of sustainability risks or opportunities that could apply to all industries.

The existing body of work on enhanced corporate reporting offers an excellent pool of issues from which to work. For this hypothetical exercise, we have drawn largely from the universe of indicators created by the Global Reporting Initiative. We have organized issues under the headings of community, customer, employees, supply chain; environment and governance (see Figure 12.7).

The advantages of starting with GRI's universe of sustainability issues are many, not the least of which is that they have emerged from a continuing multistakeholder engagement that looks beyond any single group's view of the long-term impact of corporate behavior.

Any reporting system will require periodic review of the universe of issues as new issues emerge and others fall away and as economies and societies evolve. As a multi-stakeholder, consultative organization, the GRI has incorporated review processes with organizational stakeholders that allow for the evolution of issues.

Step 2: Select an industry classification system

To facilitate comparative assessments of KPIs, you need to select a classification method to identify distinct industry groups of corporations engaged in similar activities and facing comparable ESG challenges and opportunities.

You can use the sector classification system known as the Industry Classification Benchmark (ICB). The system was developed jointly by Dow Jones Indexes and FTSE and is supported by the ICB Universe Database, which contains more than 60,000 companies and 65,000 securities worldwide.

Other classification systems, such as the Standard Industrial Classification (SIC) or the North American Industry Classification System (NAICS), could also be utilized. We recognize that there are limitations to any sector-based approach. Not every corporation fits into a sectoral definition. Indeed, large conglomerates often participate in multiple subsectors.

A KPI-based regime will have to take these complications into account and, like every classification system, will ultimately require judgment in its application.

Step 3: Establish a definition of materiality with which to test the relevance of these issues.

The next step is to extract from this universe of sustainability issues those that are most material to assessing the performance of each specific industry sector.

The definition of materiality is of crucial importance in all discussions of disclosure. Understanding the materiality of ESG issues and how materiality changes with respect to particular industry sectors is critical for successful implementation of a minimum ESG reporting scheme. Our working definition of materiality is a modified version of the materiality test developed by AccountAbility and advocated by the Global Reporting Initiative.

Our major substantive revision to the AccountAbility definition of materiality was to increase the emphasis on positive material opportunities for sustainability innovation (in business models or offerings) that might bring competitive advantage. Our definition is broader in scope than the definitions of materiality historically used by financial regulatory parties, but by no means precludes definitions of financial materiality.

Nor is it intended to replace corporate managers' responsibility to report on all financially material issues, whether or not they conform to the ESG materiality tests identified through this process. This process results in a minimum set of material issues subject to mandatory KPI reporting.

Our materiality test includes five categories of impact to be evaluated at a sector (or sub-sector) level (see Diagram 12.8). They are:

- Financial impacts/risks: Issues that may have a financial impact or may pose a risk to the sector in the short-, medium-, or long-term (e.g., product safety)
- Legal/regulatory/policy drivers: Sectoral issues that are being shaped by emerging or evolving government policy and regulation (e.g., carbon emissions regulation)
- Peer-based norms: Sustainability issues that companies in the sector tend to report on and recognize as important drivers in their line of business (e.g., safety in the airline industry)
- Stakeholder concerns and societal trends: Issues that are of high importance to stakeholders, including communities, non-governmental organizations and the general public, and/or reflect social and consumer trends (e.g., consumer push against genetically modified ingredients)
- Opportunity for innovation: Areas where the potential exists to explore innovative solutions that benefit the environment, customers and other stakeholders, demonstrate sector leadership and create competitive advantage.

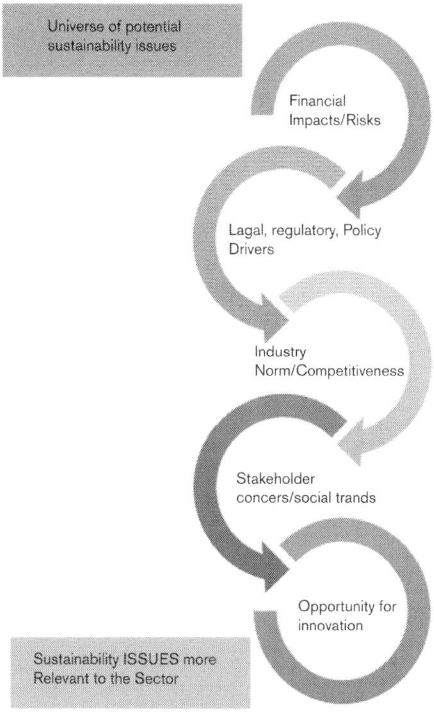

Figure 12.8. Five categories of impact to be evaluated at a sector (or sub-sector) level.

Step 4: Apply the materiality test to the sustainability issues potentially applicable to each industry sector.

To identify sector-specific material issues within the broad universe of sustainability topics, we constructed a hypothetical score for each issue on a four-point (0–3) Likert scale using each of the five materiality categories. These scores were then added together to give each issue an overall score of 0–15, with the higher scoring issues understood to be more material to the particular subsector.

Step 5: Rank the materiality of these issues within an industry and establish a threshold that defines those issues that are key.

Once the materiality tests have been applied to the broad set of sustainability issues and those issues ranked by their relative importance within a particular industry, a determination needs to be made as to where to draw the line in establishing material issues.

Step 6: Create a tailored set of key performance indicators for the most material issues for each sector.

In this final and perhaps most complicated step, it is necessary to translate the general sustainability issues into sector-specific KPIs.

Indicators

The indicators are listed in Table 12.2.

Table 12.2. Indicators Template

Environment	2020	2021	2022
Electricity Consumption			
Percentage of total workforce received training on environmental issues			
Percentage of operational sites EMS has been implemented			
Percentage of deployment of specific environmental actions the company has decided to implement.			

Labor Practices & Human Rights & Health Safety	2020	2021	2022
Percentage of all operational sites for which an employee health & safety risk assessment has been conducted (please specify) 100			
Percentage of Risk Methodology + Health and Safety Policy			
Percentage of the total workforce across all locations represented in formal joint management-worker health & safety committees			
Percentage of the total workforce across all locations who are covered by formal collective agreements concerning working conditions (please specify)			
Percentage of the total workforce across all locations who are covered by formally-elected employee representatives (please specify)			

Percentage of the total workforce across all locations who received regular performance and career development reviews (please specify)			
Percentage of the total workforce across all locations who received career- or skills-related training (please specify)			
Percentage of the total workforce across all locations who received training on preventing discrimination and human rights violations (please specify)			
Percentage of all operational sites that have been subject to human rights reviews or human rights impact assessments (please specify)			
Other indicators on the percentage of the deployment of labor or human rights actions throughout all company operations/workforce (please specify)			
Number of lost time injury events (please specify)			
Number of days lost due to injuries (please specify)			
Total number of hours worked (please specify)			
(total number of lost time injury events) x 100,000 / total hours worked (please specify)			
Percentage of disabled workers out of total workforce			
Percentage of women in top executive positions.			

Fair Business Practices	2020	2021	2022
% of the total workforce across all locations who received training (e.g., e-learning) on business ethics issues (please specify)			
% of all operational sites for which an internal audit/risk assessment concerning business ethics issues has been conducted (please specify)			
% of all operational sites with an information security management system (ISMS) certified to ISO 27000 (or other equivalent/similar standard) (please specify)			

% of all operational sites with certified anti-corruption management system (please specify)			
% of the deployment of business ethics actions throughout all company operations (please specify)			

Sustainable Procurement	2020	2021	2022
% of all suppliers who have signed the sustainable procurement charter/supplier code of conduct (please specify) *			
% of all supplier contracts that include clauses on environmental, labor, human rights, and ethical requirements (please specify) *			
% of all buyers across all locations who received training on sustainable procurement (please specify) 100% *			
% of total procurement spend which has gone through a CSR assessment or audit (please specify) 75% *			
% of total procurement spend which has gone through a CSR on-site audit (please specify) *			
% of all suppliers which has gone through a CSR assessment (e.g., questionnaire) (please specify) *			
% of all suppliers which has gone through a CSR on-site audit (please specify) * Other indicators			
% of the deployment of sustainable procurement actions throughout all company supplier base/operations (please specify)			

Conclusions about key performance indicators and methodologies:

- Key performance indicators can play a vital role in any sustainability disclosure scheme.
- A method for identifying KPIs for all industry sectors that is simple, material and transparent can be developed and implemented with a reasonable degree of up-front effort.
- KPIs are most useful when they are specific to industry subsectors.
- Substantial work has already been done in identifying a broad universe of issues that are fertile ground for identifying key issues for a given industry sector.

- Substantial work has already been done in defining criteria for the materiality of potential key issues.
- Substantial work has already been done in defining industry subsectors that will be useful in identifying comparable KPIs.
- Additional work needs to be done to identify the most material KPIs to support comparability in industry subsectors.
- KPIs can be usefully related to the key impacts of sectoral activity and the opportunities for new business strategies and models.
- Reporting on KPIs can be performance-based (quantitative) or based on management policies and business processes (qualitative).
- Certain key issues are common to many industry sectors, while others are unique to a particular sector.
- Transformation of relevant issues to sector-specific indicators is a critical step in developing KPIs that are relevant to business.
- Any method for identifying and reporting on KPIs needs to be flexible, because KPIs will vary from industry to industry, from country to country, region to region, and from time to time.
- Increased uptake in voluntary reporting, with a move towards mandatory reporting on a basic of set of KPIs is ultimately necessary to fill varying disclosure needs of our diverse societies and complete the convergence of financial and sustainability reporting.

Because sustainability disclosure is useful to governments and societies as they manage the impacts of corporations, we recommend that government regulators, stock exchanges, responsible investors, nongovernmental organizations, accounting firms, and related parties concerned with the best way to increase the availability of corporate ESG data, cooperate in the development of a full-blown method and governance structure for identifying and providing guidance to corporations regarding KPIs.

By establishing mandatory reporting on sustainability KPIs for publicly traded corporations in the United States, competition on important dimensions of sustainability can be encouraged and entire industry sectors channeled towards the creation of a more just and sustainable society.

Chapter 13

Good Business Practice Checklist

CONTENTS

13.1. WHAT ARE THE ADVANTAGES OF GOOD BUSINESS PRACTICE?

Great business practice enhances a business, in all sorts of challenges. A business that follows great practice benefits from multiple points of view, for example:

- The business is bound to be beneficial, have better income, and work with lower environment and monetary risks;
- The business is bound to practice with higher performance and efficiency rates;
- The business is better ready to draw in, hold, and propel staff, in this way improving the company's flexibility and spryness in the worldwide commercial center;
- The business can possibly separate itself and be compensated as a favored seller in a developing green store network;
- The business will have the option to separate itself in a wide-open market, making it simpler to sell the business later on, and potentially at a superior cost;
- The business might have the option to acquire environment risk protection, and potentially at a favored rate; and
- The business may think that its simpler to get to outside money, including bank loans, if necessary.

13.2. WHAT IS THE MANAGERS PART IN GUARANTEEING GREAT BUSINESS PRACTICE?

Executing great business practice includes recognizing the basic undertakings that should be done to keep a business fit as a fiddle, and having the control to guarantee that those errands are completed reliably and consistently. Great business practice requires a yearly survey at any rate; better business practice will enable you to check on regions quarterly, or even month to month. Great business practice is not just about getting your home altogether; it is tied in with setting up your business for the difficulties and opportunities it will face later on.

Managers can help their customers execute and keep up great strategic approaches as they are frequently ready to offer autonomous and master guidance. The IFAC SMP Committee has built up this agenda for use by managers, particularly professionals who work in small and medium-sized practices (SMPs), to assist them with figuring out what kind of help their private company customers may require.

An agenda like this cannot be complete. In any case, this agenda is planned to begin you pondering the particular activities your customers should take to put their business progressing nicely and keep it there.

13.3. IN WHAT MANNER CAN THIS AGENDA HELP WITH GREAT BUSINESS PRACTICE?

The agenda features great strategic approaches that private ventures ought to take a stab at consistently. In this manner, notwithstanding assisting SMPs with prompting their customers on great business practice, it can likewise be utilized by managers to guarantee their own practices are working in accordance with great strategic policies. On the off chance that you attempt the assignments in this agenda consistently, the finish of the monetary year ought not make unnecessary weight for your business, and you will be bound to have the quality data you need to oversee and develop your business, whatever conditions you face.

13.3.1. Agenda

The following are a few different ways to incorporate significant parts of this agenda into your strategic policies:

- Use the agenda as a feature of the plan in your standard workforce researches and distribute assignments so everybody understands what component of the agenda every individual is responsible for. Request standard reports on each undertaking.
- Write the agenda assignments into your schedule with the goal that you are helped to remember prerequisites at the fitting occasions.
- Build errands from the agenda into the sets of responsibilities of applicable staff.
- The agenda contains six areas as demonstrated as follows. Spaces are given, where proper, in the agenda for you to embed data pertinent to your business (Table 13.1).

1. **Financial Tasks:** Errands important to plan budget summaries should be performed routinely. Holding up until the finish of the monetary year to attempt a considerable lot of these errands will put you under tension, as various returns and structures must

be finished not long after the end of the monetary year, which may endanger the quality, and hence handiness, of monetary information. Postponing monetary assignments can likewise deny you ordinary admittance to monetary data, for example, income articulations, which can be basic to assisting you with dealing with the regular rhythmic movement of your business. Monetary undertakings are important to create budget reports, for example, an assertion of economic performance (pay/benefit and misfortune proclamation) and monetary position (asset report), which give data that encourages you to see how your business is performing and to distinguish potential territories for development.

2. **Strategic Financial Tasks:** Monetary undertakings do not end with bank compromises or asset reports. There are other monetary errands known as vital monetary undertakings that are basic in deciding the future way of your business.
3. **Strategic Management Tasks:** Occasionally, ideally at the finish of each monetary year, you should refresh your arranging, planning, and operational techniques. This way, your business will be solid and steady for the new monetary year. On the off chance that there are huge changes in your business, it is proposed that these essential administration assignments be embraced all the more routinely.
4. **Environmental Management Tasks:** There is mounting proof demonstrating that organizations that set up better control of their relationship with the climate by expanding the custom of their administration exercises profit by increments in efficiency. Thusly, there are enhancements in productivity and thriving. Better administration control can likewise upgrade consistency with legitimate necessities. Improved sustainable administration is turning into a prerequisite in inventory chains as worldwide organizations are propelled to oversee hazard and their standing, particularly when under tension from non-legislative companies (NGOs), or to meet desires for shoppers. It can assist a business withholding and draw in new clients or access abroad business sectors. Better sustainable administration is required to turn into a factor that can separate one organization from the following in a leave technique or to improve achievement in the intergenerational move; it should be thought in any progression

plan. An administration frameworks approach can both upgrade sustainable execution, for example, strength in reacting to bizarre conditions, for example, outrageous climate occasions, and offer the upper hand. See The IFAC Sustainability Framework for more data.

5. **Regulatory Requirements: Lodging Returns and Forms:** Staying up with the latest with the lodgment and installment of your legal commitments is viewed as a significant indicator of the monetary danger, wellbeing, and steadiness of your business by banks and different leasers. Consequently, recording the lodgment and installment due dates for every one of the prerequisites underneath is suggested.

6. **Individual Affairs of Business Owner:** The finish of the monetary year is likewise a significant opportunity to ensure your own issues are all together.

Table 13.1. Good Practice Checklist

1. Financial Tasks				
√	**Activity**	**Person Responsible**	**Due Date/ Regularity**	**Some Actions to Consider**
	Install financial software.		With new updates	• Ask the software vendor to list what financial statements and reports the software can produce.
				• Use the financial software to produce regular financial statements and reports.
	Enter all data promptly, and with accurate transaction dates.		Ongoing	• Regularly check data entry for quality. • If possible, separate "cash handling" from "data entry" to minimize the potential for fraud.
	Regularly review working capital products, including: • Stock/inventory balances and reconcile to physical		At least quarterly	• Recycle or dispose of old/slow-moving stock/inventory. • Write-off deadstock/inventory. • Review purchasing policies to prevent overspending on stock/ inventory. Post materials on a waste, scrap, or materials exchange.

	• Work-in-progress (for construction firms, professional practices, etc.)		At least quarterly	• Bill clients regularly or at milestones.
	• Debtors		At least quarterly	• Invoice as soon as your goods or services are delivered. • Refer bad debts to collection agents. • Review credit screening. • Renegotiate trading terms with consistently slow payers. • Contact slow payers early.
	Reconcile major accounts in balance sheet, including: • Bank and investment accounts		At least monthly	• Have two people undertake the reconciliation. These people should not be the same people who handle cash. For high volume cash businesses, reconcile daily.
	• Accounts receivable/ debtors' ledger		At least monthly	Identify customers with large outstanding amounts and follow up.
	• Accounts payable/ creditors' ledger		At least monthly	Reconcile suppliers owed money with a list of approved suppliers.
	• Property and equipment		At least quarterly	• Do an asset stock-take to ensure you still have the assets that are recorded in your accounts. • Identify obsolete, unusable, or written-off assets. Ask your accountant to adjust balances and/ or see if such assets can be turned into cash. • Do not over-invest in new capital equipment without an appropriate payback.
	• Sales/Value Added Tax (VAT)		At least quarterly	• Make adjustments quickly through the next activity statement.
	• Equity accounts (especially in partnerships) and shareholder/stockholder loans		At least quarterly	• Operate equity accounts in accordance with the partnership agreement. Try to avoid large imbalances in the amounts contributed by or retained by each partner.
	Review payroll system, including: • Annual leave entitlements		Quarterly	• Encourage staff to take leave regularly-avoid a large build-up of entitlements. Consider a reserve to fund leave liability.
	• Pension/ superannuation		Quarterly	Comply with legislation regarding frequency of payment, choice of fund and reporting to staff.

	• Income tax withholding		Monthly	• If you have an employee who is about to give birth or has given birth, visit your government's website for information on any obligations
	• Fringe benefits tax		Monthly	
	• Payroll tax		Monthly	
	• Paid parental/ maternity leave		Quarterly	
	Translate foreign exchange gains/losses.		Year-end	• Use foreign exchange rates from an official source, such as the tax authority. • Speak to your accountant about how you can manage your foreign exchange risk.
	Market valuation of certain assets.		Year-end	Involve your accountant, or a specialist valuer, as required.
	Review forward orders.		Quarterly	Review forward orders as it will help you plan for any short-term need to expand or contract your business.
	Prepare a statement of financial performance (income/profit and loss statement).		Monthly or quarterly	The profit and loss statement, balance sheet, and cash flow statement can help identify any emerging problems in time for corrective action to be taken. Your accountant can assist in their preparation.
	Prepare a statement of financial position (balance sheet).		Monthly or quarterly	
	Prepare a cash flow statement.		Monthly or quarterly	

2. Strategic Financial Tasks

√	Activity	Person Responsible	Due Date/Regularity	Some Actions to Consider
	Set targets for financial performance.		At least annually	• Ask your accountant to help you set targets relevant to your industry and your business. • Incorporate set targets into your budgets and strategic plan.

	Review and analyze financial statements.		At least annually; preferably quarterly or monthly	• Compare key ratios from your financial statements, such as working capital ratio, stock/inventory turnover ratio or profit per employee, to averages in your industry. Your accountant may be able to help you get access to such industry averages and assist with calculating and analyzing the ratios. • Compare performance against financial targets and past performance.
	Review actual performance against budget.		Monthly	Undertake variance analysis (ask yourself: What may have caused any gap between budget and actual? How can we overcome unfavorable variances?).
	Undertake sensitivity analysis.		Annually	Ask yourself: What if sales dropped 15 or 20%? Or you lost a major customer? Or a major supplier stopped selling to you? What if your chief sales staff resigned? What if your power source or water supplies were unavailable after an extreme weather event-how long could your business endure this loss? Factor answers to such questions into your forecasts.
	Set sales or production targets.		Ongoing	Undertake a break-even analysis to determine what you need to sell before you make a profit. Ask your accountant to help you with a break-even analysis if you are uncertain.
	Prepare income/ profit and loss budget.		Annually	• Make sure your budget reflects your strategic and financial targets. • Incorporate any findings from the variance analysis of the last budget, sensitivity analysis, and the break-even analysis.
	Prepare cash flow forecast.		At least annually	• Have your cash flow forecast show the projected cash flows for each month in the 12-month period. Such forecasts should be updated at least monthly. • Address any future cash shortages, for example, more cash sales, reduced expenses or external finance (such as an overdraft facility). If you decide to seek external finance for any purpose, go to your lender as soon as possible.
	Review cash flow forecast in light of actual results.		Monthly	Update cash flow forecast to reflect actual events and monitor ongoing cash positions.
	Review bank loans, leases, credit cards or other finance, ensuring you:			

	• Evaluate interest rates on your loans.		Annually	• Look at what other lenders are offering and consider whether you should switch lenders.
	• Provide historic and budgeted information to lenders.		Annually	Provide information on profit and loss, balance sheet, cash flow statement and budgets.
	• Comply with repayment schedules.		Ongoing	
	• Check compliance with debt covenants.		Ongoing	• Notify your bank immediately if you are in breach of a covenant. If you are uncertain of your covenants, ask your bank.

3. Strategic Management Tasks				
√	**Activity**	**Person Responsible**	**Due Date/Regularity**	**Some Actions to Consider**
	Create or update your strategic plan.	Owner and key staff	3–5-year horizon, updated annually	• Have a strategic plan for the owners, as well as for the business. This ensures the business complements the owners' needs. • Take time to review lessons learned from the current year and incorporate those lessons into your strategic plan.
	Review employment arrangements, ensuring you: • Conduct performance reviews.	Team leaders	At least annually	Do not wait until the formal feedback process. Provide regular informal feedback to staff.
	• Consider incentive systems or commission-based pay.	Owner and key staff	At least annually	• Make incentive systems simple, pay promptly, and link the incentives to the controllable success factors for each role. • Consider only paying commission when you have received cash from the sale and paying higher commissions for sales of higher-margin products and services.
	• Get staff to sign an employment agreement (including provisions for confidentiality obligations and ownership of intellectual property).	Owner	Commencement of employment	• Obtain legal advice to ensure employment agreements comply with the law.
	Consider if "restraint of trade" contracts is needed for key staff.		Commencement of employment	• Obtain legal advice to ensure applicable contracts are enforceable and advisable.

	Review sales contracts and customer's payment terms.		Annually	Determine whether your sales contracts protect your business. For example, in a difficult economic environment, you could protect your business by: shortening the payment terms; implementing credit limits; and seeking personal guarantees and security.
	Review suppliers' contracts or payment terms.		Annually	• Negotiate a lengthening of your payment terms of trade. • Review how goods are supplied to you (so that it better meets your needs). • See if you can reduce the minimum quantity you can order. • Look at payment discounts. • As a risk management measure, check alternative suppliers of critical products.
	Review financial commitments, such as: • Office leases		Annually	• Exercise options to renew your lease if premises meet your needs, if they do not, begin planning a move.
	• Equipment leases		Annually	Understand ownership/payout arrangements at end-of-lease.
	• Securities over assets		Annually	• Check which of your assets is security for which loan and that, where a loan no longer exists, the security is removed.
	• Hedging contracts		Annually	
	• Other		Annually	Speak to your accountant about what other forms of financing, not outlined within, that might be relevant to your business.
	Establish, update, or review your "Policies Manual," ensuring you: • Document your processes.		Annually	• A good policy manual has the potential to make your business more valuable and easier to run in your absence.
				• Use your process document as a training and quality manual.
	• Allocate specific tasks.		Annually	Separate record-keeping duties from duties involving the handling of cash and other assets to minimize the risk of fraud or theft by employees.
	• Consider fraud risk.		Annually	Speak to your accountant about establishing appropriate internal controls.

	• Review staff authority to spend money.		Annually	Consider authorizing all payments yourself for a short period as part of a cost reduction and quality assurance exercise.
	•Inform and educate staff about your policies		Annually	•Conduct random spot checks to ensure both compliance with your policies and to reduce the risk of fraud.
	Review and update IT systems, ensuring: • You have the licenses you need to use your software.		Annually	• Ensure current versions of software are being used, there are no unauthorized copies, and the number of users your license covers is sufficient for your needs.
	• Back-ups are performed frequently and held offsite.		Daily/weekly	Test whether your staff knows how to restore the back-ups and that the back-ups work.
	• Staff training needs are met.		Annually	Appoint a "champion" for each software product to enhance internal transfer of practical knowledge.
	• Disaster recovery plan documentation has been reviewed.		Annually	
	Review your intellectual property by: • Documenting procedures on how your intellectual property is used in your business		Annually	
	• Renewing trading names (including trademarks and business names) and domain names		Annually	Speak to your lawyer to see if your intellectual property is adequately covered.
	Review your insurances, including: • Types of policy required		Annually	• Does your insurance cover match your needs, for instance, insurance covering assets, business interruption, loss of attraction, life insurance, income replacement, etc.?
	• The amount of cover in place		Annually	Avoid under- and over-insurance.

	Seek ways of reducing resource use in the business. Consider: • The use of water, electricity, gas, petrol/diesel • The use of other resources • Using local suppliers if possible • Eliminating unproductive steps or processes		Annually	•Resource consideration should be part of a cost reduction strategy.
				• Consider how to operate your business if there was a disruption to the supply of electricity, gas, or water.
	Review any outstanding legal disputes.	Owner and solicitor	At least quarterly	• Keep disputes moving along. • Consider viable ways to settle disputes promptly.
	Determine whether you undertake activities (such as exporting) that may be eligible for a government grant/subsidy.		Annually	Speak to your accountant about what grants/subsidies, if any, you may be eligible for and the eligibility requirements.

4. Environmental Management Tasks					
√	Activity	Person Responsible	Due Date/ Regularity		Some Actions to Consider
	Plan to achieve better environmental management and performance, using a systems framework in which you will: • Define the scope of your business that will be included.	Owner and key personnel	Ongoing		Refer to ISO 14001:2004 for the framework upon which a robust, credible, and reliable environmental management system can be established.
			Initially, and reviewed when changes occur to location or organizational boundaries		• Ensure scope includes your facilities and covers the organization that resides under your control.

	• Identify the significant environmental aspects of your plans, activities, products, and services.		Initially, or with changes to plans, activities, products, and services		• Identify what it is you have or do that causes environmental impacts that add to or subtract from the company's environmental footprint, and can add to or reduce costs and risks, including reputation. As 80% of environmental impacts tend to be location-based, a map can help quickly identify where opportunities are situated.
	• Identify applicable legal and other requirements related to your environmental aspects.		At least annually		• Consult services that provide access to lists of environmental laws. Speak to an environmental lawyer if your need is more acute.
	• Develop an environmental policy.		Initially, and then review annually.		• Ensure it reflects the culture and nature of your business. Make sure all personnel understand it. Post it or be ready to share it upon request.
	• Set environmental objectives and targets. • Identify the resources needed to set up, maintain, and improve the management system to realize performance improvements.		At least annually Annually		• Make sure your objectives and targets support your policy. • Take into account legal and other requirements, your significant environmental aspects, technical options, financial, and business needs, and the views of interested parties when setting these. • Ask your accountant to assist in costing out objectives and targets to set priorities. • Establish a budget to ensure that you have the resources to meet your objectives and targets. Consult with your accountant for a more detailed analysis if needed.

	• Identify the education and experience needs of personnel.		Annually		Assign duties to others as required to meet your needs and any milestones. • Conduct a needs analysis to determine what training is needed to educate staff to enable the behavioral changes needed. • Determine the competencies and technical expertise required to ensure personnel can deliver on the policy and reduce the company's environmental footprint.
	• Determine the need to communicate with external stakeholders (see also activity 5 below).		Annually		• Identify the concerns of interested parties (customers, your community, investors, etc.), who are affected by your environmental performance.
					• Determine what information you will share and how you will communicate.
					• Establish procedures to inform appropriate community and regulatory agencies on matters related to emergencies and situations related to the impact of your products and services on the market.
	• Maintain sufficient documentation to ensure efficiency and effectiveness of the EMS.		Ongoing		• Document the key elements of your management activity such as your environmental policy, objectives, and targets to ensure you reduce your environmental footprint.
	• Develop procedures to prevent and respond to emergencies.		Initially, and update as appropriate		• Make sure that you and your staff understand what to do in emergencies.

					• Run periodic tests to make sure your emergency plan works.
	Do, by taking action to: • Establish procedures to prevent significant environmental impact from operations.	Owner or assigned staff	Ongoing		• Ensure that the most critical aspects of your business, which could cause significant environmental impact, are managed to avoid, or control risks like spills or air emissions. Document where there is a low to zero tolerance for failure due to absenteeism or human error.
	Check your progress, ensuring you:				
	• Establish procedures to test the tools used to determine whether indicators of your success are working.	Owner and key personnel	Annually		• Monitor and measure your performance to ensure optimum outcomes.
	• Evaluate status of compliance with legal and other requirements.		Annually		Check to make sure you are in compliance with laws and other requirements.
	• Maintain records for easy crosschecks on work performed and progress.		Ongoing		Keep records on your progress up to date, legible, and easily accessible.
	•Conduct an internal audit to ensure that the EMS is working well.		Annually		Periodically test your system to make sure it is delivering on the value you need.

	• Review the audit results and ensure other key elements of the EMS are suitable, adequate, and efficient to realize value from the environmental management system.		Annually		• Consider the results of your audit to make sure that you take advantage of the opportunity to improve and enhance your position in the market, whether it is with your customers and the supply chain in which they operate, your community, to differentiate yourself in a buyer's market if you are trying to sell the business, or simply for your own internal benefit.
	Act to:	Owner and assigned staff	Ongoing		Identify opportunities to improve your environmental performance, reduce costs,
	Ensure that you are staying current, improving, avoiding problems, resolving mistakes, and reducing impact on the environment.				lower risk, and minimize your environmental footprint.
	Assess the business risk of environmental factors that may affect your business.		Annually		• Ask your accountant to help identify and quantify these factors. • Considerations may include climate change, extreme weather, biodiversity, carbon taxes/ prices, or other environmental risks. • Opportunities to be explored could include carbon trading, carbon offsetting, or district heating (whereby a local central plant producing steam, hot water, or chilled water eliminates the need for businesses to have their own boilers or furnaces, chillers, or air conditioners).

	Monitor innovation in environmental technology and reporting.	Owner or assigned staff	At least annually		• Scan reports that provide free updates. • Subscribe to online news services that post highlights. Read environmental or corporate social responsibility (CSR) reports posted by customers or industry leaders.
	Monitor trends in enforcement.	Owner or assigned staff	Quarterly		Subscribe to news services provided by environmental lawyers on fines and court rulings on environmental offenses.
	Evaluate your succession plan and exit strategy to determine how better environmental management can differentiate your business in a buyer's market.	Owner	Annually		Involve your accountant, or a specialist adviser, as required.
	Determine the need, and value, in reporting on your company's environmental progress.		Owner	Annually, after the tasks above have been addressed	• Ensure that you report on measurable and verifiable progress. Unsubstantiated or incorrectly worded claims can cause reputational risk, lead to your reporting being labeled "greenwash," and even give rise to lawsuits. • Some form of assurance on what is reported may lend credibility to what you report. • Consult a specialist advisor or involve your accountant or lawyer to avoid misinterpretation.

5. Regulatory Requirements: Lodging Returns and Forms				
√	Requirement	Person Responsible	Due/Payment Dates	Some Actions to Consider
	Income tax return			Provide information, including financial statements, to your accountant for review; highlight large or unusual transactions.
	Corporate/business tax returns			If you have difficulties with your BAS or IAS, ask your accountant to complete it or engage a bookkeeper recommended by your accountant.
	Securities regulator annual report/return/ filing (listed companies only)			Ask your accountant to prepare these.
	Income tax withholding annual payment summary			Perform test reconciliation in the month before year-end to highlight any processing problems.
	Income tax statements (group certificate) for employees			Reconcile totals to your ledgers first.
	Payroll tax			Speak to your accountant if you are unsure of the rates and any thresholds.
	Workers' compensation insurance			• Determine your projected wages and salaries for the year. • Find out if there are any exclusions and, if so, whether they are adequately covered in another way.
	Pension/superannuation payments			Pay monthly; produce notices for staff regularly.
	Fringe benefits tax return			
	Solvency declaration—for companies only			
	Staff salaries and conditions			Review staff salaries and conditions to ensure compliance with awards (where appropriate) and legal requirements.

	Government grants			If you are in receipt of government grants, ensure you meet your obligations under the grant.
	Others (list)			
		6. Personal Affairs of Business Owner		
√	Activity	Person Responsible	Due Date/Regularity	Some Actions to Consider
	Ensure trust distributions are properly made.		At least annually	The tax treatment of trusts can be complex and is subject to change: any could expose you to large unforeseen tax bills. Speak to your adviser about your trust.
	Undertake tax and personal financial planning.		Annually (before year-end)	• Year-end presents a number of tax planning opportunities and risks. Speak to your accountant about tax and personal financial planning. • Do not invest in any year-end tax planning schemes until you speak to your accountant.
	Review any loan agreements with your business.		Annually	
	Review personal insurances.		Annually	Disability, life, and trauma
	Ensure Power of Attorney is current.		Annually	
	Review your succession/ retirement plan.	Your accountant and lawyer	Annually	Remember that your will does not take effect until you are dead, so you need a succession plan for the handing over of the business or its management if you prematurely die, as well as a will.
	Review your will, particularly if there has been a change in your circumstances.	Your accountant and lawyer	Annually	
	Review the structures you have in place to protect your personal assets.	Your accountant and lawyer	Annually	This area of law is constantly evolving. Therefore, to be safe, you should review the effectiveness of your business structures and your asset protection strategies.

Great strategic approaches will help guarantee your business is very much run. An all-around run business will help place your business in the most ideal situation to react to whatever exchanging conditions you face and help you move your business toward the path you need it to go.

In the event that your business is developing firmly, at that point, be careful about expanding fixed overheads too soon (it is prescribed you attempt to help additional outstanding task at hand through extra time or with easygoing staff until you are certain about the strength of your recuperation). Abstain from over-purchasing stock things or over-putting resources into capital hardware.

On the off chance that your business is encountering powerless or moderate development, screen intently indicators of future deals action and remain zeroed in on controlling expenses.

On the off chance that your business is attempting to develop, search for methods of expanding each selling opportunity—frequently it is as straightforward as "requesting the request" or inquiring as to whether the client "might want something different with that." A keen deals procedure does not need extreme and unsafe limited time exercises: basic deals strategies can be okay and minimal effort but profoundly powerful.

Whatever the condition of your business, search for administrations or products that are not creating a decent return—low deals or continuous issues with product backing may be helpful indicators. Your monetary framework should have the option to reveal to you whether there is next to zero gross benefit/edge from a product, or the product may tie up an excess of working capital comparative with its benefit level. When you know the wellspring of the issue, see whether it tends to be amended or whether you ought to consider done selling that product or administration.

Primary changes are regularly best made during great occasions since faculty can without much of a stretch be redeployed somewhere else for more noteworthy benefit. Notwithstanding, in the event that you need to roll out underlying improvements in less vigorous occasions, at that point, discuss transparently with the influenced individuals and ensure you treat them decently.

Regardless of whether your business is solid, powerless, or inconsistent, this agenda will help you take advantage of any circumstance and feel more in charge of your business.

Bibliography

1. (1985). Returns to education: A further international update and implications. *Journal of Human Resources, 20*(4). 583–597.
2. (1999). *Second International Congress on Technical and Vocational Education, Final Report*. Paris, UNESCO. http://unesdoc.unesco.org/images/0011/001169/116954e.pdf (accessed on 8 June 2021).
3. (2000). *UN General Assembly, United Nations Millennium Declaration*. Resolution adopted by the General Assembly. A/RES/55/2.
4. (2001). *Revised Recommendation Concerning Technical and Vocational Education*. Paris, UNESCO. http://portal.unesco.org/en/ev.php-URL_ID=13145&URL_DO=DO_TOPIC&URL_SECTION=201.html (accessed on 8 June 2021).
5. (2005). *Promoting Adult Learning, Education and Training Policy*. Paris, OECD Publishing.
6. (2005b). *Closing the Gap in Education and Technology*. Washington, DC, World Bank.
7. (2006). *OECD Thematic Review of Tertiary Education*. Country Background Report: Portugal. Paris, OECD. http://www.oecd.org/dataoecd/23/1/37745972.pdf (accessed on 8 June 2021).
8. (2006). *World Development Report 2007: Development and the Next Generation*. Washington, DC, World Bank.
9. (2006b). *Vocational Education and Training Institutions: A Management Handbook and CD-ROM*. Geneva, ILO.
10. (2007). *Education for Livelihoods and Civic Participation in Post-Conflict Countries*. Bonn, UNESCO-UNEVOC International Centre.
11. (2007). *For Debate and Guidance: Portability of Skills*. Governing Body, 298th Session, Committee on Employment and Social Policy.

Geneva, ILO. http://www.ilo.org/wcmsp5/groups/public/---ed_norm/---relconf/documents/meetingdocument/wcms_gb_298_esp_3_en.pdf (accessed on 8 June 2021).

12. (2007). *Qualifications Systems: Bridges to Lifelong Learning*. Paris, OECD Publishing.
13. (2007). *Towards More Knowledge-Based Policy and Practice in Education and Training*. 50–60.
14. (2008). *Tertiary Education for the Knowledge Society: OECD Thematic Review of Tertiary Education, Synthesis Report*. Paris, OECD Publishing. http://www.oecd.org/education/skills-beyond-school/40345176.pdf (accessed on 8 June 2021).
15. (2008a). *Enterprise Survey 2008*. Washington, DC, World Bank.
16. (2008b). *Global Economic Prospects*. Technology Diffusion in the Developing World. Washington, DC, World Bank, p. 5.
17. (2009). *Averting a Human Crisis During the Global Downturn: Policy Options from the World Bank's Human Development Network*. Washington, DC, World Bank.
18. (2009). European quality assurance reference framework for VET. *Official Journal of the European Union, C155, 52*. http://europa.eu/legislation_summaries/education_training_youth/lifelong_learning/c11108_en.htm (accessed on 8 June 2021).
19. (2009). From a vicious to a virtuous cycle: Global perspectives on skills, innovation, productivity, and shared growth. *Keynote address at the Big Skills Conference 2009*. Sydney, Australia. www.innovation.gov.au/skills/Documents/marope.ppt (accessed on 8 June 2021).
20. (2009). *Is Informal Normal? Toward More and Better Jobs*. Paris, OECD Publishing.
21. (2009). *Rural Skills Training a Generic Manual on Training for Rural Economic Empowerment (TREE)*. Geneva, ILO.
22. (2009). *The Shift to Learning Outcomes: Policies and Practices in Europe*. Reference series 82. Luxembourg, Office for Official Publications of the European Communities. www.cedefop.europa.eu/EN/Files/3054_en.pdf (accessed on 8 June 2021).
23. (2009). Thematic studies. *Qualifications That Count: Strengthening the Recognition of Qualifications in the Mediterranean Region*. Luxembourg, Office for Official Publications of the European Communities.

24. (2009a). Bonn declaration. *UNESCO World Conference on Education for Sustainable Development*. Bonn, UNESCO. http://unesdoc.unesco.org/images/0018/001887/188799e.pdf (accessed on 8 June 2021).

25. (2009b). *CAQA Organization: Rationale and Brief Functional Description.* Working paper. Amman, ETVET Council (Jordan).

26. (2009b). Report by the director-general on the implementation of the program adopted by the general conference. *Progress on the Implementation of the Strategy for Technical and Vocational Education and the Revised Version of the Strategy*. EX 182 EX/INF.5.

27. (2010). *Developing Observatory Functions: Information Systems for Education and Labor Market Reforms*.

28. (2010). *Population Facts 2010/6*. International Migrants by Age. New York, UN Department of Economic and Social Affairs (UNDESA), Population Division.

29. (2010). *Trends, Drivers and Qualitative Scenarios in Europe 2020: For Education and Training Policy Makers Engaged with Meeting Skills Needs*. Report prepared for Warwick University/CEDEFOP.

30. (2010a). *Enterprise Survey 2010*. Washington, DC, World Bank.

31. (2010a). *Key Indicators of the Labor Market*. Geneva, ILO.

32. (2010a). *PISA 2009 Results: What Students Know and Can Do: Student Performance in Reading, Mathematics and Science* (Vol. 1). Paris, OECD Publishing.

33. (2010a). *Reaching the Marginalized.* EFA Global Monitoring Report. Paris, UNESCO. http://unesdoc.unesco.org/images/0018/001866/186606E.pdf (accessed on 8 June 2021).

34. (2010a). *Skills Supply and Demand in Europe*. Medium-term forecast up to 2020. Luxembourg, Publications Office of the European Union.

35. (2010a). *The Real Wealth of Nations: Pathways to Human Development, 20th Anniversary edn*. New York, United Nations Development Program.

36. (2010b). *Changing Qualifications: A Review of Qualifications Policies and Practices*. Luxembourg, Office for Official Publications of the European Communities. www.cedefop.europa.eu/EN/Files/3059_en.pdf (accessed on 8 June 2021).

37. (2010b). *Concept Note for the World Bank Education Strategy 2020.* Washington, DC, World Bank.

38. (2010b). *Learning for Jobs: Synthesis Report of the OECD Reviews of Vocational Education and Training*. Paris, OECD Publishing.
39. (2010b). *Operational Guide to the Integrated Disarmament, Demobilization and Reintegration Standards*. New York, United Nations Development Program.
40. (2010b). *Teachers and Trainers for the Future-Technical and Vocational Education and Training in a Changing World*. Geneva, ILO.
41. (2010b). *TVET Policy Review Malawi*. Paris, UNESCO. 39–70.
42. (2010c). *Linking Credit Systems and Qualifications Frameworks: An International Comparative Analysis*. Luxembourg, Office for Official Publications of the European Communities. http://www.cedefop.europa.eu/EN/Files/5505_en.pdf (accessed on 8 June 2021).
43. (2010c). *Philippines Skills Report: Skills for the Labor Market in the Philippines*. 49–70.
44. (2010c). *Recognizing non-Formal and Informal Learning: Outcomes, Policies and Practices*. Paris, OECD Publishing. http://www.oecd.org/document/0,3343,en_2649_39263294_44870941_1_1_1_1,00.html (accessed on 8 June 2021).
45. (2010d). *A Bridge to the Future: European Policy for the Vocational Education and Training 2002–2010*. Luxembourg, Office for Official Publications of the European Communities. http://www.cedefop.europa.eu/EN/Files/3058_en.pdf (accessed on 8 June 2021).
46. (2011). *Building Skills in the Informal Sector*. Paper commissioned for the EFA Global Monitoring Report. Paris, UNESCO.
47. (2011). *Enterprise Survey 2011*. Washington, DC, World Bank.
48. (2011). *The Role of Skills Development in Overcoming Social Disadvantage*. Background paper prepared for the Education global monitoring report 2012. Paris, UNESCO.
49. (2011). Work-based learning. Why? How? *Revisiting Global Trends in TVET: Reflections on Theory and Practice* (pp. 164–203). Bonn, Germany, UNESCO-UNEVOC International Centre for Technical and Vocational Education and Training.
50. (2011). *World Migration Report 2011: Communicating Effectively About Migration*. Geneva, International Organization for Migration.
51. (2011a). *Employment-Related Mobility and Migration, and Vocational Education and Training*. Working Paper 9. Luxembourg, Office for

Official Publications of the European Communities. http://www.cedefop.europa.eu/EN/Files/6109_en.pdf (accessed on 8 June 2021).

52. (2011a). *Global Employment Trends 2011: The Challenge of a Jobs Recovery*. Geneva, ILO.

53. (2011a). *Population Prospects: The 2010 Revision, Vol. 1: Comprehensive Tables*. New York, UNDESA, Population Division.

54. (2011a). *UNESCO Future Forum-Global Water Futures 2050+*. https://www.soroptimistinternational.org/unesco-future-forum-global-water-futures-2050/ (accessed on 8 June 2021).

55. (2011b). *International Migration in a Globalizing World: The Role of Youth*. Technical Paper No. 2011/1, New York, UNDESA, Population Division.

56. (2011b). *New ILO Study Says Greener Economies Will Require Development of New Green Job Skills*. http://www.ilo.org/global/about-the-ilo/newsroom/news/WCMS_166870/lang--en/index.htm (accessed on 8 June 2021).

57. (2011b). *The Hidden Crisis: Armed Conflict and Education*. EFA Global Monitoring Report. Paris, UNESCO. http://unesdoc.unesco.org/images/0019/001907/190743e.pdf (accessed on 8 June 2021).

58. (2011b). *Working and Aging: Guidance and Counseling for Mature Students*. Luxembourg, Office for Official Publications of the European Communities. https://www.cedefop.europa.eu/en/news-and-press/news/working-and-ageing-guidance-and-counselling-mature-learners (accessed on 8 June 2021).

59. (2012). *Better Skills Better Jobs Better Lives – OECD: A Strategic Approach to Skills Policies*. Paris, OECD Publishing. http://www.oecd-ilibrary.org/education/better-skills-better-jobs-better-lives_9789264177338-en (accessed on 8 June 2021).

60. (2012). *Enterprise Survey 2012*. Washington, DC, World Bank.

61. (2012). *Intergenerational Solidarity*. Luxembourg, Publication Office of the European Union. http://www.eurofound.europa.eu/pubdocs/2012/38/en/1/EF1238EN.pdf (accessed on 8 June 2021).

62. (2012). *Rethinking Education: Investing in Skills for Better Socio-Economic Outcomes*. Strasbourg, France, European Commission.

63. (2012). *The Future We Want, Resolution Adopted by the General Assembly on 27 July 2012*. United Nations Conference on Sustainable Development, Rio +20 Declaration. http:// www.un.org/ga/search/

view_doc.asp?symbol=A/RES/66/288&Lang=E (accessed on 8 June 2021).

64. (2012). *Torino Process*. Luxembourg, Office for Official Publications of the European Communities.
65. (2012a). *Global Employment Trends 2012: Preventing Deeper Jobs Crisis*. Geneva, ILO.
66. (2012a). Shanghai Consensus. *Recommendations of the Third International Congress on TVET: Transforming TVET: Building Skills for Work and Life*. Shanghai. http://unesdoc.unesco.org/images/0021/002176/217683e.pdf (accessed on 8 June 2021).
67. (2012a). *Trends in VET Policy in Europe 2010–12: Progress Towards the Bruges Communiqué.* Luxembourg, Office for Official Publications of the European Communities. http://www.cedefop.europa.eu/EN/Files/6116_en.pdf (accessed on 8 June 2021).
68. (2012b). *Draft National Strategy for Promotion of Gender Equality in TVET*. Dhaka, ILO. http://www.ilo.org/wcmsp5/groups/public/---asia/---ro-bangkok/---ilo-dhaka/documents/publication/wcms_222688.pdf (accessed on 8 June 2021).
69. (2012b). *Permeable Education and Training Systems: Reducing Barriers and Increasing Opportunity*. Luxembourg, Office for Official Publications of the European Communities.
70. (2012c). *Working Towards Sustainable Development: Opportunities for Decent Work and Social Inclusion in a Green Economy*. Geneva, ILO. http://www.ilo.org/wcmsp5/groups/public/---dgreports/---dcomm/---publ/documents/publication/wcms_181836.pdf
71. (2013). *Education at a Glance 2013: OECD Indicators*. Paris, OECD Publishing. http://dx.doi.org/10.1787/eag-2013-en (accessed on 8 June 2021).
72. (2013). *School-to-Work Transition Information Bases*. Bangkok. UNESCO-Bangkok. http://unesdoc.unesco.org/images/0021/002166/216661e.pdf (accessed on 8 June 2021).
73. (2013). *Skills Development for Inclusive and Sustainable Growth in Developing Asia-Pacific*. Manila, Asian Development Bank and Springer. https://www.adb.org/publications/skills-development-inclusive-and-sustainable-growth-developing-asia-pacific (accessed on 8 June 2021).
74. (2013). *Status of TVET in the SADC Region*. Paris, UNESCO.

75. (2013). *The Global Competitiveness Report 2013–2014*. Geneva, World Economic Forum.

76. (2013). *The Reform of the National Vocational Training System: Guidance Document and Plan of Operations 2014–2018*. Tunis, Republic of Tunisia.

77. (2013a). *Skills for a Low-Carbon Europe: The Role of VET in a Sustainable Energy Scenario*. Synthesis report. Luxembourg, Office for Official Publications of the European Communities.

78. (2013b). *Analysis and Overview of NQF Level Descriptors in European Countries.* Luxembourg, Office for Official Publications of the European Communities. http://www.cedefop.europa.eu/en/publications/21919.aspx (accessed on 8 June 2021).

79. (2014). Improving the equity of quality and learning in education: A systemic approach. Varghese, N.V., (ed.), *From Schooling to Learning: A Report from the IWGE* (pp. 55–79). Paris, IIEP- UNESCO.

80. Adams, A. V., (2009). Skills development in the informal sector of sub-Saharan Africa. In: Maclean, R., & Wilson, D., (eds.), *International Handbook of Education for the Changing World of Work: Bridging Academic and Vocational Education, UNESCO-UNEVOC* (Vol. 6, pp. cxiii–cxxxiii). New York, Springer.

81. Adams, A. V., Razmara, S., & Johansson, D. S. S., (2013). *Improving Skills Development in the Informal Sector: Strategies for Sub-Saharan Africa.* Washington, DC, World Bank.

82. ADEA, (2012). *Promoting Critical Skills for the Accelerated and Sustainable Development of Africa: The Key Messages of the ADEA Triennale*. Ouagadougou, Burkina Faso.

83. African Union, (2007). *Strategy to Revitalize Technical and Vocational Education and Training in Africa*. Addis Ababa, African Union. https://www.academia.edu/25379014/Strategy_to_Revitalize_Technical_and_Vocational_Education_and_Training_TVET_in_Africa_Final_Draft (accessed on 8 June 2021).

84. Aguinis, H., (2004). *Regression Analysis for Categorical Moderators*. New York: Guilford.

85. Aguinis, H., (2009). *Performance Management* (2nd edn.). Upper Saddle River, NJ: Pearson Prentice Hall.

86. Aguinis, H., & Branstetter, S. A., (2007). Teaching the concept of the sampling distribution of the mean. *J. Manag. Educ., 31*, 467–483.

87. Aguinis, H., & Pierce, C. A., (2008). Enhancing the relevance of organizational behavior by embracing performance management research. *J. Organ. Behav., 29*, 139–145.
88. Aguinis, H., Beaty, J. C., Boik, R. J., & Pierce, C. A., (2005). Effect size and power in assessing moderating effects of categorical variables using multiple regression: A 30-year review. *J. Appl. Psychol., 90*, 94–107.
89. Aguinis, H., Mazurkiewicz, M. D., & Heggestad, E. D., (2009). Using Web-based frame-of-reference training to decrease biases in personality-based job analysis: An experimental field study. P*ers. Psychol.* In press.
90. Aguinis, H., Sturman, M. C., & Pierce, C. A., (2008). Comparison of three meta-analytic procedures for estimating moderating effects of categorical variables. *Organ. Res. Methods, 11*, 9–34.
91. Akoojee, S., (2011). Private TVET provision in Africa. *Preserving Traditional Forms Differently- Managing Novel Ones Creatively: Understanding Current Private Provision in Africa and Policy Implications*. Background paper commissioned by UNESCO Education Sector.
92. Allais, S., (2010). *The Implementation and Impact of National Qualifications Frameworks: Report of a Study in 16 Countries*. Geneva, Skills and Employability Department, ILO.
93. Alliger, G. M., Tannenbaum, S. I., Bennett, W. Jr., Traver, H., & Shotland, A., (1997). A meta-analysis of the relations among training criteria. *Pers. Psychol., 50*, 341–358.
94. Anda, M. L. D., (2009). *Qualifications Frameworks: Implementation and Impact: Background Case Study on Mexico.* Geneva, Skills and Employability Department, ILO.
95. Aragon, S., ´ anchez, A., Barba-Arag ´ on, I., & Sanz-Valle, R., (2003). Effects of training on business results. ´ *Int. J. Hum. Resour. Manag., 14*, 956–980.
96. Arandarenko, M., & Bartlett, W., (2012). *Labor Market and Skills in the Western Balkans*. Belgrade, FREN.59–70.
97. Arthur, W. J., Bennett, W. J., Edens, P., & Bell, S. T., (2003). Effectiveness of training in organizations: A meta-analysis of design and evaluation features. *J. Appl. Psychol., 88*, 234–245.
98. ASEAN, (2009). *Cha-Am Hua Hin Declaration on Strengthening*

Cooperation on Education to Achieve an ASEAN Caring and Sharing Community. 17–52.

99. Asian Development Bank, (2009). *Education and Skills: Strategies for Accelerated Development in Asia and the Pacific.* Manila, Asian Development Bank.
100. Bacchetta, M., & Jansen, M., (2011). *Making Globalization Socially Sustainable*. Geneva, ILO and WTO.
101. Baethge, M., Achtenhagen, F., Arends, L., Babic, E., Baethge-Kinsky, V., & Weber, S., (2006). *PISA- VET: A Feasibility-Study.* Stuttgart, Germany, Steiner.
102. Baranzini, D., Bacchi, M., & Cacciabue, P. C., (2001). A tool for evaluation and identification of training needs in aircraft. *Hum. Factors Aerosp. Saf., 1*, 167–193.
103. Barber, J., (2004). Skill upgrading within informal training: Lessons from the Indian auto mechanic. *Int. J. Train. Dev., 8,* 128–139.
104. Bartels, F. B., & Lederer, S., (2009). *Outsourcing Markets in Services: International Business Trends, 47–81.*
105. Bartlett, K. R., & Rodgers, J., (2004). HRD as national policy in the Pacific Islands. *Adv. Dev. Hum. Resour., 6,* 307–314.
106. Basu, C. K., & Majumdar, S., (2010). The role of ICT and TVET in rural development and poverty alleviation. *International Handbook of Education for the Changing World of Work* (Vol. 1, pp. 1923–1934). UNESCO-UNEVOC. Dordrecht, Springer.
107. Becker, G., (1962). Investment in human capital: A theoretical analysis. *J. Pol. Econ., 70*(5, Pt. 2), S9–49.
108. Becker, G., (1964). *Human Capital: A Theoretical and Empirical Analysis, With Special Reference to Education.* New York: Columbia Univ. Press.
109. Bell, B. S., & Kozlowski, S. W. J., (2002). Adaptive guidance: Enhancing self-regulation, knowledge, and performance in technology-based training. *Pers. Psychol., 55*, 267–306.
110. Ben, S. H., (2009). *Études De Cas: La Tunisie. Enseignement Supérieur Et Marché Du Travail Dans Le Monde Arabe.* Beyrouth, Institut français du Proche-Orient.
111. Benson, G., Finegold, D., & Mohrman, S. A., (2004). You paid for the skills, now keep them: Tuition reimbursement and voluntary turnover.

Acad. Manag. J., 47, 315–331.

112. Besley, T., & Cord, L., (2006). *Delivering on the Promise of Pro-Poor Growth Insights and Lessons from Country Experiences*. Basingstoke, UK/New York/Washington, DC, Palgrave Macmillan, and World Bank.
113. Bewick, T., & Abbott, P., (2010). *Think Global, Act Sectoral*. London, International Network of Sectoral Skills Organizations.
114. Bhawuk, D. P. S., & Brislin, R. W., (2000). Cross-cultural training: A review. *Appl. Psychol.: An Int. Rev., 49*, 162–191.
115. Bhorat, H., & Lundall, P., (2002). *Employment, Wages and Skills Development: Firm-Specific Effects-Evidence from Two Firm Surveys in South Africa, Working Paper No. 02/68*. Cape Town, South Africa, University of Cape Town Development Policy Research Unit.
116. Bhorat, H., Lundall, P., & Rospabe, S., (2002). *The South African Labor Market in a Globalizing World: Economic and Legislative Considerations*. Geneva, ILO.
117. Biggs, T., Miller, M., Otto, C., & Tyler, G., (1996). *Africa Can Compete! Export Opportunities and Challenges for Garments and Home Products in the European Market*. Washington, DC, World Bank.
118. Blake, D., & Gallagher, D., (2009). Examining the development of the Victorian certificate of applied learning and its implications in schools and teacher education in Australia. *Journal of Applied Learning in Higher Education* (Vol. 1, pp. 49–71). Missouri Western State University.
119. Blanchard, P. N., & Thacker, J. W., (2007). *Effective Training: Systems, Strategies, and Practices* (3rd edn). Upper Saddle River, NJ: Pearson Prentice Hall.
120. BMBF, (2015). *Reform of Vocational Education and Training*. 23–68.
121. Bozell, M., & Liston, C., (2010). *Building Effective Green Energy Programs in Community Colleges*. New York, Workforce Strategy Center.
122. Brown, K. G., (2001). Using computers to deliver training: Which employees learn and why? *Pers. Psychol., 54,* 271–296.
123. Brown, K. G., (2005). Examining the structure and nomological network of trainee reactions: A closer look at "smile sheets." *J. Appl. Psychol., 90*, 991–1001.
124. Brown, K. G., & Van, B. M. E., (2007). Applying a social capital perspective to the evaluation of distance training. In: Fiore, S. M.,

& Salas, E., (eds.), *Where is the Learning in Distance Learning? Towards a Science of Distributed Learning and Training* (pp. 41–63). Washington, DC: Am. Psychol. Assoc.

125. Brown, M., (2012). Developing green skills through a regional TAFE institute. *Paper presented at the 15th AVETRA Conference*. Canberra. 38–61.

126. Brown, P., Green, A., & Lauder, H., (2001). *High Skills: Globalization, Competitiveness, and Skill Formation*. Oxford, Oxford University Press.

127. Brown, P., Lauder, H., & Ashton, D., (2011). *The Global Auction: The Broken Promises of Education, Jobs, and Incomes*. Oxford, Oxford University Press.

128. Brown, T. C., (2005). Effectiveness of distal and proximal goals as transfer-of-training interventions: A field experiment. *Hum. Resour. Dev. Q., 16*, 369–387.

129. Campbell, J. P., (1971). Personnel training and development. *Annu. Rev. Psychol., 22*, 565–602.

130. CANTA, (2013). *Regional TVET Strategy for Workforce Development and Economic Competitiveness*. Port of Spain, CANTA. 17–52.

131. Cascio, W. F., & Aguinis, H., (2005). *Applied Psychology in Human Resource Management* (6th edn.). Upper Saddle River, NJ: Pearson Prentice Hall.

132. Cascio, W. F., & Aguinis, H., (2008). Staffing twenty-first-century organizations. In: Walsh, J. P., & Brief, A. P., (eds.), *Academy of Management Annals* (Vol. 2, pp. 133–165). Mahwah, NJ: Erlbaum.

133. Castejon, J. M., Coles, M., Chakroun, B., Deij, A., & McBride, V., (2011). *Developing Qualifications Frameworks in EU Partner Countries: Modernizing Education and Training*. London, Anthem Press.

134. CEDEFOP and European Commission, (2010). *European Inventory on Validation of Non-Formal and Informal Learning*. 14–25.

135. CEDEFOP, (2008). *Social Partners and Sectoral Training Funds: Mobilizing Resources*. Briefing note 3/2008 http://www.cedefop.europa.eu/EN/Files/8560_en.pdf (accessed on 8 June 2021).

136. Chakroun, B., (2008). What can we learn from policy learning? In: Chakroun, B., & Sahlberg, P., (eds.), *ETF Yearbook 2008: Policy Learning in Action* (pp. 11–18). Luxembourg, Office for Official

Publications of the European Communities.

137. Chakroun, B., & Jimeno, S. E., (2010). TVET reforms in the Arab region: The 'push' and 'pull' in policy development. In: Mazawi, A. E., & Sultana, R. G., (eds.), *Education and the Arab 'World': Political Projects, Struggles, and Geometries of Power* (pp. 59–76). New York, Routledge.

138. Chakroun, B., & Sahlberg, P., (2008). *ETF Yearbook 2008: Policy Learning in Action*. Luxembourg, Office for Official Publications of the European Communities.

139. Chen, G., Thomas, B., & Wallace, J. C., (2005). A multilevel examination of the relationships among training outcomes, mediating regulatory processes, and adaptive performance. J. *Appl. Psychol., 90*, 827–841.

140. Cheng, I. H., (2010). Case studies of integrated pedagogy in vocational education: A three-tier approach to empowering vulnerable youth in urban Cambodia. *International Journal of Educational Development, 30*(4), 438–446.

141. Cheng, K., & Marope, P. T. M., (2010). 21st-century development challenges and opportunities: Demands on education systems. Developing knowledge, skills, competencies, and values for the 21st century. *14th UNESCO-APEID International Conference*. Plenary Session I. Bangkok, UNESCO Bangkok.

142. Chiaburu, D. S., & Marinova, S. V., (2005). What predicts skill transfer? An exploratory study of goal orientation, training self-efficacy and organizational supports. *Int. J. Train. Dev., 9*, 110–123.

143. Chinien, C., (2005). *The Use of ICTs in Technical and Vocational Education and Training: South-Eastern Europe: Analytical Survey*. Moscow, UNESCO Institute for Information Technologies in Education.

144. Chinien, C., Boutin, F., McDonald, C., & Searcy, C., (2004). *Skills to Last: Broadly Transferable Sustainable Development Literacy for the Canadian Workforce*. Ottawa, National Center for Workshop Development.

145. Chitolie-Joseph, E., (2008). T*he Development and State of the Art of Adult Learning and Education (ALE): National Report of Saint Lucia*. Castries, Ministry of Education and Culture.

146. Cho, E., & McLean, G. N., (2004). What we discovered about NHRD

and what it means for HRD. *Adv. Dev. Hum. Resour., 6*, 382–393.

147. Cho, J., (2012). *Innovation of National Education Administration System in Korea.* Presentation at KRIVET-Africa TVET Experts Workshop.

148. Clardy, A., (2005). Reputation, goodwill, and loss: Entering the employee training review equation. *Hum. Resour. Dev. Rev., 4,* 279–304.

149. Collett, K., (2008). *Vocational Training for Excluded Groups: Success Stories*. London, Centre for Skills Development, City and Guilds.

150. Collins, D. B., & Holton, E. F., I. I. I., (2004). The effectiveness of managerial leadership development programs: A meta-analysis of studies from 1982 to 2001. *Hum. Resour. Dev. Q., 15*, 217–248.

151. Colquitt, J. A., LePine, J. A., & Noe, R. A., (2000). Toward an integrative theory of training motivation: A meta-analytic path analysis of 20 years of research. *J. Appl. Psychol., 85*, 678–707.

152. COMEDAF, (2007). Strategy to revitalize technical and vocational education and training (TVET) in Africa. *Presented at the Meeting of the Bureau of the Conference of Ministers of Education of the African Union (COMEDAF II+)*. Addis Ababa.

153. Commission Staff Working Document SEC, (2007). 1098 Luxembourg, Office for Official Publications of the European Communities. 22–65.

154. Condon, L., & Rickard, A., (2009). Australia: The role of partnerships, industry skills councils and training packages. In: Fien, J., Maclean, R., & Park, M. G., (eds.), *Work, Learning and Sustainable Development* (pp. 279–294). London, Springer.

155. Council of Australian Governments, (2009). *Green Skills Agreement*. Australian Government, Department of Education, Employment and Workplace Relations.

156. Cullen, J., & Turnbull, S., (2005). A meta-review of the management development literature. *Hum. Resour. Dev. Rev., 4,* 335–355.

157. Cunha, F., & Heckman, J., (2007). The technology of skill formation. *American Economic Review, 97*(2), 31–47.

158. Darch, H., & Lucas, T., (2002). Training as an e-commerce enabler. *J. Workplace Learn.,14,* 148–155.

159. Davis, F. D., & Yi, M. Y., (2004). Improving computer skill training: Behavior modeling, symbolic mental rehearsal, and the role of knowledge structures. *J. Appl. Psychol., 89*, 509–523.

160. Day, D. V., (2000). Leadership development: A review in context. *Leadersh. Q., 11*, 581–614.

161. Decker, P. J., & Nathan, B. R., (1985). *Behavior Modeling Training: Principles and Applications*. New York: Praeger.

162. Demobilization & Reintegration' Programs. Geneva, Centre d'études et de recherches internationales, Sciences Po, Graduate Institute of International Studies. 50–57.

163. Department for Education and Skills, (2003). *Aiming High: Raising the Achievement of Gypsy Traveler Pupils: A Guide to Good Practice.* London, Department for Education and Skills.

164. Derksen, D., (2014). *Reintegrating Armed Groups in Afghanistan: Lessons from the Past*. United States Institute of Peace (USIP) Brief 168.Washington, DC, USIP.

165. DeRouin, R. E., Fritzsche, B. A., & Salas, E., (2004). Optimizing e-learning: Research-based guidelines for student-controlled training. *Hum. Resour. Manag. Rev., 43*, 147–162.

166. Driskell, Hall, J. J., & Salas, E., (2001). Does stress training generalize to novel settings? *Hum. Factors, 42*, 99–110.

167. Dvir, T., Eden, D., Avolio, B. J., & Shamir, B., (2002). Impact of transformational leadership on follower development and performance: A field experiment. *Acad. Manag. J., 45,* 735–744.

168. ECOTEC, (2008). *A European Inventory on Validation of Non-Formal and Informal Learning*. Birmingham, ECOTEC Research and Consulting.

169. Edkins, G. D., (2002). A review of the benefits of aviation human factors training. *Hum. Factors Aerosp. Saf., 2,* 201–216.

170. Education Development Centre, (2011). *The Maldivian National Curriculum Framework (Fifth Working Draft)*. Malé, Ministry of Education of the Maldives.

171. Eichhorst, W., Escudero, V., Marx, P., & Tobin, S., (2010). *The Impact of the Crisis on Employment and the Role of Labor Market Institutions.* Discussion Paper 5320. Bonn, Germany, IZA. http://ftp.iza.org/dp5320.pdf (accessed on 8 June 2021).

172. Ellis, A. P. J., Bell, B. S., Ployhart, R. E., Hollenbeck, J. R., & Ilgen, D. R., (2005). An evaluation of generic teamwork skills training with action teams: Effects on cognitive and skill-based outcomes. *Pers. Psychol., 58*, 641–672.

173. Employers' Forum on Disability, (2009). *What Does the Research Say are the Commercial Benefits?* 38–52.

174. ETF and World Bank, (2005). *Reforming Technical Vocational Education and Training in the Middle East and North Africa: Experiences and Challenges*. Luxembourg, Office for Official Publications of the European Communities.

175. ETF, (2008). *Peer Review Report: National Qualifications Framework (NQF) Development in Egypt*. 48–51.

176. ETVET Council & Leney, T., (2009). *CAQA Organization: Rationale and Brief Functional Description*. Unpublished paper.

177. EU High-Level Group, (2012). *EU High-Level Group of Experts on Literacy: Final Report*. Luxembourg, European Commission.

178. Eurofound. (2010). *European Company Survey 2009*. Dublin, Euro found.

179. European Alliance for Apprenticeships, (2013). *Work-Based Learning in Europe: Renewing Traditions: Background Information.* Bonn, International BIBB Conference 2013.

180. European Commission, (1999). *Convergences and Divergences in European Education and Training Systems.* Education, Training, Youth research project commissioned by the ECDG22.

181. Fares, J., & Puerto, S., (2009). *Towards Comprehensive Training*. Social protection, Discussion paper no. SP 0924. Washington, DC, World Bank. http://documents.worldbank.org/curated/en/2009/11/11510314/towards-comprehensive-training (accessed on 8 June 2021).

182. Faust, M., Voskamp, U., & Wittke, V., (2004). *Globalization and the Future of National Systems: Exploring Patterns of Industrial Reorganization and Relocation in an Enlarged Europe*. Gottingen, Organizations Beratung Importgut Exportschlager (OBIE). 14–72.

183. Fien, J., (2013). *Education for Sustainable Development in Technical and Vocational Education and Workplace Training*. Background paper prepared for Decade for Education for Sustainable Development Final Report.

184. Fien, J., & Maclean, R., (2009). Introduction: The legacy of the Bonn declaration. In: Fien, J., Maclean, R., & Park, M. G., (eds.), *Work, Learning and Sustainable Development* (p. xix). Dordrecht, Springer.

185. Fien, J., & Wilson, D., (2005). *Promoting Sustainable Development in TVET: The Bonn Declaration, Prospects, 35*(3), 273–288.

186. Fiol, C. M., O'Connor, E. J., & Aguinis, H., (2001). All for one and one for all? The development and transfer of power across organizational levels. *Acad. Manag. Rev., 26*, 224–242.
187. Ford, J. K., & Kraiger, K., (1995). The application of cognitive constructs and principles to the instructional systems model of training. Implications for needs assessment, design, and transfer. In: Cooper, C. L., & Robertson, I. T., (eds.), *International Review of Industrial and Organizational Psychology (*10, 1–48). Chichester, UK: Wiley.
188. Ford, J. K., & Schmidt, A. M., (2000). Emergency response training: Strategies for enhancing real-world performance. *J. Hazard. Mater., 75*, 195–215.
189. Fowlkes, J. E., Salas, E., Baker, D. P., Cannon-Bowers, J. A., & Stout, R. J., (2000). The utility of event-based knowledge elicitation. *Hum. Factors, 42*, 24–35.
190. Fox, A., (2003). Training budgets are said to be withstanding companies' economic troubles. *HR Mag., 48*(7):32, 38.
191. Frayne, C. A., & Geringer, J. M., (2000). Self-management training for improving job performance: A field experiment involving salespeople. *J. Appl. Psychol., 85*, 361–372.
192. Frese, M., Beimel, S., & Schoenborn, S., (2003). Action training for charismatic leadership: Two evaluations of studies of a commercial training module on inspirational communication of a vision. *Pers. Psychol., 56*, 671–697.
193. G20, (2013). *G20 Leaders' Declaration*. Saint Petersburg.
194. Gajaweera, G. A. K., (2010). *Qualifications Frameworks: Implementation and Impact Background.* Case Study on Sri Lanka. Geneva, Skills and Employability Department, ILO.
195. Gasskov, V., (2006a). *Mechanisms of financing TVET*. Presentation for GTZ symposium, Addis-Ababa. 128–132.
196. Gaudine, A. P., & Saks, A. M., (2004). A longitudinal quasi-experiment on the effects of post-training transfer interventions. *Hum. Resour. Dev. Q., 15*, 57–76.
197. Gereffi, G., (2005). *The New Off-Shoring of Jobs and Global Development*. Geneva, IILS. 187–190.
198. Global Commission on International Migration, (2005). *Migration in an Interconnected World: New Directions for Action*. Geneva, ILO.

199. Goeters, K. M., (2002). Evaluation of the effects of CRM training by the assessment of non-technical skills under LOFT. *Hum. Factors Aerosp. Saf., 2*, 71–86.

200. Goldstein, I. L., (1980). Training in work organizations. *Annu. Rev. Psychol., 31*, 229–272.

201. Goldstein, I. L., & Ford, J. K., (2002). *Training in Organizations* (4th edn.). Belmont, CA: Wadsworth.

202. Government of Mauritius, (2001). *Mauritius Qualifications Authority Bill 2001, No. XXXIX*, 11, 12.

203. Government of New South Wales, (2013). *Department of Environment, Climate Change and Water.* website. https://www.environment.nsw.gov.au/research-and-publications/publications-search/department-of-environment-climate-change-and-water-nsw-annual-report-2009–10 (accessed on 8 June 2021).

204. Graziosi, A., (2011). *Training Institutions and Labor Market Needs: Bridging the Gap.* Geneva, ILO.

205. Grootings, P., & Nielsen, S., (2008). Policy learning: Applying the changing learning paradigm for policy advice on TVET reforms in transition countries. In: CEDEFOP, (ed.), *Modernizing Vocational Education and Training* (Vol. 2). Fourth report on vocational education and training research in Europe: Background report. Luxembourg: Office for Official Publications of the European Communities.

206. GTZ, (2006). *Implementation Issues of Diversified Financing Strategies for TVET.* Eschborn, GTZ. 21–63.

207. Guerrero, S., & Barraud-Didier, V., (2004). High-involvement practices and performance of French firms. *Int. J. Hum. Resour. Manag., 15*, 1408–1423.

208. Hakim, G. L., (2011). *Does TVET Promote Social Mobility?* Background paper commissioned by UNESCO Education Sector.

209. Hammonds, K. H., (2005). *Why we Hate HR* (Vol. 97, p. 40). Fast Co.

210. Handel, J. M., (2008). *Measuring Job Content: Skills, Technology, and Management Practices*. Institute for Research for Poverty Discussion Paper No. 1357–08.

211. Hanushek, E., Woessmann, L., & Zhang, L., (2011). *General Education, Vocational Education and Labor-Market Outcomes Over the Life-cycle*. Bonn, Institute for the Study of Labor.

212. Hargroves, K., & Smith, M. H., (2005). *The Natural Advantage of*

Nations: Business Opportunities, Innovation and Governance in the 21st Century. London, Earthscan. 160–170.

213. Härtl, M., (2009). Germany: Policy-making strategies and project experiences. In: Fien, J., Maclean, R., & Park, M. G., (eds.), *Work, Learning and Sustainable Development*. Dordrecht, Springer.
214. Heart Trust, N. T. A., (2009). *Policy on Competency-Based Education and Training*. Draft Concept Paper. Kingston, HEART Trust NTA.
215. Heimbeck, D., Frese, M., Sonnentag, S., & Keith, N., (2003). Integrating errors into the training process: The function of error management instructions and the role of goal orientation. *Pers. Psychol., 56*, 333–361.
216. Hill, C. E., & Lent, R. W., (2006). A narrative and meta-analytic review of helping skills training: Time to revive a dormant area of inquiry. *Psychother. Theory Res. Pract., 43*, 154–172.
217. Hiromichi, K., (2011). *Trends in Technical and Vocational Education and Training.* Background paper commissioned by UNESCO Education Sector.
218. Holladay, C. L., & Quinones, M. A., (2003). Practice variability and transfer of training: The role of self-efficacy generality. *J. Appl. Psychol., 88*, 1094–1103.
219. Holmes, K., (2009). The reform and governance of public TVET institutions: Comparative experiences. In: Maclean, R., & Wilson, D., (eds.), *International Handbook of Education for the Changing World of Work: Bridging Academic and Vocational Learning* (pp. 905–919). Dordrecht, Springer.
220. Holton, E. F. III., Bates, R. A., & Ruona, W. E. A., (2001). Development of a generalized learning transfer system inventory. *Hum. Resour. Dev. Q., 11*, 333–360.
221. Holton, E. F. III., Chen, H. C., & Naquin, S. S., (2003). An examination of learning transfer system characteristics across organizational settings. *Hum. Resour. Dev. Q., 14*, 459–482.
222. Holton, E. F., I. I. I., (2003). Cycle time: A missing dimension in HRD research and theory. *Hum. Resour. Dev. Rev., 2,* 335, 336.
223. Holton, E. F., I. I. I., (2005). Holton's evaluation model: New evidence and construct elaborations. *Adv. Dev. Hum. Resour., 7,* 37–54.
224. Huint, H., & Saks, A. M., (2003). Translating training science into practice: A study of managers' reactions to post-training transfer

interventions. *Hum. Resour. Dev. Q., 14*, 181–198.

225. Ibarrarán, P., & Rosas-Shady, D., (2008). *Evaluating the Impact of Job Training Programs in Latin America: Evidence from IDB Funded Operations*. Washington, DC, IADB.
226. ILO and CEDEFOP, (2011). Skills for green jobs. *A Global View: Synthesis Report Based on 21 Country Studies.* Geneva, ILO. http://www.ilo.org/wcmsp5/groups/public/---dgreports/---dcomm/---publ/documents/publication/wcms_159585.pdf (accessed on 8 June 2021).
227. ILO and IILS, (2011). *World of Work Report 2011: Making Markets Work for Jobs*. Geneva, ILO.
228. ILO. (2006). Changing patterns in the world of work, report of the director-general. *International Labor Conference, 95th Session.* Geneva, ILO.
229. Inter-Agency Working Group on TVET Indicators, (2012). *Proposed Indicators for Assessing Technical and Vocational Education and Training.* Working document.
230. International Fund for Agricultural Development, (2010). *Rural Poverty Report 2011: Enabling Poor Rural People to Overcome Poverty.* Rome, IFAD.
231. International Organization for Migration, (2010). *World Migration Report 2010: The Future of Migration: Building Capacities for Change.* Geneva, International Organization for Migration.
232. International Skills Standards Organization, (2010). *Think Global Act Sectoral*. London, INSSO. 15–19.
233. Jacinto, C., (2011). *Technical and Vocational Education and Training in the Last Decade in Latin America.* Background paper commissioned by UNESCO Education Sector.
234. Jacobsen, J., Lindekaer, A. L., Ostergaard, H. T., Nielsen, K., Ostergaard, D., Laub, M., et al., (2001). Management of anaphylactic shock evaluated using a full-scale anesthesia simulator. *Acta Anaesthesiol. Scand., 45,* 315–319.
235. Jacoby, S. M., (2004). *Employing Bureaucracy* (2nd edn.). Mahwah, NJ: Erlbaum.
236. Janjua, S., (2011). Is skill training a good investment for the poor? The evidence from Pakistan. *International Journal of Training Research, 9*, 95–109.
237. Jaramillo, A., & Angel-Urdinola, D., (2011). Higher Education,

productivity, and labor market insertion: Are MENA countries getting results? In: Jaramillo, A., & Melonio, T., (eds.), *Breaking Even or Breaking Through: Reaching Financial Sustainability While Providing High Quality Standards in Higher Education in the Middle East and North Africa* (pp. 1–12). Washington, DC, World Bank.

238. Johanson, R. K., & Adams, A. V., (2004). *Skills Development in Sub-Saharan Africa*. Washington, DC, World Bank.
239. Johanson, R., (2009). *A Review of National Training Funds, SP Discussion Paper No. 0922*. Washington, DC, World Bank Social Protection Unit.
240. Kaufman, R., & Guerra, I., (2001). A perspective adjustment to add value to external clients (including society). *Hum. Resour. Dev. Q., 12*, 319–324.
241. Kearns, P., (2009). What are the limits of ICTs and media in the delivery of TVET? An Australian focus. In: Maclean, R., & Wilson, D., (eds.), *International Handbook of Education for the Changing World of Work*. Dordrecht, Springer.
242. Keevy, J., (2011). *The Recognition of Qualifications Across Borders: The Contribution of Regional Qualifications Frameworks*. Background paper commissioned by UNESCO. Pretoria, South African Qualifications Authority.
243. Keevy, J., Chakroun, B., & Deij, A., (2010). *Transnational Qualifications Frameworks.* Luxembourg, Publications Office of the European Union.
244. Keith, N., & Frese, M., (2005). Self-regulation in error management training: Emotion control and metacognition as mediators of performance effects. *J. Appl. Psychol., 90*, 677–691.
245. Keith, N., & Frese, M., (2008). Effectiveness of error management training: A meta-analysis. *J. Appl. Psychol., 93*, 59–69.
246. Khan, S., (1999). *Towards Sustainability: A Guide for Colleges*. London, Further Education Development Agency.
247. King, K., & McGrath, S., (2002). *Globalization, Knowledge and Enterprise*. Oxford, Symposium.
248. King, K., & Palmer, R., (2010). *Planning for Technical and Vocational Skills Development.* Fundamentals of Educational Planning, No. 94. Paris, UNESCO International Institute for Educational Planning.

249. Klein, H. J., Noe, R. A., & Wang, C., (2006). Motivation to learn and course outcomes: The impact of delivery mode, learning goal orientation, and perceived barriers and enablers. *Pers. Psychol., 59*, 665–702.

250. Kontoghiorghes, C., (2004). Reconceptualizing the learning transfer conceptual framework: Empirical validation of a new systemic model. *Int. J. Train. Dev., 8*, 210–221.

251. Kozlowski, S. W. J., & Salas, E., (1997). An organizational systems approach for the implementation and transfer of training. In: Ford, K., Kozlowski, S. W., Kraiger, K., Salas, E., & Teachout, M., (eds.), *Improving Training Effectiveness in Work Organizations* (pp. 247–287). Mahwah, NJ: Erlbaum.

252. Kozlowski, S. W. J., Brown, K. G., Weissbein, D. A., Cannon-Bowers, J. A., & Salas, E., (2000). A multi-level perspective on training effectiveness: Enhancing horizontal and vertical transfer. In: Klein, K. J., & Kozlowski, S. W. J., (eds.), *Multilevel Theory, Research, and Methods in Organizations* (pp. 157–210). San Francisco, CA: Jossey-Bass.

253. Kozlowski, S. W. J., Gully, S. M., Brown, K. G., Salas, E., Smith, E. M., & Nason, E. R., (2001). Effects of training goals and goal orientation traits on multidimensional training outcomes and performance adaptability. *Organ. Behav. Hum. Decis. Process., 85*, 1–31.

254. Kraak, A., (2011). *Cross-Sectoral State Coordination, TVET Policies and Economic Development: Lessons from South Africa Finland, Ireland, and Malaysia.* Background paper commissioned by UNESCO Education Sector.

255. Kraak, A., Jewison, R., Pillay, P., Chidi, M., Bhagwan, N., Sebolelo, N., & Blanche, E., (2014). *Review of the Current Skills Development System and Recommendations Towards the Best Model for Delivering Skills in the Country*. Human Resource Development Council for South Africa.

256. Kraiger, K., (2002). Decision-based evaluation. In: Kraiger, K., (ed.) *Creating, Implementing, and Maintaining Effective Training and Development: State-of-the-Art Lessons for Practice* (pp. 331–375). San Francisco, CA: Jossey-Bass.

257. Kraiger, K., (2003). Perspectives on training and development. In: Borman, W. C., Ilgen, D. R., & Klimoski, R. J., (ed.), *Handbook of Psychology: Volume 12, Industrial and Organizational Psychology*

(pp. 171–192). Hoboken, NJ: Wiley.

258. Kraiger, K., & Aguinis, H., (2001). Training effectiveness: Assessing training needs, motivation, and accomplishments. In: London, M., (ed.), *How People Evaluate Others in Organizations: Person Perception and Interpersonal Judgment in I/O Psychology* (pp. 203–219). Mahwah, NJ: Erlbaum.
259. Kraiger, K., & Jerden, E., (2007). A new look at student control: Meta-analytic results and directions for future research. In: Fiore, S. M., & Salas, E., (EDS.), *Where is the Learning in Distance Learning? Towards a Science of Distributed Learning and Training* (pp. 65–90). Washington, DC: APA Books.
260. Kraiger, K., Ford, J. K., & Salas, E., (1993). Application of cognitive, skill-based, and effective theories of learning outcomes to new methods of training evaluation. *J. Appl. Psychol., 78*, 311–328.
261. Kraiger, K., McLinden, D., & Casper, W. J., (2004). Collaborative planning for training impact. *Hum. Resour. Manag. Rev., 43,* 337–351.
262. Latham, G. P., (1988). Human resource training and development. *Annu. Rev. Psychol., 39*, 545–582.
263. Lauterbach, U., (2009). The pedagogy of apprenticeship. In: Maclean, R., & Wilson, D., (eds.), *International Handbook of Education for the Changing World of Work* (pp. 1653–1668). Dordrecht, Springer.
264. Lave, J., & Wenger, E., (1991). *Situated Learning.* Cambridge, Cambridge University Press.
265. Lee, M., (2004). National human resource development in the United Kingdom. *Adv. Dev. Hum. Resour., 6*, 334–345.
266. Leney, T., (2009a). *Qualifications that Count: Strengthening the Recognition of Qualifications in the Mediterranean Region.* Thematic Study. Turin, Italy, ETF. http://www.etf.europa.eu/web.nsf/(RSS)/C125782B0048D6F6C125768200396FB6?OpenDocument&LAN=EN (accessed on 8 June 2021).
267. Leney, T., Ammerman, P., Brandsma, J., Bewhringeer, F., Coles, M., Feenstra, B., Grollmann, P., et al., (2005). *Achieving the Lisbon Goal: The Contribution of VET.* Brussels, European Commission.
268. Lievens, F., Harris, M. M., Van, K. E., & Bisqueret, C., (2003). Predicting cross-cultural training performance: The validity of personality, cognitive ability, and dimensions measured by an assessment center

and a behavior description interview. *J. Appl. Psychol., 88*, 476–489.

269. Lim, D. H., & Morris, M. L., (2006). Influence of trainee characteristics, instructional satisfaction, and organizational climate on perceived learning and transfer training. *Hum. Resour. Dev. Q., 17*, 85–115.

270. Linou, N., & Kontogiannis, T., (2004). The effect of training systemic information on the retention of fault-finding skills in manufacturing industries. *Hum. Factors Ergon. Manufacturing, 14*, 197–217.

271. Lippold, K., Nichols, A., & Sorensen, E., (2011). *Strengthening Families Through Stronger Fathers: Final Impact Report for the Pilot Employment Programs*. New York, Urban Institute. http://www.urban.org/publications/412442.html (accessed on 8 June 2021).

272. Littrell, L. N., Salas, E., Hess, K. P., Paley, M., & Riedel, S., (2006). Expatriate preparation: A critical analysis of 25 years of cross-cultural training research. *Hum. Resour. Dev. Rev., 5*, 355–388.

273. Lotz-Sisitka, H., & Raven, G., (2009). South Africa: Applied competence as the guiding framework for environmental and sustainability education. In: Fien, J., Maclean, R., & Park, M. G., (eds.), *Work, Learning and Sustainable Development: Opportunities and Challenges* (pp. 309–318). Dordrecht, Springer and UNEVOC.

274. Mabey, C., & Ramirez, M., (2005). Does management development improve organizational productivity? A six-country analysis of European firms. *Int. J. Hum. Resour. Manag., 16*, 1067–1082.

275. Maclean, R., & Lai, A., (2011). The future of technical and vocational education and training: Global challenges and possibilities. *International Journal of Training Research*, 2–15.

276. Maclean, R., & Pavlova, M., (2011). *Vocationalization of Secondary and Higher Education: Pathways to the World of Work* (pp. 40–85). UNESCO-UNEVOC, Revisiting Global Trends in TVET: Reflections on Theory and Practice. Bonn, Germany, UNESCO-UNEVOC International Centre for Technical and Vocational Education and Training.

277. Maclean, R., Jagannanthan, S., & Sarvi, J., (2011). Main issues, concerns and challenges regarding TVET in Asia and the Pacific. In: Maclean, R., Jagannanthan, S., & Sarvi, J., (eds.), *Skills Development for Inclusive and Sustainable Growth in Developing Asia-Pacific* (pp. 3–27). Manila, Asian Development Bank and Springer.

278. Marks, M. A., Sabella, M. J., Burke, C. S., & Zaccaro, S. J., (2002). The impact of cross-training on team effectiveness. *J. Appl. Psychol., 87*, 3–13.

279. Marock, C., (2010). *Qualifications Frameworks: Implementation and Impact, Background Case Study on Mauritius*. Geneva, ILO Skills and Employability Department.

280. Marope, P. T. M., (2005). *Namibian Human Capital and Knowledge Development for Economic Growth with Equity*. Africa Region Human Development Working Paper Series No. 84. Washington, DC, World Bank.

281. Marope, P. T. M., & Goldberg, I., (2009). *Closing the Skills and Technology Gap in South Africa*. Concept note prepared for a World Bank study.

282. Martin, R., Villeneuve-Smith, F., Marshall, L., & McKenzie, E., (2008). *Employability Skills Explored*. London, Learning and Skills Network (LSN).

283. Martinaitis, Z., (2012). Building on skills forecasts: Comparing methods and applications. *Building on Skills Forecasts: Comparing Methods and Applications; Conference Proceedings, No. 18* (pp. 97–108). Luxembourg, Office for Official Publications of the European Union.

284. Mattson, B., (2005). Using the critical outcome technique to demonstrate financial and organizational performance results. *Adv. Dev. Hum. Resour., 7*, 102–120.

285. McGrath, S., (2011). Skills for development? Rethinking the kind of development, we want TVET to support. In: King. K., (ed.), *Towards a New Global World of Skills Development*? (pp. 8–11). TVET's Turn to Make its Mark. NORRAG News 46.

286. McGrath, S., (2012). Vocational education and training for development. A policy in need of a theory? *International Journal of Educational Development, 32*(5), 623–631.

287. McGrath, S., & Akoojee, S., (2010). Regulating private vocational education and training (VET) in South Africa: The national development imperative. *Africa Education Review, 7*, 16–33.

288. McGrath, S., & Lugg, R., (2012). Knowing and doing vocational education and training reform: Evidence, learning and the policy process. *International Journal of Educational Development, 32*, 696–

708.

289. McGrath, S., King, K., Leach, F., & Carr-Hill, R., (1995). *Education and Training for the Informal Sector*. London, Overseas Development Administration.

290. McGuire, D., Cross, C., & O'Donnell, D., (2005). Why humanistic approaches in HRD will not work. *Hum. Resour. Dev. Q., 16*, 131–137.

291. Meek, L. V., (2000). Understanding diversity and differentiation in higher education: An overview. *Higher Education Policy, 13,* 1–6.

292. Mertaugh, M., & Hanushek, E. A., (2005). Education and training. In: Barr, N., (ed.), *Labor Markets and Social Policy in Central and Eastern Europe: The Accession and Beyond* (pp. 207–242). Washington, DC, World Bank.

293. Ministry of Education and Human Resources Development (MEHRD) and KERIS, (2007). *Adapting Education to the Information Age*. Seoul, MEHRD and KERIS.

294. Ministry of Education Finland, (2010). *Noste Program: Final Report*. (In Finnish). 24–65.

295. Ministry of Education, Republic of Serbia, (2010). *Vocational Education and Training Reform Program: Teacher Training and Human Resource Development (Belgrade)*. www.vetserbia.edu.rs/humanresourcedevelopment.htm (accessed on 8 June 2021).

296. Mishra, S., & Pulist, S. K., (2013). *eLearning in Commonwealth Asia 2013*. New Delhi, Commonwealth Educational Media Centre for Asia.

297. Misola, N., (2010). *Improving the Participation of Female Students in TVET Programs Formerly Dominated by Males*. Bonn, Germany, UNESCO-UNEVOC International Centre.

298. Morey, J. C., Simon, R., Jay, G. D., Wears, R. L., Salisbury, M., et al., (2002). Error reduction and performance improvement in the emergency department through formal teamwork training: Evaluation results of the MedTeams project. *Health Serv. Res., 37*, 1553–1581.

299. Morgan, R. B., & Casper, W. J., (2000). Examining the factor structure of participant reactions to training: A multidimensional approach. *Hum. Resour. Dev. Q., 11*, 301–317.

300. Morgeson, F. P., & Campion, M. A., (1997). Social and cognitive sources of potential inaccuracy in job analysis. *J. Appl. Psychol., 82*, 627–655.

301. Morris, M. A., & Robie, C., (2001). A meta-analysis of the effects of

cross-cultural training on expatriate performance and adjustment. *Int. J. Train. Dev., 5*, 112–125.

302. Murray, F., & Hsi, H., (2007). *Knowledge Workers in Biotechnology: Occupational Structures, Careers and Skill Demands.* Paper prepared for the National Academies Workshop on Research Evidence Related to Future Skill Demands. 129–137.
303. Nielsen, S., (2011). *TVET Teachers and Trainers*. Background paper commissioned by UNESCO Education Sector.
304. Nielsen, S., & Nikolovska, M., (2007). European training foundation. *ETF Yearbook 2007. Quality in Vocational Education and Training.* Luxembourg, Office for Official Publications of the European Communities.
305. Noe, R. A., (2008). *Employee Training and Development* (4th edn.). Boston, MA: Irwin-McGraw.
306. O'Connor, P., Flin, R., & Fletcher, G., (2002). Techniques used to evaluate crew resource management training: A literature review. Hum. *Factors Aerosp. Saf., 2*, 217–233.
307. OECD, (2003). *Beyond Rhetoric: Adult Learning Policies and Practices*. Paris, OECD Publishing.
308. Paradise, A., (2007). *State of the Industry: ASTD's Annual Review of Trends in Workplace Learning and Performance*. Alexandria, VA: ASTD.
309. Phillips, J. J., & Phillips, P., (2007). Measuring return on investment in leadership development. In: Hannum, K. M., Martineau, J. W., & Reinelt, C., (eds.), *The Handbook of Leadership Development Evaluation* (pp. 137–166). Hoboken, NJ: Wiley.
310. Pidd, K., (2004). The impact of workplace support and identity on training transfer: A case study of drug and alcohol safety training in Australia. *Int. J. Train. Dev., 8*, 274–288.
311. Pires, A. L. O., (2010). *Country Report: Portugal*. Torino, CEDEFOP. www.cedefop.europa.eu (accessed on 8 June 2021).
312. Population Reference Bureau, (2013). *The World's Youth 2013 Data Sheet*. Washington, DC, Population Reference Bureau.
313. Pouligny, B., (2004). Les anciens combattants d'aujourd'hui, désarmement, démobilisation et réinsertion: *The Politics and Anti-Politics of Contemporary 'Disarmament.'*
314. Psacharopoulos, G., (1981). Returns to education: An updated

international comparison. *Comparative Education, 17*, 321–341.

315. Raffe, D., & Spours, K., (2007). Three models of policy learning and policy-making in 1419 education. In: Raffe, D., & Spours, K., (eds.), *Policy-Making and Policy Learning in 14–19 Education*. Bedford Way Papers. London, Institute of Education.
316. Rao, T. V., (2004). Human resource development as national policy in India. *Adv. Dev. Hum. Resour., 6*, 288–296.
317. Ravallion, M., (2004). *Pro-Poor Growth: A Primer*. World Bank Policy Research Working Paper No. 3242. Washington, DC, Development Research Group, World Bank.
318. Republic of Tunisia, (2011). Rapport De La Consultation Nationale Sur L'emploi. Tunis, Republic of Tunisia.
319. Richman-Hirsch, W. L., (2001). Post-training interventions to enhance transfer: The moderating effects of work environments. *Hum. Resour. Dev. Q., 12*, 105–119.
320. Rivera, R. J., & Paradise, A., (2006). *State of the Industry: ASTD's Annual Review of Trends in Workplace Learning and Performance*. Alexandria, VA: ASTD.
321. Robertson, I. T., (1990). Behavior modeling: Its record and potential in training and development. *Br. J. Manag., 1*, 117–125.
322. Rodrik, D., (2006). *Understanding South Africa's Economic Puzzles*. CID Working Paper No. 130.
323. Rowold, J., (2007). The impact of personality on training-related aspects of motivation: Test of a longitudinal model. *Hum. Resour. Dev. Q., 18*, 9–31.
324. Sackett, P. R., & Mullen, E. J., (1993). Beyond formal experimental design: Towards an expanded view of the training evaluation process. *Pers. Psychol., 46*, 613–627.
325. SACMEQ, (2010). *SACMEQ III Project Results: Pupil Achievement Levels in Reading and Mathematics*. Working Document No. 1. http://www.sacmeq.org/downloads/sacmeqIII/WD01_SACMEQ_III_Results_Pupil_Achievementpdf (accessed on 8 June 2021).
326. SADC and UNESCO, (2011). *Final Report: Status of TVET in the SADC Region* (p. 10). Gaborone, SADC.
327. Salas, E., & Cannon-Bowers, J. A., (2001). The science of training: A decade of progress. *Annu. Rev. Psychol., 52*, 471–499.

328. Salas, E., Burke, C. S., Bowers, C. A., & Wilson, K. A., (2001). Team training in the skies: Does crew resource management (CRM) training work? *Hum. Factors, 42*, 641–674.

329. Salas, E., Wilson, K. A., & Burke, C. S., (2006). Does crew resource management training work? An update, an extension, and some critical needs. *Hum. Factors, 48*, 392–412.

330. Salzano, E., (2005). *Technology-Based Training for Marginalized Girls*. Paris, UNESCO.

331. Satterfield, J. M., & Hughes, E., (2007). Emotion skills training for medical students: A systematic review. *Med. Educ., 41*, 935–941.

332. Schmidt, A., & Ford, J. K., (2003). Learning within a student control training environment: The interactive effects of goal orientation and metacognitive instruction on learning outcomes. *Pers. Psychol., 56*, 405–430.

333. Second Reading.

334. Sen, A., (1999). *Development as Freedom*. Oxford, Oxford University Press.

335. Seyfried, E., (2011). *Quality Assurance in TVET*. Background paper commissioned by UNESCO Education Sector.

336. Shaikh, N., (2007). *The Present as History: Critical Perspectives on Global Power*. New York, Colombia University Press.

337. Shemyakina, O., (2011). *The Labor Market, Education and Armed Conflict in Tajikistan*. Working Paper 5738. Washington, DC, World Bank.

338. Shiohata, M., (2011). *Skills Acquisition Among Lao Women Textile Weavers in a Changing Economy*. Case study prepared for UNESCO Education Sector.

339. Singh, K., (2012). *Report of the Special Rapporteur on the Right to Education*. Sixty-seventh session of the United Nations General Assembly. Document Number A/67/31. http://www.right-to-education.org/sites/right-to-education.org/files/resource-attachments/UNSR_TVET_2012.pdf (accessed on 8 June 2021).

340. Sirianni, P. M., & Frey, B. A., (2001). Changing a culture: Evaluation of a leadership development program at Mellon financial services. *Int. J. Train. Dev., 5*, 290–301.

341. Sitzmann, T., Bell, B., & Kraiger, K., (2008). A multi-level analysis of the effect of prompting self-regulation in technology-delivered

instruction. *Pers. Psychol. Manuscr*. (under review).

342. Sitzmann, T., Brown, K. G., Ely, K., & Kraiger, K., (2008). Motivation to learn in a military training curriculum: A longitudinal investigation. *Mil. Psychol. Manuscr*. (under review).
343. Sitzmann, T., Kraiger, K., Stewart, D., & Wisher, R., (2006). The comparative effectiveness of Web-based and classroom instruction: A meta-analysis. *Pers. Psychol., 59*, 623–664.
344. Smith, E. M., Ford, J. K., & Kozlowski, S. W. J., (1997). Building adaptive expertise: Implications for training design. In: Quinones, M. A., & ˜Ehrenstein, A., (EDS.), *Training for a Rapidly Changing Workplace: Applications of Psychological Research* (pp. 89–118). Washington, DC: APA Books.
345. Smith, J., (2008). *Off-Shoring, Outsourcing and the 'Global Labor Arbitrage.'* Working Paper. Procida Italy, International Initiative for Promoting Political Economy. 180–190.
346. Spencer, H., (1859). What knowledge is of most worth? *Westminster Review, 141*, 1–23.
347. Spitzer, D. R., (2005). Learning effectiveness measurement: A new approach for measuring and managing learning to achieve business results. *Adv. Dev. Hum. Resour., 7*, 55–70.
348. Stanley, J., (2013). *Global Validation Workshop on Policies and Practices on TVET Teachers and Instructors in the Arab Region, a Regional Study*. Final Report. Paris, UNESCO. 17–92.
349. Strietska-Ilina, O., Hofmann, C., Haro, D. M., & Shinyoung, J., (2011). *Skills for Green Jobs: A Global View: Synthesis Report Based on 21 Country Studies*. Geneva, International Labor Office, Skills and Employability Department. http://www.ilo.org/wcmsp5/groups/public/---dgreports/---dcomm/---publ/documents/publication/wcms_159585.pdf (accessed on 8 June 2021).
350. Sugrue, B., & Rivera, R. J., (2005). *State of the Industry: ASTD's Annual Review of Trends in Workplace Learning and Performance*. Alexandria, VA: ASTD.
351. Swanson, R. A., (2001). *Assessing the Financial Benefits of Human Resource Development*. Cambridge, MA: Perseus.
352. Sweet, R., (2009). *European Training Foundation, Work-based Learning Programs for Young People in the Mediterranean Region*. Luxembourg, Office for Official Publications of the European

Communities.

353. Switzer, K. C., Nagy, M. S., & Mullins, M. E., (2005). The influence of training reputation, managerial support, and self-efficacy on pretraining motivation and perceived training transfer. *Appl. HRM Res., 10*, 21–34.

354. Szalkowski, A., & Jankowicz, D., (2004). The development of human resources during the process of economic and structural transformation in Poland. *Adv. Dev. Hum. Resour., 6*, 346–354.

355. Tannenbaum, S. I., & Woods, S. B., (1992). Determining a strategy for evaluating training: Operating within organizational constraints. *Hum. Resour. Plann., 15*(2), 63–81.

356. Tannenbaum, S. I., & Yukl, G., (1992). Training and development in work organizations. *Annu. Rev. Psychol., 43*, 399–441.

357. Taylor, P. J., Russ-Eft, D. F., & Chan, D. W. L., (2005). A meta-analytic review of behavior modeling training. *J. Appl. Psychol., 90*, 692–709.

358. TESDA, (2015). *SICAT – Trainers Methodology Level 1 Online Training Program*. www.sicattesda.ph (accessed on 8 June 2021).

359. Tharenou, P., Saks, A. M., & Moore, C., (2007). A review and critique of research on training and organizational-level outcomes. *Hum. Resour. Manag. Rev., 17*, 251–273.

360. Towler, A. J., (2003). Effects of charismatic influence training on attitudes, behavior, and performance. *Pers. Psychol., 56,* 363–381.

361. Tracey, J. B., Hinkin, T. R., Tannenbaum, S., & Mathieu, J. E., (2001). The influence of individual characteristics and the work environment on varying levels of training outcomes. *Hum. Resour. Dev. Q., 12*, 5–23.

362. Trow, M., (1995). *Diversity in higher education in the United States of America*. Paper presented at the CVCP Seminar on Diversity in Higher Education. London.

363. Tuck, R., (2007). *An Introductory Guide to National Qualifications Frameworks: Conceptual and Practical Issues for Policy Makers*. Geneva, ILO Skills and Employability Department.

364. Twitchell, K., Holton, E. III., & Trott, J. W. Jr., (2000). Technical training evaluation practices in the United States. *Perform. Improv. Q., 13*(1), 84–109.

365. Ubeda, G. M., (2005). Training and business performance: The Spanish case. *Int. J. Hum. Resour. Manag., 16*, 1691–1710.

366. UNCTAD, (2011). *Foreign Direct Investments in LDCs: Lessons*

Learned from the Decade 2001–2010 and the Way Forward. Geneva, United Nations Conference on Trade and Development.

367. UNDP, (2009). *Capacity Development: A UNDP Primer*. New York, UNDP. 56–71.
368. UNEP, (2008). *Green Jobs: Towards Decent Work in a Sustainable, Low Carbon World*. New York, UNEP. 39–53.
369. UNEP, (2011). *Towards a Green Economy: Pathways to Sustainable Development and Poverty Eradication*. http://www.unep.org/greeneconomy/ (accessed on 8 June 2021).
370. UNESCO-Bangkok. (2011). *TVET in Asia and the Pacific Region: Overview of the Regional Background Paper on TVET: Asia and the Pacific Region*. Unpublished background paper.
371. UNESCO-UNEVOC, (2004). *Bonn Declaration on Learning for Work, Citizenship and Sustainability*. UNESCO International Meeting of Technical and Vocational Education and Training Experts. Bonn, Germany. http://www.unevoc.unesco.org/fileadmin/user_upload/pubs/SD_BonnDeclaration_e.pdf (accessed on 8 June 2021).
372. UNESCO-UNEVOC, (2012). *UNEVOC in Action, Biennial Report 2010–2011*. Bonn, Germany, UNESCO-UNEVOC International Centre for Technical and Vocational Education and Training.
373. UNESCO, (1989). *Convention on Technical and Vocational Education*. Paris, UNESCO. http://portal.unesco.org/en/ev.php-URL_ID=13059&URL_DO=DO_TOPIC&URL_SECTION=201.html (accessed on 8 June 2021).
374. UNIDO, (2009). *Industrial Development Report 2009: Breaking in and Moving Up: New Industrial Challenges for the Bottom Billion and the Middle-Income Countries*. Vienna, UNIDO.
375. United Nations, (1992). *Report of the United Nations Conference on Environment and Development* (A/CONF.151/26 Vol.1), Rio de Janeiro, UN General Assembly.
376. UNSTT, (2012). *Realizing the Future, we Want for All*. Report to the Secretary-General. New York, United Nations System Task Team. 45–60.
377. Valente, C., (2011). *What Did the Maoists Ever do for us? Education and Marriage of Women Exposed to Civil Conflict in Nepal*. Working Paper 5741.Washington, DC, World Bank.
378. Van, D. K. M., Gielen, E., & Nauta, C., (2001). Supervisory support

as a major condition to enhance transfer. *Int. J. Train. Dev., 5*, 52–63.

379. Van, L. M. J., & Van, P. B. M., (2002). The costs and benefits of lifelong learning: The case of the Netherlands. *Hum. Resour. Dev. Q., 13*, 151–168.
380. Vancouver, J. B., & Day, D. V., (2005). Industrial and organization research on self-regulation: From constructs to applications. *Appl. Psychol., 54*, 155–185.
381. Varghese, N., & Puttmann, V., (2011). *Trends in Diversification of Post-Secondary Education*. Paris, UNESCO-IIEP.
382. Veal, K., (2008). *Once Were Warriors: Reintegrating Ex-Combatants*. Supplement to UNESCO- UNEVOC Bulletin, No. 14.
383. Walther, R., (2007). *Vocational Training in the Informal Sector*. Paris, Agence Française de Développement.
384. Wang, G. G., & Wilcox, (2006). Training evaluation: Knowing more than is practiced. *Adv. Dev. Hum. Resour., 8*, 528–539.
385. Wang, G. G., Dou, Z., & Li, N., (2002). A systems approach to measuring return on investment for HRD interventions. *Hum. Resour. Dev. Q., 13*, 203–224.
386. Wang, G., (2002). Control groups for human performance technology (HPT) evaluation and measurement. *Perform. Improv. Q., 15*(2), 34–48.
387. Watts, A. G., & Fretwell, D., (2004). *Public Policies for Career Development*. Washington, DC, World Bank.
388. Welsh, E. T., Wanberg, C. R., Brown, K. G., & Simmering, M. J., (2003). E-learning: Emerging uses, empirical results, and future directions. *Int. J. Train. Dev., 7*, 245–258.
389. Wesson, M. J., & Gogus, C. I., (2005). Shaking hands with a computer: An examination of two methods of organizational newcomer orientation. *J. Appl. Psychol., 90*, 1018–1026.
390. Wexley, K. N., (1984). Personnel training. *Annu. Rev. Psychol., 35*, 519–551.
391. Wilson, R., & Zuckersteinova, A., (2011). *Anticipating Changing Skills Needs: A Master Class*. Technical Reference Document for New Skills. University of Warwick IER/CEDEFOP.
392. Woods, P., (2004). *Environmental Education for a Sustainable Future: Formal Schooling*. curriculum leadership. http://www.curriculum.edu.

au/leader/environmental_education_for_a_sustainable_future:_,4695.html (accessed on 8 June 2021).

393. World Bank and DfID, (2003). *Knowledge and Skills in the New Economy: Knowledge and Skills in the MENA Region, Tunisia*. Washington, DC, World Bank.
394. World Bank, (2005a). *World Development Report 2006: Equity and Development*. Washington, DC, World Bank.
395. World Commission on Environment and Development, (1987). *Our Common Future*. Oxford, Oxford University Press.
396. World Conference on Education for All, (2000). *The Dakar Framework for Action: Meeting our Collective Commitments to Education for All*. Paris, UNESCO.
397. World Economic Forum, (2008). *The Global Competitiveness Report 2008–2009*. Geneva, World Economic Forum, pp. 34, 35.
398. World Resources Institute, (2011). *A Compilation of Green Economy Policies, Programs, and Initiatives from Around the World.* The Green Economy in Practice: Interactive Workshop 1. 12–19.
399. Yang, J., & Valdes-Cotera, R., (2011). *Conceptual Evolution and Policy Development in Lifelong Learning*. Bonn, Germany, UNESCO Institute for Lifelong Learning.
400. Yarnit, M., (2004). *Regeneration and All That: Learning and Skills and Sustainability*. London, Learning and Skills Development Agency.
401. Zhao, Y., Lei, J., Lai, B. Y. C., & Tan, H. S., (2005). What makes the difference? A practical analysis of research on the effectiveness of distance education. *Teach. Coll. Rec., 107*, 1836–1884.

INDEX

C

D

E